Political Transition

Political Transition

Politics and Cultures

Edited by
Paul Gready

Pluto Press

LONDON • STERLING, VIRGINIA

First published 2003 by Pluto Press
345 Archway Road, London N6 5AA
and 22883 Quicksilver Drive, Sterling, VA 20166-2012, USA

www.plutobooks.com

British Library Cataloguing in Publication Data
A catalogue record for this book is available from
the British Library

ISBN 0 7453 2042 2 hardback
ISBN 0 7453 2041 4 paperback

Library of Congress Cataloging in Publication Data
Political transition : politics and cultures / edited by Paul Gready.
        p. cm.
     ISBN 0–7453–2042–2 (hc) — ISBN 0–7453–2041–4 (pb)
   1. Political culture—Case studies. 2. Political science. I. Gready,
Paul.
     JA75.7 .P6627 2003
     306.2'09'0511—dc21

                                                      2002154508

10   9   8   7   6   5   4   3   2   1

Designed and produced for Pluto Press by
Chase Publishing Services, Fortescue, Sidmouth, EX10 9QG England
Typeset from disk by Stanford DTP Services, Towcester, England
Printed and bound in the European Union by
Antony Rowe, Chippenham and Eastbourne, England

Contents

1 Introduction

Paul Gready

Memory, identity, space/place and voice are central to the vocabularies, politics and cultures of political transition. These keywords are mutually informing. Policy decisions in relation to justice, truth and reconciliation imply as well as create a value system for these terms. Similarities and divergences in the way the quartet are understood can reflect converging or fundamentally different understandings of the lived-through past and the desired future. They provide some of the crucial fault lines of transition and primary moral and political sites of nation-building.

The post-Cold War rhetorical mainstreaming of human rights has entrenched a legal/quasi-legal orthodoxy as the preferred way to come to terms with the past. Official mechanisms such as truth commissions and war crimes tribunals are, nonetheless, only ever part of the story of the post-oppression or post-conflict era and also themselves structure and restructure memory, identity and space/place and privilege certain voices while suppressing others. Ross and Mertus, for example, detail in this volume how such institutions have misrepresented the lives and concerns of women. Mertus (2000) has argued elsewhere that war crimes tribunals are most likely to address the interests of the international community and least likely to satisfy survivors, while Mamdani (2000) has persuasively claimed that institutions such as truth commissions re-make conflicts in a single image (of individual victims and perpetrators, of civil and political rights violations).

Officially sanctioned memories, identities, spaces/places and voices are challenged and resisted from within civil society by the marginalised, disenfranchised and disenchanted, by minorities, political opponents and past perpetrators. Other agents from civil society – the media, human rights groups, academics – have also helped to define the profile of who gets to be heard, where and what is remembered, in ways that can reinforce or undermine official agendas. Furthermore, a number of countries have chosen the path of forgetting or of non-legal and non-institutional responses to a traumatic past, and in all transitions local civil society and non-

1

governmental responses co-exist with any state- or internationally-sponsored initiatives. These different approaches to the past impact upon the content and form of memory, identity, space/place and voice, and therefore on the cultures and politics of transition.

Transition, as it is understood here, implies a change in political regime and culture towards greater democratisation, post-repression, post-colonialism, post-war. Institutional mechanisms define and delimit transition in a particular way: in largely political and legal terms, as temporally and spatially delimited (in part by the institutions themselves), as a historical stage or way-station in a narrative of progress. Transition as it emerges in this volume is somewhat different. It is a contested and intrinsically incomplete process, shot through with considerations of politics and power, mobilised as a demand and a promise, and characterised by continuity as well as multi-faceted, if often uneven, change. Patterns from the past are often reconfigured rather than radically altered in the present. Resistance, for example, does not end where transition begins – as Buur notes in this collection, transition creates its own victims.

Ignatieff (1996) writes of societies characterised by a simultaneity of the past and/in the present which means that the past is 'not past at all' (121). While acknowledging an inevitable and desirable temporal simultaneity, there is a need to liberate the present and future from the burden of the past that threatens to overwhelm them. To come to terms with the past means superimposing serial time on simultaneous time; it means reactivating the movement of time. Transition involves moving on while claiming ownership of the full temporal range, forgetting as well as remembering.

There is a geographical as well as a temporal dimension to transition. Transition is spatialised, it re-maps geographical relationships, public and symbolic places – as such it re-makes geographies as well as histories, discourses of transition unravelling unevenly across time and space. Furthermore, as Mertus (2000) illustrates, tensions between global, national and local priorities are played out in transitional societies. This book attempts to capture something of the dialectic between the global and the local, top down and bottom up, official and unofficial.

In short, transition is understood in this collection of essays to be a rhetorical device or political strategy as well as a layered and often fractured political and cultural reality. More specifically, it is a politics and culture built on the foundations of memory, identity, space/place and voice, and it is here that critical and comparative perspectives are sought in this collection.

The regions of Europe, Latin America and Southern Africa have been chosen for comparative analysis in this volume because they have been central to the macro discourses about justice and truth, influencing policies in an increasingly global exchange and, it is suggested here, will perform a similar role in relation to the debates about memory, identity, space/place and voice. The collection, therefore, juxtaposes different country and regional experiences and historical eras or phases of transition. It is also multidisciplinary, with individual contributions often drawing on a range of disciplinary approaches.

The sub-divisions of the book – 'The Politics of Memory', 'Identities', 'Re-making Space' and 'Testimony and Voices' – are by no means watertight, so debates can be traced within and between the sections. The approach taken in the collection to these four concerns is introduced below.

THE POLITICS OF MEMORY

This is an over-used and under-theorised term in the literature on political transition. For example, in one study that carries the term as its title, it is a rather thinly conceptualised and partially applied cloak for a discussion primarily focusing on mainstream transitional justice and accountability measures.

> It can be said that the politics of memory is two things. Narrowly conceived, it consists of policies of truth and justice in transition (*official or public memory*); more widely conceived, it is about how a society interprets and appropriates its past, in an ongoing attempt to mould its future (*social memory*). (de Brito et al. (eds) 2001:37)

Other similarly titled books fail to define their key term at all (Amadiume and An-Na'im (eds) 2000). This collection begins to develop a more comprehensive definition, stretching beyond the confines of transitional justice initiatives.

Some components of the definition are overtly political: the use of memory in electoral politics (Sylvester); the nature of official, insti-tutionalised memory, such as that enshrined in truth commissions, war crimes tribunals and other criminal prosecutions, strictly cir-cumscribed by politics and power (Sanford, Buur, Ross, Mertus); the nationalisation and 'ownership' of memory by the state or party (Sylvester) or, conversely, its privatisation, which can democratise memory and/or constitute an abdication of state/party responsibility (Jelin); selective, partial memories and the struggle between opposing memories of the past (Sylvester, Jelin, Pogány); memory's reach and its mobilisation within the politics of the present (Sylvester, Jelin, Sanford, Pogány): 'memory on-call, an all-purpose memory, a memory for all seasons' (Zertal 2000:120). Struggles over the meaning of the past are also struggles over power in the present – Jelin, for example, in her chapter in this collection notes the possibility that the original reason for commemoration becomes a 'pre-text' for present struggles. The politics of memory is interwoven with the repetition and recasting of past divisions and conflicts, as the past continues to influence, sometimes literally exploding into, ongoing societal disputation (Sylvester, Jelin, Sanford, Dawson, Buur, Hackeling, Tanner Hawkins).

The politics of memory must also address broader issues and struggles, such as whether to remember (Pogány), what to remember and control of memory (Sylvester, Jelin, Sanford, Pogány, Tanner Hawkins), when to remember (O'Dwyer), and the history of memory itself (Jelin). Crucial to the politics being outlined here are disputed lines of inclusion and exclusion, solidarity and fracture, memory and forgetting. Examples of these contests range from controversies around the issue of 'victims' in Northern Ireland and South Africa (Dawson, Buur, Ross), to disputes over the selection and meaning of specific commemorative dates and events (Jelin), attempts to enforce invisibility, silence and forgetting in the war zones of Angola (Nordstrom), and to the re-working of the profile of debate and democracy in new forms of technology such as the internet (Tanner Hawkins). Another line of tension underpinning many contributions to this book is the relationship between official memory (state-sponsored efforts at memory creation and dissemination), collective memory,[1] and individual memory:[2] what Jelin (1998) calls the 'layers and levels' of memory.

Memory carries an almost overwhelming set of political expectations during transitions that frame its form and delivery: an emancipatory potential often ascribed in the idea that even those without and outside history still have memory (although this notion is interestingly countered by Pogány's suggestion that for the Roma memory is a luxury given ongoing deprivation and persecution); a final, even ultimate, victory for resistance and liberation; a form of deterrence; a leading role in the policy arenas of truth and justice; a walk-on part in reconciliation, democratisation and reconstruction; the raw material of catharsis and healing; the facilitator of continuity within new beginnings. Alongside the sophisticated politics of memory is an equally sophisticated politics of forgetting (Cohen 2001). The ideal for the politics of memory is a move from private memory to public acknowledgement, accountability, debate and 'ownership', and a combination of the past- and future-oriented functions of memory.

IDENTITIES

This book looks at transitional identity in a way that complements the dominant discourse in this field (nationalism), by highlighting various trajectories of identity: the politics of victimhood, the link between identity and recognition/resources (Dawson, Buur, Ross), between identity, recovery and action (Marsh, Sanford); interrelationships and divisions between individual, group and nation/state (Dawson, Buur, Marsh); identity as a reaction to another time and another place (Andrews); lines of continuity as well as change, grand narratives alongside the everyday (Andrews, Buur, Ross). These provide the contours of a politics of identity, inextricably linked to the politics of memory.

Just as memory during transition is plural, so there is a diversity of identity possibilities within a transitional context. As Ignatieff (1996) writes: 'nations ... do not have a single identity ... National identity is a site of conflict and argument, not a silent shrine for collective worship' (116). Transition typically involves a search for new identities, the challenge of dealing with curtailed, fixed (Ross) and proliferating identities (Andrews) – crucially informed by 'rhetorical frames' and 'imaginable possibilities' (Cruz 2000). It is with such frames and possibilities that this book is concerned.

Memory and forgetting are implicated in identity formation at all layers/levels, and vice versa. 'The core meaning of any individual or group identity, namely, a sense of sameness over time and space, is sustained by remembering; and what is remembered is defined by the assumed identity' (Gillis 1994:3). A further important component of the memory–identity linkage is that both are relational, fundamentally forged in, defined by and in turn defining, relationships and social interaction. Both can be collective. Novick (2001), echoing Gillis, talks of 'a circular relationship between collective identity and collective memory. We choose to center certain memories because they seem to us to express what is central to our collective identity. Those memories, once brought to the fore, reinforce that form of identity' (7).

The danger arises when identity is run through with essentialist discourses (a 'chosen people') and 'other', memories of atrocity and the desire for revenge, and narratives ascribing guilt and innocence, infamy and glory. Ethnic nationalism is hard to explain without addressing the mutually enforcing relationship between collective memory and collective identity. Stripped of the fossilising force of Cold War politics, nationalism has become central to political transitions, as both a means and an end. 'A collective memory that denies full humanity to the out-group allows for various shades of "getting rid of"' (Cohen 2001:97). Memory of atrocity becomes self-duplicating. But it is important to note that democratically forged collective memory can be an agent of inclusion and reconciliation (Tanner Hawkins). Further, this is only one identity strand within transition – collectivism battles pluralism and identities collapse inwards and expand outwards – and one way in which identity bears memory into the future in terms of rhetorical frames and imagined possibilities.

One key, and related, rhetorical frame relates to the identity status of victimhood. As part of wider trends often associated with a postmodern identity politics, and politically loaded identity-naming during transition (victims, survivors, perpetrator-victims, bystanders, beneficiaries, etc.), the politics of victimhood takes a particular form in transitional states. It can be a means of self-help, seeking redress, reclaiming voice and critiquing new forms of marginalisation, forgetting and power. It can also take on a more sinister guise. Although the different faces of victim politics are not always easy to distinguish, the process of identity formation is more likely to be dangerous if it produces a group, national or diaspora identity-politics dominated by the embrace of exclusive and intolerant victim claims. Such identities can be competitive and fragmentary, dominated by grievance, history, a sense of injustice, and the pursuit of recognition and resources. Sometimes such identities are based on ethnicity or religion.

Chapters in this book examine the politics of victimhood in Northern Ireland and South Africa as it affects a range of issues: 'hierarchies of victimhood' as they inform an uneven remembering of the past and access to resources and recognition in the present;

the way in which such identity categories are claimed, constructed, assigned, contested, essentialised, rejected; the danger of fragmentary, mutually hostile claims; and victimhood as a site of political mobilisation, a form of oppositional politics, a re-working of political frameworks from the past and the generator of new conflicts.

In the context of a victim culture it is possible to talk of too much memory, and too much identity, but also of too little: victimhood alone makes a person/group stand out, it alone stakes a claim to attention and resources. Perhaps the most damaging reason for this is that societies lose the capacity to generate multiple, alternative identifications and faith dies in 'transformative politics', 'a future orientation', in a broader collective, national project (Maier 1993). Whether this results in claims for a new nation-state based on race or religion, or not, a dream has died. This is a profoundly negative implication of transitional victim politics.

A final (already mentioned) identity theme is the coexistence of continuity and change. In the arena of identity, legacies from the past include persistent rhetorical frames – such as the (Berlin) Wall in the East German psyche (Andrews) – and the frustration of imagined possibilities, the re-working and renewing of opposition and the continuities of daily life and human experience. In short, identity is additive rather than substitutive and influenced but not exclusively determined by transitional political change (Andrews, Dawson). Identity formation can replace one grand narrative with another (nationalism, nation-building) and/or retreat to, uncover, rediscover the intimacy of subjectivities of the ordinary and everyday.

RE-MAKING SPACE

If transition is a spatial as well as a temporal phenomenon, then its spaces are real and symbolic (social, ideological, economic, narrative). In part the story told here is about people as geographical agents attempting to secure for themselves an element of flexibility and freedom in their daily lives under oppression (Hackeling), about contesting official, transitional narratives of space from the local (street names) to the national (the new national, democratic space (Marsh)), and about the invisible, linked spaces of local wars and global economics and politics, creating people without memory, identity and voice (Nordstrom). Transition takes place in, over, through and across particular spaces, appropriates and re-makes spaces that include the very local, the national and the global – this is the politics of space, clearly linked to the politics of memory and identity.

One of the most important geographies of transition relates to sites of commemoration, which serve as key locations of struggle for the keywords of this volume (Jelin, Henri). For example, in their planning and reception such sites concentrate and bring to the fore debates about memory.

> All over the world, commemorations of atrocities have turned into memory wars, the forces of denial and acknowledgement literally battling it out over territory. With each political oscillation, statues are pulled down, street names changed, and public holidays abolished. (Cohen 2001:234)

Such sites speak to the need for externalisation, or what Jelin (1998) calls the 'materialization' (27), of memory, identity and voice. Memory needs to be 'deposited' somewhere, thereby turning individual memory into public and collective memory (28). Henri makes similar remarks in his chapter in this book about the need to externalise experience, '[i]t is almost as if one places this memory in a respectful place outside of oneself. In doing that, this memory finds a place inside oneself that is not only destructive.' This placing outside can be done in both time and space, resulting in a concentration of meaning and the balm of distance. Dawsons' caution, that commemoration is double-edged with the potential to fuel conflict or its resolution, is also worth noting.

In a not dissimilar vein, many of the contributors also allude to a narrative space of memory, identity and voice. Both physical and narrative spaces are moved between, transformed, occupied, reclaimed, named, linked; and central to both is a transgressive movement from the private to the public and the personal to the political. Michael Taussig (1992) writes about 'the violent silencing enacted by State terror' in Latin America, in relation to 'disappearances', that the aim is not to destroy memory: 'Far from it. What is aimed at is the *relocation and refunctioning of collective memory*' (48). The aim is to keep the memory of resistance and its destruction alive, but fragmented and in retreat within the private sphere where it feeds an incapacitating fear. Organisations such as the Mothers of the Disappeared are so important because they re-engage with, re-occupy, the public sphere and recuperate collective memory.

Chapters in this collection also stress the significance of community reclamation of public spaces that are thereby re-made, turned into sites of popular memory (Marsh, Sanford). Sanford refers to the need for community spaces in which to transform what Veena Das describes as 'poisonous knowledge'; issues and actions are not silenced by violence but held in suspension until communities can reconstruct memory in a public place. Turning repression into resistance, O'Dwyer suggests that the silencing of voice and memory has become a counter-strategy in Ireland used against the British state, the safe space is within as voice and memory await their appointment with history. The spaces to be liberated are inside as well as out. While, obviously, spaces of exclusion and silencing remain – Nordstrom refers to globalisation's foot-soldiers in Angola's war economy – processes linking narrative, physical and political space contest their geographies of control.

If official, institutional spaces are of great significance to memory, identity and voice, equally vital are 'civil times and civil spaces' (Gillis 1994:20). Jelin's chapter in this volume suggests that commemorations, whether official or 'societal', provide 'public occasions, open spaces' for various voices and divergent memories to be articulated. Characterised by alternating hegemonies, disagreement, dialogue or its absence, such moments and spaces unmask the construction of collective and official memories. Powerful contemporary official spaces also include trials (Osiel 2000) and truth commissions. A space of public debate can be reclaimed, defined and extended by such events and the media coverage they engender. Boraine (2000) has described the victims' hearings of the South African Truth and Reconciliation Commission as a 'liberated zone' (99). Both individual voice and public debate were liberated.

Unfortunately, the liberated zone was surrounded by a zone that was in some ways decidedly unliberated. Outside the confines of the hearing, for example, Henri's testimony ceased to be his own. It was appropriated, edited, interpreted, re-interpreted, re-told, sold in a way that impacted profoundly on his life. This is one example of a more general concern. One of the problems facing the Video Archive for Holocaust Testimonies at Yale University, according to Hartman (2000), is that the 'testimonial alliance', community and mutual trust that characterised the interview could potentially be undermined by 'postproduction procedures': 'the impersonal, market forces of electronic recall and dissemination', the conversion of 'archives of conscience' into 'megabytes of information, electronic warehouses of knowledge', and the transgression of the line between 'diffusion' and 'commodification' serving to 'banalize ... a new representational genre (the video testimony), or Holocaust memory itself'. The issue here is how to link liberated zones or safe places – which as Henri notes are essentially 'artificial' – with the state and society, how to expand their reach and range, beyond victims, while still respecting victims.

Civil society spaces, at a local level and operating longer term, are needed, unofficial, inventive, alternative, subversive spaces. Hackeling writes instructively of the various spaces of negotiation and dissent in East Germany. Sanford, Dawson, Mertus and Henri identify the need for safe, supportive spaces of reflection, articulation, engagement, and healing. The imperative, ultimately, as Boraine alludes (2000:420), is to create 'liberation zones' that transcend societal divisions, and it is just such spaces that Tanner Hawkins (in her chapter about the Pinochet arrest and the internet as a narrative space of memory) and Henri (outlining the work of the Direct Action Centre for Peace and Memory and Western Cape Action Tour Project (WECAT)) describe.

There is an irrepressible dynamic being outlined in this volume: as Sanford argues, one voice creates space for other voices, individual testimony represents an expansion of agency, a chorus of voices creates community space for political action. So the issue of space, its manufacture and transgression, is closely linked to the fusion of testimony and agency.

TESTIMONY AND VOICES

Transition, at both an individual and collective/national level, is about being able to tell one's story and/or having a new story to tell. It is a testimonial moment. It announces an end to the era of silence, whether imposed or 'chosen', ended by a multifaceted process of negotiation and articulation. This volume identifies various platforms for voice (exhumations, public spaces, people's tribunals, the internet) as well as itself providing such a platform through the frequent use of testimony and interviews.

Werbner (1998) talks of a 'right of recountability' (1). But as the experience of Henri and others suggest this is not enough: 'The right to narration is not merely the right to tell one's story, it is the right to control representation' (Slaughter 1997:430). Serious questions are raised by Henri about the ethics and politics of public testimony and its dissemination, about the 'ownership' and uses of life stories. For Henri, writing has become an important way to reclaim voice and agency, to take back his right to comment on and explain his own testimony: 'the right to claim memory with honour, to live with it in dignity on one's own terms'. The underlying questions here – apart from how testimony, one's own past and story, can be truly 'owned' – are: how can the individual story be respectfully placed within the broader context of societal and official narratives, and what is the most desirable relationship between voice, interpretation and representation, the oral and the written, word and image?

Sylvester, Sanford, Marsh, Mertus, Henri and O'Dwyer all suggest questions relating to power and narrative layering in their chapters. Can the local appropriate national/global discourses? Can the subaltern insinuate him-/herself within dominant discourses and spaces? Can personal narrative subvert the legal anti-narrative? Is to speak from within another's discourse to speak in an occupied voice? Is there a need, as Henri suggests, to theorise the relationship between layers of voices, listeners/readers, mediations, and disseminations? Who ultimately is appropriating whom?

Despite, or perhaps precisely because of, these complexities, sites and spaces of voice need to be 'real' and 'virtual', local/national, as outlined in the section on 'Re-making Space' above, and international – there are many ways to transcend divisions, to expand the reach and range of liberated zones. International human rights law, for example, which is often of increasing relevance for transitional states, is cast in this light by Slaughter (1997). Having characterised human rights abuse as an infringement on a subject's ability to narrate his or her story, he states:

> If human rights abuses exist on a continuum of narratability ... human rights instruments and norms can be evaluated and promoted for their effectiveness in addressing that continuum and providing a public, international space that empowers all human beings to speak. (ibid: 413)

International human rights law becomes

> a commitment to the voice ... the tool to guarantee recourse to individual narration. Human rights law implicitly, although often explicitly as well, commits contemporary states to an ideological

understanding of human subjectivity that privileges the power of speaking oneself. (429)

And yet here too caution is needed. Mertus argues in this collection that women's court testimony regarding rape at the International Criminal Tribunal for the Former Yugoslavia re-violated women by not allowing them to tell the stories they wanted to tell.

It is important to deny neither the complex ethics and politics nor the extraordinary power of voice. Voice is central, again at many different levels, to identity and memory, as a vehicle of subjectivity and remembering. It is also a form of agency/action, traversing public/private and personal/political divisions.

Testimony and/as agency as portrayed in this collection resonates with the literature on the genre of *testimonio*. This genre typically captures the voice of the marginalised, details a context of political urgency, seeks to effect societal change, demands justice, challenges official discourse, blurs clear lines between the individual and the collective. Thus, in this volume, voice and testimony are political, words and narratives inform action, demand action, create the space for action, are action. But their meaning also needs to be dissected in a more nuanced and context-specific ways. They are, in addition, profoundly unsettling, inverting and challenging expectations (Pogány, Andrews); airing awkward perspectives (Dawson); owning victimhood (Dawson, Buur); struggling with the difficulties and dangers of 'naming harm' (Ross); speaking, if at all, in a stuttering, repetitious, occupied voice, forcibly detained *and* secured in a safe house awaiting their transitional moment (O'Dwyer).

The contents of the four sections of this book are outlined in more detail in the chapter summaries below.

THE POLITICS OF MEMORY

These chapters speak most directly to the theme of the politics of memory outlined above.

Chapter 2 by Christine Sylvester, 'Remembering and Forgetting "Zimbabwe": Towards a Third Transition', plots the contested and fragmented chronology of post-colonial memory in Zimbabwe. The author identifies elections as having punctuated three eras of transition, signalling contests over memory and airing contending mythologies about the 'true' post-colonial Zimbabwe. The ruling ZANU(PF) has enacted a politics of memory and mythology in which the party *is* Zimbabwe – it is the source of liberation and patronage, the saviour from colonialism and oppression, the custodian of national identity and memory. Increasingly, memory of the past has been marshalled in order to forget the hardships and failures of the present.

Sylvester argues that ZANU(PF) has engaged in colonial mimicry by resorting to an invented ideal time of itself and to colonial-style violence, to the dream of development and the reality of repression. As a further dimension of mimicry, in a deferred politics of the present, the 'now' is subsumed by a permanent and variously manifested transitional 'not yet' or 'will be', by the past and future, with ZANU(PF) insisting that it is the sole custodian of this circular, back-to-the-future, post-colonial journey. However, the return to the issues (the rural peasantry, land, war, colonialism) and methods of the past and attempts to appropriate and manage alternative memories have not gone uncontested. The Movement for Democratic Change (MDC), launched as a party in September 1999, epitomises the rise of alternative memory claims and the return to a different past, the hope-filled early independence era. Memory and forgetting are thus being contested, notably between political parties, urban and rural areas, and between historical eras of transition. Sylvester concludes by stating that the MDC must not in turn mimic ZANU(PF), but rather proliferate the 'inappropriate' (for example, through gender sensitivity and inclusivity and a more diverse and open-ended remembering and imagining of Zimbabwe).

Chapter 2 outlines the continuities as well as discontinuities between colonial and post-colonial memory, the tensions that develop over time within the post-colonial era over which past to lay claim to and be judged by, and the extent to which, in Zimbabwe at least, politics has been conducted through the differential mobilisation of memory and forgetting, or put another way, 'ownership' of memory has become a crucial political issue.

Chapter 3 by Elizabeth Jelin, 'Contested Memories of Repression in the Southern Cone: Commemorations in a Comparative Perspective', is also about the contested politics of memory over time, the disputed role of the past in an evolving present, but taking commemorative practice as its starting point. It deals with public struggles about the meaning of the past – the memories of the repressive dictatorships established in the 1950s, 1960s and 1970s in the Southern Cone of South America (Argentina, Brazil, Chile, Paraguay and

Uruguay). These are countries with 'a long history of a transnational social life', including processes of oppression, resistance and within transition. The chapter takes the study of the disputes about the selection and meaning of specific dates and commemorative practices as an 'entry point to approach the elusive core of memory and oblivion'. Such memory markers in public time and space exemplify the way in which public memories are produced, contested and appropriated in increasingly vocal transitions.

The commemorative practices during the past decades in the five countries are presented briefly. Contrasts and commonalities are analysed in terms of the relative strength of various social and political actors, and in terms of the interpretive frameworks and meanings of the past that these actors bring to the public arena. Jelin, for example, shows that the same date may have different meanings for the various actors and forces that frame their current struggles and identities in relation to these dates. The chapter concludes with some reflections on the relationship between past and present. How to secure the inter-generational transmission of memories; whether, as the meanings of dates of commemoration change over time, the past can become simply a 'pre-text' for struggles of the present; and, given the dominance of social actors in the region as the main challengers to military narratives and the limited role of political parties and the state in public commemorations, whether the post-dictatorship state can be brought back into the public sphere to engage with the interrelated issues of legitimacy, responsibility and demands for justice?

Chapter 4 by Victoria Sanford, '"What is Written in Our Hearts": Memory, Justice and the Healing of Fragmented Communities', provides an ethnographic study of local mobilisations for truth, healing and justice, following massacres of Maya in Guatemala, which are driven by processes of exhumation and reburial. The body and its artifacts take on multiple meanings: the body in need of a proper burial; as a means of identification; as a source of truth and restored belief in justice; as a deterrent; as a means of resurrecting cultural practices and place as a social, living space.

Public processes such as exhumations, burials and trials act as an avenue of empowerment, a form of agency, a sign that fear and forgetting have been overcome, and link truth to power. In this context, collective recovery of community memory can begin to create new public spaces for community mobilisation. Safe community spaces for people to speak and be heard facilitate recuperation and the redefinition of collective identity in a context where collective identity is crucial to recovery. Although profound challenges remain – a history of forced civilian, mostly Maya, participation in civil patrols and therefore counter-insurgency violence, cultures of vertical and local impunity, with forensic anthropologists, who are potentially expert witnesses in forthcoming trials, under 24-hour protection against intimidation and death threats – the chapter documents the way in which public processes and places (a municipal plaza, a church, a clandestine cemetery) have been re-taken and re-made into sites of popular memory and action, seeking justice but also breaking onto an ever-widening range of issues.

As the chapters in this section illustrate, in part the contest over memory is one over whether there should be memory at all, the desirability of memory or at least certain kinds of highly politicised memory, and whose memory should prevail. Chapter 5 by Istvan Pogány, 'Memory and Forgetting: The Roma Holocaust', focuses on the Roma Holocaust or *Porajmos*, 'devouring' in Romani. He asks why such a disparity exists in the attention received by parallel crimes, the Jewish and Roma Holocausts. Interestingly, in the context of debates about the exceptionality of the Jewish Holocaust, Pogány analyses Nazi policies towards the Jews and the Roma for differences and similarities, wrestling with the question of how one finds a moral vocabulary for such a comparison. The author concludes that despite local variations, 'at its worst, the persecution of the Roma was indistinguishable from that of the Jews', and that in many parts of Europe 'in all probability' it would satisfy 'the definition of genocide or of complicity in genocide'. So he returns to the question: why has such suffering remained, on the whole, unacknowledged?

In attempting to understand why the Roma Holocaust remained largely forgotten until recently, the author concentrates on the attitudes of the Roma themselves. The chapter argues that the Roma are preoccupied with the immediate concerns, needs and injustices of the present, lack an interest in or desire to assert their often tragic past, and have no tradition of commemoration. Socioeconomic and political factors have also contributed to a lack of voice (poverty, illiteracy, social and cultural marginalisation, suspicion of authority, political impotence and the absence of a powerful state or diaspora). While silence may represent a conscious decision to put the past behind them, the voicing of a reluctant memory also takes on a particular inflection. The Roma, it is claimed, see themselves as lucky, shaping memory as a somewhat undemanding narrative of survival and good fortune. Such considerations sketch out areas of difference between the Roma and Jews in the aftermath of genocide. These themes are illustrated using interview material, which consistently upsets expectations. Pogány concludes by noting an increasingly vocal Roma public voice, demanding recognition of and compensation for the *Porajmos*, contesting the collective memory of the past, and, more worryingly, claiming an equivalence of victimisation alongside the Jews during the Holocaust.

IDENTITIES

The section on 'Identities' examines the sites and strategies of identity construction during political transition.

In Chapter 6 'Continuity and Discontinuity of East German Identity Following the Fall of the Berlin Wall: A Case Study', Molly Andrews raises a series of important questions about what happens to national identity during political transition. A past ambivalence towards an 'official' East German identity was replaced by a proliferation of other forms of East German identification as new spaces opened up for people to experience their common past and present. On the basis of interviews conducted in 1992 with leaders in the citizens' movements that led the 1989 revolution, Andrews plots 'a revolution of memory and identity'.

As one example of identity continuity and discontinuity, the destruction of the Berlin Wall coincided with a strengthening of an inner, mental wall, as differences between the two Germanies became increasingly recognised and even entrenched. A self-confident East German identity was embraced after the decline of East Germany, between the coming-down of the wall and unification: a nation proved its right of historical existence by freeing, and in effect eliminating, itself. There has also been an ambivalence towards, and rejection of, an East German identity and past alongside a reaction against the forced appropriation into a new identity epitomised by rapid unification (which occasioned a new identity crisis) and a perceived erasure or discrediting of the East German past, culture, and identity. An East German identity has been forged at the intersection of shared commonalities (history, experiences, culture), the rediscovery of difference and reassertion of self-respect. Sometimes still reactive, always relational, the post-communist East German identity is perhaps most importantly a revitalising of oppositional culture and identity. Identity and meaning, therefore, are much more complex and layered than a simplistic sourcing in a lost (or new) nation would suggest – in important ways they are additive rather than substitutive, and draw on universal human experiences and qualities. Andrews calls for researchers of identity to capture this complexity.

Several chapters in the book examine the construction and contestation of victim identities and victimhood. Chapter 7 by Graham Dawson, 'Mobilising Memories: Protestant and Unionist Victims' Groups and the Politics of Victimhood in the Irish Peace Process', is about the politics of Protestant/Unionist victimhood in Northern Ireland. Dawson argues that the Labour government's attempt, 'from above', to integrate the issue of victims within the framework of an inclusive peace process, thereby attempting to establish for itself a leadership and neutral arbiter role, was followed by a flowering 'from below' of victims' groups seeking to give victims a voice and present their interests. Among the results of this twinned, contested process were a variety of new political developments: for example, a framework for representation and recognition of victims, possibilities for reparation and redress, efforts to organise a new kind of public voice, and a contested politics of victimhood involving competing claims and hierarchies, as constituencies have found ways of 'fighting the war by other means'.

The bulk of the chapter draws on fieldwork with loyalist groups which experienced violence mainly at the hands of nationalist paramilitaries. These groups have mobilised memory work towards a range of objectives such as telling their side of the story (linking memory and identity, for example, in claims of 'ethnic cleansing' and 'genocide'), and seeking release, support, redress, recognition and acknowledgement in both private and public arenas. The author highlights the paradoxical impacts of such work for any possible future peace. For example, memory informs a new politics of perceived betrayal and injustice within the peace process and a 'hierarchy of victims' which effectively appropriates the category while rejecting any moral equivalence for Republican victims. Dawson concludes by arguing that victim groups are important because they constitute a new kind of public voice in Northern Ireland that both reproduces and challenges its politics of identity and because of their intrinsic value to the communities and individuals with which they work. The challenge is how to mobilise the energies released by such groups both for the psychological/emotional work of reparation and healing and for the political work of building peace.

Lars Buur, in Chapter 8, '"In the Name of the Victims": The Politics of Compensation in the Work of the South African Truth and Reconciliation Commission', looks at the emergence of 'victim' as a category and identity in the context of the South African Truth and Reconciliation Commission (TRC), where people from being victims of apartheid have become victims of the TRC in various ways, and thereby of transition itself. However, as Buur argues, people have also used the identity of victimhood to mobilise as political actors, within a sometimes fractious victim politics. He argues that crucial to the emergence of victims as a contested category was a complex interaction between various 'vectors': 'objectification' based on a rational/statistical system of knowledge-creation, identification and selection; an evolving and institutionally inconsistent 'taxonomy' of gross human-rights abuses; and the possibility of 'release', notably in the eventual use of the promise of reparations as an inducement to increase statement numbers.

These processes created tensions between victim expectations, TRC promises/recommendations and ANC policy commitments. Buur argues that the TRC and the ANC have clashed over the question of representivity, the complex relationship between representative group identities and entitlements. The ANC has marshalled various arguments – that South Africa is a nation of victims, that the struggle was not about money – to question the TRC's construction of the identity of victim and avoid/delay making reparation payments. Symbolic reparation for all is possible through the TRC's representative sample of victims, but in relation to material compensation to privilege the needs of a representative sample appear unjust. In this way the TRC, which was supposed to lay the foundation for peace and justice, in fact re-cast the conflict of the past and generated new conflicts that open onto a series of broader contemporary issues: how are limited resources to be allocated and to whom? How can the tensions be reconciled between a new dispensation that suggests the possibility of formal equality and the reality of deprivation and growing inequality? Buur concludes that what is at stake is nothing less that the legitimacy not only of the TRC, but of the new South Africa.

Fiona Ross, in Chapter 9, 'The Construction of Voice and Identity in the South African Truth and Reconciliation Commission', examines the construction of women's voice and identity, specifically women as victims, in the TRC's work. The TRC equated voice, being able to tell one's story, with the restoration of human and civil dignity, personal and national healing and with the creation of post-apartheid identities. But, the author asks, what happens if 'speaking pain' is not straightforward and simple? At the TRC's victim hearings a pattern became apparent in which women bore witness to the experience of others, generally husbands and sons, rather than talking about themselves. The operational definitions of the TRC seemed to preclude an analysis of the full range of apartheid's effects and their gendered nature. Gross violations of human rights focused on 'bodily integrity rights' which, the author argues, privileged the experiences of men, and more generally the 'spectacular' dimensions of apartheid rather than its more widespread impacts on experience and subjectivities. Furthermore, it was difficult personally, socially and culturally for women to testify about their experiences, especially about violations of a sexual nature, while others objected to the TRC's governing rationale and ethos.

Although there were attempts to remedy these shortcomings – explicit encouragement to women to talk about their own experience, the holding of a series of women's hearings, a separate chapter dedicated to women in the final report – the author argues that the emergence of 'women' as a category in the Commission's work carried with it assumptions about the nature and severity of particular harms, notably privileging sexual violence while silencing other kinds of experience. Ross discusses the validity of identifying 'women' as a category needing particular attention, as a 'supplementary intervention', arguing that 'women' became a category of essential difference while at the same time variance within the category was homogenised. The TRC, it is argued, generated and fixed a range of identities, simplifying complex subjectivities and social relationships. This narrow focus may serve to sanitise apartheid, reinscribe gender differences, and downplay agency and resistance.

RE-MAKING SPACE

The chapters in this section illustrate that oppression and resistance, authoritarianism and political transition, war and peace, have a spatial as well as a temporal dynamic. Further, transitions involve intersections between a variety of real and symbolic spaces (physical, social, ideological, economic, narrative – the local, national and global).

Joan Hackeling in Chapter 10, 'Remembering Ordinary Agency Under East German State Socialism: Revelations of the Rostock District Record, 1978–89', outlines a particular geography of life under oppression. It addresses local conflicts and ordinary agency in the Rostock District of the former East Germany between 1978 and 1989. The author contests the picture of ordinary life under communism as uniform and conformist or deeply fragmented and private, and argues from an examination of city and district records that conflicts and negotiations between residents and the authorities often took a geographical form. For example, residents demanded resource equality between different places and sought to manipulate private/public, personal/political and local/national differences and divisions for their own ends.

The chapter explores in greater detail the less discursive forms of geographical negotiation. For example, people moved controversial activities or indeed moved themselves, thereby exploiting differences between places in relation to levels of scrutiny and rule enforcement, bypassed local bureaucracies to petition more distant or higher state officials directly and negotiated the terms of their public attendance and participation (at work, school, in elections and state-sanctioned leisure and social activities). Both state control and the negotiation of differences with the authorities were, in part, place-based. Hackeling's argument is that ordinary residents acted on ordinary conflicts as geographical agents, in an attempt to create some flexibility in their lives. While such 'unheroic' practices should neither be romanticised nor exaggerated, they do provide a legacy of life in East Germany, a crucial prehistory to the events of 1989 and bequeath to East Germans a familiar precedent for active engagement in the public life of post-unification Germany.

Chapter 11 by Steven Marsh, 'Insinuating Spaces: Memories of a Madrid Neighbourhood During the Spanish Transition', also resonates with themes of geographical agency. In post-Franco Spain, he argues that the discourse of democracy and the device of transition have been used to construct and bind the population to a new national project, a new 'time' and social 'space' called 'democratic' Spain. Drawing on the work of de Certeau, the author insists on the agency of the subaltern and local to transgress, re-make the dominant official/national narratives of time and space, to tactically 'insinuate' themselves and their agendas within the ideological and physical space of dominant groups.

To illustrate this thesis, the chapter draws on oral testimony from Vallecas, a working-class part of Madrid, the most deprived areas of which were at the forefront of resistance to Franco in the late 1960s and 1970s. Residents' associations provided a training ground for a generation of future democratic political leaders. Furthermore, both during and post-Franco, they tactically used whatever resources were available – the church, the political left, the monarchy – to secure basic needs and human rights and then to gain political control over the contested 'space' of the district (to (re-)construct their homes and neighbourhoods, engage in a battle for the streets around the issue of naming, expose cuts in public spending and contest the relocation of the new Madrid regional parliament from the centre of the city to the margins). In the struggle over the re-making of the area, within the broader discourses of democracy and transition, the author argues that the city has been turned 'inside out'.

Carolyn Nordstrom in Chapter 12, 'Public Bad, Public Good(s) and Private Realities', addresses the layered spaces and politics of invisibility that characterise Angola's permanent war/transition. Here people inhabit private realities that are publicly erased and politically denied – invisible people and places, outside time, space, history, without memory, identity and voice. These invisibilities and erasures, the author argues, are crucial to the processes of global economics and politics. The chapter follows a journey that identifies linked layers of invisibility, parallel economic and political spaces, ascending from the no-man's-lands between the warring factions of the MPLA government and UNITA to global arenas of profit and power. Local networks of exchange, war and survival are set within global networks of exchange that loot the country and fuel the war.

In the resource-rich war zone, the MPLA and UNITA respectively control the urban areas/consumer goods and rural/food-producing regions. No-man's-lands are zones of obscene extremes, traversed by the invisible – such as women-traders whose children are held ransom for their return – oiling the system for government officials, assorted soldiers and traders, profiteers, racketeers and mafias. The more closed-off the borders and spaces, the more there is a need to trade and the more political trade becomes. Linking the local and the global are basic foodstuffs, minerals, weapons and the most unlikely luxury items; survival and death, misery and money/power, war and economics, periphery and centre are interwoven. Similarly, the informal (black-market, smuggling), illegal, extra-state shadow economy dwarfs, becomes more reliable than, and is inextricably linked to, the formal, legal and state; and in both war and peace money buys power. Nordstrom states that next to nothing is known about these eclipsed lives and economies and that this in itself is a very political act.

TESTIMONY AND VOICES

Huge expectations are placed on testimony/voice during political transition, as they both transcend divisions between, and knit together, the personal/private and public/political. Chapters in this section identify various sites or spaces of testimony and voice and plot linkages between voice and agency. All engage with the ethics, politics and power of voice. None more so that the last two chapters which contain first-person testimonies from South Africa and Ireland.

Julie Mertus, in Chapter 13, 'The Politics of Memory and International Trials for Wartime Rape', examines what prospects adversarial tribunals such as the International Criminal Tribunal for the Former Yugoslavia (ICTY) hold for women who see themselves as active agents of change seeking to use international advocacy as a personal and political tool. Mertus contends that war crimes trials alone cannot serve the various needs and interests of victims of sexual violence. She explores the limits of such tribunals for wartime rape through an analysis of the Foca case, decided by the ICTY in February 2001. The case resulted in the sentencing of three ethnic Serbs to imprisonment for their abuse of women at a 'rape camp' near Foca, a Bosnian town south-east of Sarajevo. Was this a landmark victory for the international women's human rights movement and/or a source of disappointment and re-traumatisation for the survivors?

Trials are never designed to tell the stories victims want to tell. Narratives are re-worked into what Mertus calls the legal 'anti-narrative' of segments, linearity, consistency, narrow legal definitions, sterile language and euphemism. Courts mistrust the natural voice of the survivor. The narrative is perpetrator-driven. The prosecution reduces the witness to the role of victim, relevant not as an agent but only insofar as her actions demonstrate something about the perpetrator. Survivors are not asked about their experiences of themselves and their survival. Defence lawyers seek to cast blame and discredit survivors. Rape survivors asserted their agency, but in a mute and distorted form, against the grain of legal process. Mertus concludes that survivors need space and opportunity to choose their narrative voice and form, which requires alternative and complementary witness/survivor-focused processes to international war crimes tribunals.

Eliza Tanner Hawkins, in Chapter 14, 'Networks of Memory: Chileans Debate Democracy and the Pinochet Legacy over an Internet Forum', discusses the online forum created by the Chilean

Newspaper *La Tercera* in the aftermath of the arrest of General Pinochet in London in October 1998. She argues that this event laid bare the unresolved tensions and divisions within Chilean society. In this context, the online forum created a public sphere or space, a communications network for debate for Chileans all over the world about the meaning and legacy of the Pinochet dictatorship. The chapter is based on a study of 1670 letters sent to *La Tercera*'s online forum between October 1998 and January 1999.

Tanner Hawkins outlines the distinctive characteristics of the online public space as including accessibility (related to wealth and class but unrestricted in other important ways, for example, geography), a new freedom to communicate, the way people communicate (exchanges of views, standards of civility), and the content of discussions. Specifically highlighted in the chapter are debates about the definition and quality of Chilean democracy. The internet provided a platform for a multitude of voices and a crash course in a culture of democracy. The consequences of such a space are identified as the formation of public opinion and of collective memories. Participants tried to understand the past in order to make sense of the present, specifically events surrounding the arrest of Pinochet. Supporters of Pinochet recalled problems during the Allende years casting Pinochet as the saviour of Chile, while his opponents stressed the human rights abuses of his tenure, called for justice and viewed the sharing of experiences and judicial actions as a form of vindication of their experiences and memories. This discussion is part of the process of re-writing (official) history, of the forging of a still contested, but perhaps increasingly consensual, collective identity and memory.

Yazir Henri is a former combatant and torture survivor whose life became caught up in the traumatic 'choiceless choice[s]' (Langer cited in Langer 1991:26) of political struggle. He states in Chapter 15, 'Reconciling Reconciliation: A Personal and Public Journey of Testifying Before the South African Truth and Reconciliation Commission', that the opportunity to testify before the TRC provided a (previously lacking) space to speak out in his own voice, to confront his past and reclaim his dignity. Outside the safe space of the TRC, however, was an unprotected public space in which Henri's story took on a life of its own as it was variously appropriated by others (the media, individual commentators, the TRC report).

> Since testifying ... I have been called many names, placed within several stories, given several histories and the most harmful of narratives ... have now become a part of my public face ... the agonised confessor ... the betrayer.

Henri's attempt to reclaim himself was undermined as his story/self was dismembered, re-told into the very narrative he went to the TRC to question, re-told into the lives/deaths, in the voice and narrative, of others. Henri delivers various other criticisms of the TRC, but perhaps his central question concerns the ethics and politics of voice.

Today Cape Town is a deeply divided city, characterised by the legacy of apartheid: violence, socioeconomic deprivation and segregation, white privilege. Henri argues that there remains a need for supportive spaces where South Africans can explore their mutual humanity. One such supportive space is provided by the Direct Action Centre for Peace and Memory and the Western Cape Action Tour Project (WECAT). It started as a self-help network motivated by the need to break the cycle of victimhood in the context of demobilisation, post-traumatic stress disorder and unemployment. Henri describes WECAT's 'heritage tours', designed to facilitate encounters with the historical and present-day life of marginalised and traumatised communities. Encounters occur around places that have witnessed immense pain; place transforms and is transformed, situating recognition, commemoration and acknowledgement. Henri talks of creating a 'memorial marker [that] is human, alive and dialogic'. Reconciliation for this author is crucially about such encounters, about responsibility and resurrecting hope.

Ella O'Dwyer testifies to a story that is both personal and political, private and public. Imprisoned in England as an Irish Republican prisoner, O'Dwyer describes herself as having studied the processes of institutionalisation and control through literature, informed by the work of Foucault, from within the confines of prison and Empire. In Chapter 16, 'Empire Dies for Irish Freedom: Silence and Amnesia in Anglo-Irish Talks', she unpacks the strategic deployment of language and discourse as weapons in the context of incarceration and the Irish conflict: the war of words encompassing silence, statement, amnesia (say and sign nothing); slogan and repetition; creative annihilation and compulsive control; agreement and treaty. Within the frame of prison, colony and Empire, the subaltern struggles to speak at all, has her voice interned, embargoed, stammers a disjointed, disjunctive discourse, is only able to speak from within another's discourse in an occupied voice. O'Dwyer finds an analogy in Samuel Beckett's Molloy, moving 16 stones around his person so that he can suck each one on a perfectly consecutive basis. This, she argues, can be seen to bear a striking resemblance to the Irish interface with Empire as Molloy personifies both inadequate expression and the compulsion to control.

O'Dwyer states that a history of treaties and agreements cannot indefinitely intern contradictions, disagreement, fear and resistance within the national voice or narrative. The colonist comes to fear both the known and the unknown, agreement and silence. She concludes with the suggestive proposition that silence and amnesia are agents of vision, in that they have protected voice and memory in secure places. They await their opportunity to make history, both as the story of the past but also as the strategic architect of the future. In the words of Barbara Harlow (1996), the dilemma now is a classic of the transitional move from interrogation to negotiation: when to talk and when not to talk.

NOTES

1. Collective (or social) memory, as stories and practices about the past told and enacted by society or groups within society, to themselves and others, can be said to incorporate but transcend, be shaped by and in turn shape, individual experiences and official narratives through various kinds of communicative sharing and contestation (of experience, knowledge, emotion, reaction). It reworks memories through collaboration, corroboration and dispute, providing an evolving template for comparison, identification, evaluation and debate.

2. Individual memory combines psychological processes of recall, learning and forgetting with an insistence that even the most personal and private memories are socially, culturally and politically informed. There is a context to each act of remembrance. Individual memory in various ways spans the private and public domains, the psychological, experiential and the social/interactive.

REFERENCES

Amadiume, Ifi and Abdullahi An-Na'im (eds). 2000. *The Politics of Memory: Truth, Healing and Social Justice*. London: Zed Books.

Boraine, Alex. 2000. *A Country Unmasked: Inside South Africa's Truth and Reconciliation Commission*. Oxford: Oxford University Press.

Cohen, Stanley. 2001. *States of Denial: Knowing About Atrocities and Suffering*. Cambridge: Polity Press.

Cruz, Consuelo. 2000. 'Identity and Persuasion: How Nations Remember Their Pasts and Make Their Futures', *World Politics* 52:275–312.

de Brito, Alexandra, Carmen Gonzaléz-Enríquez and Paloma Aguilar. 2001. 'Introduction', in Alexandra de Brito et al. (eds) *The Politics of Memory: Transitional Justice in Democratizing Societies*. Oxford:Oxford University Press.

Gillis, John. 1994. 'Memory and Identity: The History of a Relationship', in John Gillis (ed.) *Commemorations: The Politics of National Identity*. Princeton: Princeton University Press.

Harlow, B. 1996. *After Lives: Legacies of Revolutionary Writing*. London: Verso.

Hartman, Geoffrey. 2000. 'Memory.com: Tele-Suffering and Testimony in the Dot Com Era', *Raritan* 19(3):1–18.

Ignatieff, Michael. 1996. 'Articles of Faith', *Index on Censorship* 25(5):110–22.

Jelin, Elizabeth. 1998. 'The Minefields of Memory', *NACLA* 32(2):23–9.

Langer, Lawrence. 1991. *Holocaust Testimonies: The Ruins of Memory*. New Haven: Yale University Press.

Maier, Charles. 1993. 'A Surfeit of Memory? Reflections on History, Melancholy and Denial', *History and Memory* 5(2):136–52.

Mamdani, Mahmood. 2000. 'The Truth According to the TRC', in Ifi Amadiume and Abdullahi An-Na'im (eds) *The Politics of Memory: Truth, Healing and Social Justice*. London: Zed Books.

Mertus, Julie. 2000. 'Truth in a Box: The Limits of Justice Through Judicial Mechanisms', in Ifi Amadiume and Abdullahi An-Na'im (eds) *The Politics of Memory: Truth, Healing and Social Justice*. London: Zed Books.

Novick, Peter. 2001. *The Holocaust and Collective Memory: The American Experience*. London: Bloomsbury.

Osiel, Mark. 2000. *Mass Atrocity, Collective Memory, and the Law*. New Brunswick: Transaction Publishers.

Slaughter, Joseph. 1997. 'A Question of Narration: The Voice in International Human Rights Law', *Human Rights Quarterly* 19:406–30.

Taussig, M. 1992. *The Nervous System*. New York: Routledge.

Werbner, Richard. 1998. 'Introduction: Beyond Oblivion: Confronting Memory Crisis', in Richard Werbner (ed.) *Memory and the Postcolony: African Anthropology and the Critique of Power*. London: Zed Books.

Zertal, Idith. 2000. 'From the People's Hall to the Wailing Wall: A Study in Memory, Fear, and War', *Representations* 69:96–126.

Part I
The Politics of Memory

2 Remembering and Forgetting 'Zimbabwe': Towards a Third Transition

Christine Sylvester

Commenting on Zimbabwe's 1990 elections, Jonathan Moyo (1992), then a lecturer at the University of Zimbabwe, attributed a three-seat parliamentary loss for the ruling party 'to the unpopularity of ZANU(PF) rather than to the popularity of the opposition' (145). The party was unpopular, he said, because it was trying to establish a *de jure* one-party state that would ban opposition parties and unseat their elected members of parliament. Ten years later, seemingly forgetting the ruling party's old sources of unpopularity – and the new ones it had since cultivated – Moyo directed ZANU (PF)'s election effort against a vigorous new party – the Movement for Democratic Change (MDC) – which did seem to be popular. ZANU (PF) just won, but the outcome of election 2000 was significant as its automatic two-thirds parliamentary majority was now gone. One measure of ZANU (PF)'s relative unpopularity in 2000 could be seen in the ousting of several key incumbents; but even more than this, the margins of defeat by ZANU (PF) candidates running in Harare and Bulawayo were stunning and unprecedented.[1]

The 2000 election contest culminated ZANU (PF)'s long-time efforts to shape national memories to downplay its ambivalent and worsening governance record and play up its historic role as the founding party of Zimbabwe. This time its candidates and spokespersons repeatedly revisited the realm of anti-colonial memory, asking voters to bear in mind how things had been in Rhodesia and how instrumental ZANU (PF) forces had been in rescuing the country. Despite an intervening 20 years, despite Mugabe's advanced age, ZANU (PF) was young again – at least in its campaign pitches. It was 'progressive' again on issues of land redistribution and fierce once more towards all practices it deemed colonial. The MDC countered by presenting ZANU (PF) as an incompetent, corrupt and quasi-terrorist organisation of old men. ZANU (PF) did not respond directly; it steered clear of its 'now' and conjured up a time when it was promising but 'not yet' in power. That strategy enabled it to shift blame for public policy failings onto a variety of colonial/imperial ghosts, chiefly white farmers, Britain and the International Monetary Fund (IMF). By looking backwards as a way of managing an unpopular present, ZANU (PF) hoped to write a ticket to the future, and to do so with its everyday failings as a government in full public view.

Vote ZANU (PF), it said, and 'Zimbabwe Will Never Be a Colony Again.'[2] But what would it be? That is the debate in Zimbabwe today and the question I consider here by revisiting the country's post-colonial history in light of ZANU (PF)'s self-glorifying myths about making 'Zimbabwe'. Three periods of transition from colonialism can be discerned and sketched.

The first period (1980 to 1990) brought socialist promises, growth with equity economics, and some indigenous well-being. It emptied into the second period of transition (1990–97) of structural adjustment economics and a politics of the belly that threatened all previous achievements (Bayart 1993). A third period began with the rise of civil society claims on the state in 1997 and continues with the present struggle between democratic and sharply autocratic tendencies. Within these eras, national elections serve as moments when a range of contending mythologies about 'the true' post-colonial Zimbabwe can be heard. Of particular concern are the myths ZANU (PF) built about itself relative to its performance in office and relative to the view of it presented by competing parties, the media and members of civil society.

REMEMBERING THE 'NOT YET' AND FORGETTING THE 'NOW'

Memory has become an important analytic tool for studying the constitution, representation and manipulation of history and identity in many contexts. It has been a key tool in post-colonial analytic efforts to answer back to imperial images of colonies as places we need remember only in the context of western history. At the risk of simplifying a diverse body of research, one can say that post-colonial analysis remembers, recovers, theorises and evokes details of daily life that manifest agency, victimhood and interpenetrated cultures and knowledges. These are precisely the factors that tend to be omitted from imperial histories and often from tales of nationalist heroics. Post-colonial scholarship has been conducted around ordinary women, workers and peasants (Ranger 1985, Barnes and Win 1992, Schmidt 1992, Raftopoulos and Yoshikuni (eds) 1999). It has reported on people injured by nationalist guerrillas in the struggle to free Zimbabwe from colonial control (Staunton (ed.) 1990, Kriger 1992) and has showcased resistance and the ironic choices people make in the face of colonial policy.[3]

Dipesh Chakrabarty's recent post-colonial work helps us theorise Zimbabwe's memory politics. He argues that colonial history consigned non-western societies to 'an imaginary waiting room of history' (2000:8), a period of 'not yet' being ready to govern themselves. European overlords were the 'now' – fully in the modern present and engaged in an ethical and scientific project of shaping the world for everyone. Anti-colonial movements demanded their time, their movements, their voting rights, their states. Once in power, however, to extend Chakrabarty's point, some acted as though average citizens, in the 'now' by virtue of being given the franchise, were nonetheless 'not yet civilized enough to rule themselves' (ibid.). New regimes often invented 'the people' both as active agents of history and as automatic followers of a few heroic men. Robert Mugabe has been adept at billing himself as indispensable to the 'not yet' era of late colonial Rhodesia, to the post-colonial 'now' of Zimbabwe *and* to what 'will be' in the future. Heroic indispensability is insisted on through force and through manipulations of historical memory to immortalise some anti-colonial movements and cast out a range of others. The process leads to 'scriptualized memory' (Werbner (ed.) 1998:15), and stands as a reminder of Homi Bhabha's (1994) simple statement that 'remembering is never a quiet act of introspection or retrospection' (63).[4]

ZANU (PF) administered a large dose of scriptualised memory to Zimbabweans in the lead-up to the 2000 parliamentary elections. Yet its engagement in memory politics was not new. Previous research shows that each national election period in Zimbabwe saw efforts to define, fix in people's minds, and render hegemonic one guiding myth of Zimbabwe and one proper set of citizen–state relations (Sylvester 1986, 1990, 1995). ZANU (PF)'s use of remembering and forgetting in the 2000 elections was more intense, transparent and cynically nostalgic. Yet despite its efforts – as well as the violence, and intimidatory tactics it used – large numbers of the electorate walked out on the ZANU (PF) performance of anti-colonial yesterday. Many refused to forget the pain of the 'now' (high inflation, prices and unemployment; fuel shortages; farm seizures; and epidemic levels of HIV/Aids) for a remembered 'not yet' of ZANU (PF) parading itself as the 'will be' of Zimbabwe's future. We could also say that there was some refusal among the electorate, bringing Wole Soyinka's (2000) poetic words to bear, to 'lose itself in the labyrinths of the past' (21) – labyrinths that promised ways forward but often delivered only memories of those promises.

TRANSITIONING 'ZIMBABWE'

There are two periods of ZANU (PF)-led transition from colonial to post-colonial political economy and a third that has been emerging since around 1997. Although each period can be demarcated, there is overlap such that no one period offers one unmistakable, wholly dominant trend. What we see in Zimbabwe is the sense Chakrabarty offers of the 'not yet' bound up to futures that both already 'are' (futures inescapably interacting with pasts in fragmented daily ways) and that the regime insists 'will be' made in the image it wants. To construct a 'will be' in this context, political mythologies and memories work upon each other. Leonard Thompson (1985) notes that political mythology is a cluster of tales told about the past that 'reinforce one another and jointly constitute the historical element in the ideology of the regime or its rival' (1). The tales can narrate events leading to the foundations of a state or radically discredit the past or a particular set of practices in the present. Parts of the mythology need not be logically consistent to be effective. Thompson found the Ceausescu government of Romania, a regime the ZANU (PF) government admired, weaving tales of a pre-Christian monarchy into a socialist/patrimonial *mélange*. Similarly, Zimbabwe's first ten years saw Marxist proclamations about the importance of peasants and proletarians harnessed to ZANU (PF)'s determination to define and direct the country single-handedly, even if that meant killing certain proletarians and peasants. The country then underwent free market adjustments and increasing degrees of freeloading by many ZANU (PF) patrons; and yet the party maintained a vague socialist style and never stopped enacting itself as the always already indispensable wisdom of Zimbabwe. We see these aspects of memory and myth operating across the three periods of transition.

FROM THE NATIONALIST 'NOW' TO A COMPROMISED MARXIST 'WILL BE'

The first decade of ZANU (PF) rule saw Marxism dominating the rhetoric of state, liberal socialism working through a mostly autarkic economy and authoritarian tendencies catching average Zimbabweans accused of opposing ZANU (PF)'s power or plans (Sylvester 1991). The mix had a history in the armed struggle and settler colonial rule, the climate of governance at independence and a combination of two post-colonial models common in the 1970s: democracy *cum* economic liberalism versus Marxian political economy. ZANU (PF) maintained that it alone could guide the 'now' into the 'what will be' because it had singular responsibility for removing the settler regime and sole entitlement to 'reap the ripe peaches we have tended'.[5]

ZANU (PF)'s stated plan was to lead a two-stage process of transition from capitalism to socialism. Peasants and proletarians would initially benefit from policies of redistributive economic justice and bourgeois political rights. These moves would consolidate the post-colony, bring democracy to the entire population and begin to redress an inequitable history. In a vague second stage, ZANU (PF) would restructure the national economy so that inherited capitalist elements would give way to socialist forms of production (ZANU (PF) 1984, Government of Zimbabwe 1982). The government made some progress in enacting first-stage promises. Its investments in education and health care significantly improved conditions for black Africans over those remembered from colonial days. Discriminatory legislation fell before new laws that granted African women as well as men majority status at age 18, and changed colonial employment practices.

Facing a global recession in the early 1980s, which affected Zimbabwe's mineral exports, and a high post-war population growth rate (3.3 per cent), government issued investment guidelines in 1982 but put off investors by refusing to sign an overseas private investment insurance agreement, by keeping a tight rein on foreign exchange and by maintaining radical rhetoric. Other compromises cut deeper into the Marxist dream. Insisting it would resettle 162,000 peasant families on land either abandoned by fleeing owners during the armed struggle or purchased under the constitutional terms of willing buyer/willing seller (with donor money), the government had settled only 70,000 families by the end of the 1980s. Socialist co-operatives were started but not provided with resources (Makumbe 1996: Chapter 3); meanwhile, party officials grabbed expensive homes, farms and cars.

On it went like this. Government then unleashed the infamous North Korean-trained Fifth Brigade against the heartland of the only viable opposition in the country – PF-ZAPU. We now know that its targets extended far beyond the estimated 300 to 3,000 ZAPU loyalists accused of sabotaging the new state (estimate from Kriger 1995:149). The large-scale atrocities of the *Gukurahundi* (washing away the beaten chaff) aimed to ensure that ZAPU and other 'misreadings' of Zimbabwe would be erased from the 'will be'. National memories were to be forcibly adjusted in the direction of ZANU (PF); but the futures that already 'are' were wrapped in memories of slaughter that would weaken ZANU (PF)'s claim to lead all of Zimbabwe. Opposition, harshly dealt with in the first transition, was neither forgotten over 20 years nor superseded. That this was so became clear in the 1990s, when the government was forced to open the Fifth Brigade activities to investigation.[6]

Elsewhere in the political economy the policies tilted less towards Marxist promises than to pragmatic ends couched in ZANU (PF)'s self-memorialising rhetoric (see Sylvester 1985). Take reconciliation. Mugabe famously pronounced the 'now' as a time of reconciliation between the races (perhaps as a first-stage accommodation with capital), and it did seem that EuroZimbabweans had it easier in the immediate post-colonial years than many Black Zimbabweans. They were often berated humiliatingly by the government; but they were not hunted, nor were their heroes decapitated (Kriger 1995:139–62). Yet Nathan Shamuyarira, then Minister of Information, spoke of 'reconciling us to the reality of our independence, the death of colonialism and the national aspirations of the people' (see ibid. 141). The 'death of colonialism' suggested the harsher, anti-EuroZimbabwean side of the first transitional promises of reconciliation.

That some of those (Zimbabwean as opposed to colonial Rhodesian) 'people' might be forced to reconcile to a 'will be' that did not fit their preferences became somewhat clearer after the *Gukurahundi* and the forced merger of ZANU and ZAPU in 1987; so did the sense of who would articulate 'the' memory (reality) of 'our' independence. Absent the effort to record the undersides of colonial rule through a truth and reconciliation commission, and against the backdrop of unreconciliatory farm invasions 20 years later – which hit out against EuroZimbabwean farm owners *and* black farm workers – some try to remember reconciliation in the 1980s only to forget details of its enunciation.[7] Add ZANU (PF)'s extreme sensitivity to opposition of all kinds and the pragmatic transition within the Marxist transition gets inscribed with Marxist, liberal and authoritarian myths and memories that ZANU (PF) cannot fully control. By the time of the 1990 elections, ZANU (PF)'s effort to have the country forget PF-ZAPU, and a history of more inconsequential would-be parties and agendas, would fall in on itself as a renegade ZANU (PF) member established a new party – Zimbabwe Unity Party (ZUM). Despite plentiful weaknesses, ZUM won three seats and nearly 30 per cent of the vote.

FROM A MARXIST 'NOT YET' TO A NEO-LIBERAL 'NOW'

By the 1990 elections, parliamentary seats reserved for whites had been overturned constitutionally, PF-ZAPU was part of ZANU (PF), and the party-government had replaced the Westminster model with a presidential system that gave the head of state more autonomy from parliament and more power. Marxism was recited at official ZANU (PF)'s levels as 'adapted to our own objective and historical circumstances' (ZANU (PF) 1990:3–4). One adaptation was to be a unified, dissidence-absent 'povo' (people) led by ZANU (PF). Another would materialise slightly later as a full-blown, neo-liberal economic agenda.

The unity theme was not new, but the single-mindedness of the message was. With ZAPU officially absorbed, ZANU (PF) slated itself to become the centrepiece of all Zimbabwean memory and action, and hoped to finalise this 'inevitability' through the election. The plan was for ZANU (PF) to sweep every seat and turn Zimbabwe into a *de facto* one-party state in time for the tenth anniversary of the country on 18 April 1990 (Moyo 1992:144). ZANU (PF) would be 'educating the people and creating *for them* concrete experiences which help them to identify more and more with national goals and programmes' (Mugabe 1989:347, emphasis added). Here was the colonial 'not yet' raising its head again, this time as the self-proclaimed font of knowledge and national identity. Mugabe justified national unity as 'the capacity and power to sublimate ... inferior and divisive energies into a superior and transcendent spirit ... a nobler social outlook' (ibid.:356). ZANU (PF) alone defined nobility. Unity around ZANU (PF) would also be fun, organic, and safe, 'one open political forum, one family of free and active participants' (ibid.:356). ZANU (PF) would provide the fencing around the family playground.

Jonathan Moyo (1992) maintained at the time that 'ZANU(PF) destroyed its own case for a legislated one-party state' in 1990 by increasingly tolerating violations of its leadership code and by reacting aggressively whenever the Zimbabwe Congress of Trade Unions (ZCTU) and University of Zimbabwe students lashed out against 'inflation, unemployment, shortage of transport and shortage of housing which had become ubiquitous' (31–2). The world had changed too – not just in the fall of a Cold War bloc but with the release of Nelson Mandela in South Africa and challenges to the single-party credo across Africa. ZANU (PF) was late for the single-party train; but the memory kept running down its track long after the last puff of smoke disappeared.

What followed the elections in the economy came as something of a surprise to many Zimbabweans: the Marxist myth *cum* pragmatic emphasis on growth with equity deflated and spun into outright liberalisation and adjustment.[8] A structural adjustment programme was enacted that the government initially described as 'homegrown', meaning not dictated by the IMF or World Bank or beholden to their conditionalities, though their monies were involved. A government that had mouthed Marxist axioms a few months earlier had reason to lay down the memory of ESAP as our 'will be' not theirs. However, as Austin Chakaodza (1993) points out, investment-geared 'trade liberalisation policy introduced by the government was one of the major conditionalities demanded by the IMF-World Bank before granting Zimbabwe new borrowings' (61). The demands then widened to include liberalising foreign currency allocations, reforming parastatals, ending protection for non-productive import-substituting industries and increasing profit remittance abroad.

All this activity eventuated in retrenchments, higher prices for consumer goods, and widespread user-pays fees in education and health. Having undercut government's claims about one-party democracy, Moyo condemned structural adjustment as the 'avarice and usury of vested interests in politics and business' (Chakaodza 1993:64). The Social Dimensions of Adjustment Programme introduced in 1993 provided help for very poor households earning less than Z$400 per month, some training courses and loans for new businesses. There were few other safety nets, however, in what has been described as the shift (or transition) 'from state paternalism to donor paternalism'.[9] ZANU (PF) lost the hazy homegrown plot to the international financial institutions.

Then Minister of Mines, Eddison Zvobgo, speaking on the Zimbabwe Broadcasting Service ('Election 1995', 5 April 1995) boasted during the 1995 election campaign that ZANU (PF) had brought Zimbabwe the economic structural adjustment programme. It is important to point out, however, that the ZANU (PF) election manifesto did not mention ESAP. Other than the odd, openly stated turnabout in the politics of memory, such as this one, the ZANU (PF) campaign was noteworthy for covering its insecurities and silences with a rah-rah spirit, while a flimsy and divided opposition mostly huffed and puffed. That fractured opposition, though thoroughly undistinguished, did introduce a theme to the electorate that would recur in a stunning way five years later – constitutional reform. It hammered at the issue of a constitution that was effectively keeping opposition out of office, through the device of presidentially appointed seats in parliament and the first-past-the-post system. Although this scope of complaint was narrow, a window opened to view the legal document ZANU (PF) had amended and reconstructed over the years, ostensibly to improve governance of the country but increasingly, it was said, to perpetuate itself as the 'will be' of Zimbabwe.

As for the actual 1995 election, it was a dismal affair in which, yet again, it seemed Zimbabwe could not produce a viable opposition to challenge ZANU (PF). Opposition was around but not in a form that could win elections and lead a new transition out of ESAP hardships and stale Marxist promises (Sylvester 1995:403; also Darnolf 1997). When Zimbabweans turned out in low numbers for an election that was not a contest,[10] we might say that by 1995 ZANU (PF) had attained some hegemony through the pretences of its indispensable memory and its superb talent at co-opting dissent and offering side-payments to supporters. But that hegemony was thin and brittle (see Scott 1990), for what ZANU (PF) was not successful at pulling off was the notion that it alone was the receptacle of *all* post-colonial memory and nationhood. There were generational splits in ZANU (PF) by 1995 as well as fights outside it over who should get the spoils from the system (see Sylvester 1995). Most telling, the party could not compete in an election without engaging painful memories of its vengeful, authoritarian streak. John Makumbe said at the time that '[t]he public is all the time looking over its shoulders when it comes to discussing political views that are contrary to those of the ruling party' (Makumbe 1994:1). ZANU (PF) thus could not end social conflict, corral all loyalty or determine the values in its own house. All it could effectively do – and it was very good at this – was wear its liberation halo and hand out prizes, such as commercial farms destined for resettlement, to cronies. By late 1997 there was a sense in the country, articulated by Sithole (1998), that 'Zimbabwe is on the brink of losing national integrity' (19).

A THIRD TRANSITION: BACK TO THE FIRST 'WILL BE'?

Sithole made his comment in the context of what some think of an ironic turning point in (formal) opposition-less ZANU (PF) rule in 1997: the rise of pluralism through the unlikely vehicle of harsh war-veteran power. Events began in 1997 when the War Veterans Association, led by the late Chenjerai 'Hitler' Hunzvi, a man who had had only minimal liberation experience, challenged the party outright time and again. Re-running memories of the early 1980s, veterans under him claimed that the victorious party-state had inadequately compensated those who had secured Zimbabwe for it, despite the demobilisation allowances paid in 1980. In August 1997, after violent protests, the government granted military-trained ex-combatants a Z$50,000 lump sum pension and Z$2,000 monthly payments – all tax-free. In addition, it promised a comprehensive package of free education and health services for the veterans, as well as funds to start businesses. The one additional promise would be twisted three years later into a war veterans' campaign against EuroZimbabwean farmers: Mugabe pledged that 20 per cent of resettlement lands would go to ex-combatants.

Despite veterans receiving unprecedented allowances, which the government could ill afford – indeed, their compensations came out of workers' pay, an issue that galvanised the ZCTU – their clamour continued. Hundreds who could not meet the terms of the awards, because they could not prove formal military training or that they had participated consistently and persistently in the struggle between January 1962 and March 1980, demonstrated and rioted in subsequent months. Sithole (1998) explains that a political war then began with rippling effects. Guerrilla ex-combatants, from ZANLA and ZIPRA, and then the *mujibhas* and *chimbwidos* who had linked the communities to the guerrillas during the war, widows of heroes, victims of *Gukurahundi* and all others who could remember the promises of liberation, were part of that political war. These people felt cut out of what he calls the 'independence dividend'. They wanted 'the forgetful political class' (14) to remember them. The timing of these memory flashbacks corresponded to the sharp decline of the Zimbabwean economy throughout the 1990s and the sense that no effective opposition party would arise after the 1995 elections to take ZANU (PF)'s 'now' to one that could include ordinary Zimbabweans.

In July 1997 the government established a National Economic Consultative Forum to discuss the state of the economy, and among the invitees was the ZCTU. The labour movement refused to attend. 'Our position as the ZCTU is very clear', said then Secretary-General, Morgan Tsvangirai, 'we are not participating at this circus' (*Financial Gazette* 22 January 1998:3). It claimed that the government had stolen its idea and was now seeking to control the Forum for its own cynical ends. Thereafter the ZCTU set itself in an increasingly adversarial position to a government that had initiated the union movement and once controlled it (see Schiphorst 2001). It participated actively in the newly formed National Constitutional Assembly (NCA), a front of human rights groups, non-governmental organisations and labour seeking constitutional reforms and a change of government as the answer to state excesses. The ZANU (PF) government tried to pre-empt the NCA by appointing a Constitutional Commission to draft a legal document for the new millennium.

A resurgent land issue was another consequence of civil society awakenings appropriating ZANU (PF) plans. Resettlement had been on the ZANU (PF) agenda since the earliest days of independence. However, despite the availability of donor funds to buy out white farms and/or to install proper rural infrastructures, the government had not moved ahead much except to distribute some farms in patronage schemes for its supporters. Sam Moyo (1999) remembers the 1980s as the problem period for land, writing that 'redistribution and restitution issues were insufficiently treated in critical policy making or academic discourses of human, basic or legal rights in Zimbabwe' (1). Land became a neglected issue, he said, for all major donors except Britain, which provided funds and technical support to acquire and resettle land. By the 1990s a politics of remembering land was possible and ZANU (PF) began to orchestrate it as a way both of managing unruly war veterans and of preserving the myth it had created about itself as the champion of rural Zimbabweans.

There was disagreement on the contours of the resources-to-the-people situation in the late 1990s, and on remedies to halt an unfolding transition from structural adjustment to economic meltdown. On the war compensation issue, Sithole (1997a), for one, argued that everyone had suffered in the Zimbabwean anti-colonial war and therefore 'any reward system would be divisive and should not be attempted' (16). On the land issue, he wrote late in 1997 that 'those who are asking the land question are asking the wrong question: rather they should be asking the "factory question"' (1997:7). Sithole saw Zimbabweans as urban or peri-urban aspirants, and '[p]easants are a class in exit ... The answer for most of our people is in more factories, not the elusive "promised land"' (ibid.:8).

In January 1998 food riots occurred when the prices of basic foods increased sharply. For the first time since taking office, the ZANU (PF) government ordered the troops out to quell mobs that were looting shops for food and other items. Over 800 people were arrested and schools and businesses closed for at least three days. Elsewhere, government offices were targeted by citizens who had been on the housing waiting list since the early 1960s or who were still waiting for telephone lines nearly 20 years after independence.

Opposition also continued to exist within ZANU (PF). In April 1999, a ZANU (PF) parliamentarian attacked Mugabe's leadership and was hauled before the party disciplinary committee. There was some outcry within the party at this move and at the detention and torture of two journalist critics who had reported on an attempted military coup; yet the government defied a court order to release them. Opposition then extended to the international community. The US froze aid money to Zimbabwe, claiming the government had developed a poor record on human rights and was disregarding the rule of law. The IMF had taken a similar move seven months earlier for reasons of the government's poor fiscal performance. Italy would later pull aid for an electrification project, and the Dutch, citing economic mismanagement and the country's involvement in the Congo war, would drop new aid initiatives as well. No matter. The ZANU (PF) government committed itself fully to the war in the Democratic Republic of Congo, appropriating over one billion dollars to fund its share of the war effort. In August 1999 it brazenly gave cabinet ministers and deputies a 182 per cent pay increase. ZANU (PF)'s memory of itself as unpopular in the 1990 and 1995 elections was short and its arrogance grand.

The main response within Zimbabwe to months of shocking decisions by the ZANU (PF) government was the formation of the MDC. An estimated 20,000 Zimbabweans gathered in Harare's Rufaro Stadium in September 1999 for the official launch of the movement into a party. Successive speakers pledged to remove the government from office and take Zimbabwe into a social democratic transition, away from economic instability, unemployment, land problems, closed government and corruption. In effect, the pledges were to return Zimbabwean memory to early post-colonial days, before ZANU (PF) had done serious damage to the country. The old agenda of reconciliation was on the MDC agenda too, as it put together a coalition of seemingly opposed memory holders: labour, the intelligentsia, activists, EuroZimbabweans (many of them politically inactive from 1990 on), and urban dwellers in general. Sithole (1999) remarked at the time that the strength of MDC is in the workforce (1), a workforce that was urban, class spanning and irritable.

Mugabe lashed out at the new party, the ZCTU and Britain, where he had met a rough reception in October 1998 for – on top of all else – his homophobic attitudes. Accusing donors and the British of financing the MDC 'enemy of Zimbabwe', he countered by trying to take back 'the' national 'now' and 'will be' that the MDC was threatening to fragment. In the face of a 25 per cent AIDS rate, unemployment at more than 50 per cent, inflation running to nearly 70 per cent, a fuel shortage, hospitals with few medicines and a depleted stock of foreign exchange, the party and president did not labour to develop a recovery plan for the country and publicise its merits. Rather, it tried to shove the present of the entire country into a ZANU (PF) script of past glory.

The event that begot that strategy in earnest was the constitutional referendum. After several months of government-led work on a new constitution, which included extensive national canvassing and participation by civil society (geared to pre-empt the NCA from leading the process itself), the ZANU (PF)-heavy draft came to a referendum vote. On 16 February 2000, 55 per cent of the few (half million out of 5 million registered) Zimbabwean voters who turned out rejected the proposed constitution. In a rehearsal for the 2000 parliamentary elections, the electorate in Harare and Bulawayo swung the vote towards 'no'. The MDC had campaigned vigorously against the constitution, and ZANU (PF) for it, through the reborn Jonathan Moyo. Analysts argued once again that the outcome of the constitutional referendum was more an artefact of ZANU (PF)'s unpopularity and perceived masterminding of the Commission than a rejection of the document (Raftopoulos 2000:11–12). But this time that unpopularity translated into votes and the first defeat the ruling ZANU (PF) party had faced since independence.

It also signalled the rise of cities as centres of Zimbabwean political activity again, a phenomenon not seen with such force since the early nationalist movement in the 1960s. One could call it a swing of memory ownership: heretofore, Rhodesians and then ZANU (PF) had portrayed Zimbabwe as a rural, peasantry-based country. Urbanites, plentiful and growing, were objects of ZANU (PF) suspicion, since many had voted for opposition parties throughout the late 1970s and early 1980s. In the 1990s, urbanites tended to stay away from elections altogether. The referendum marked a change, the urban claim to Zimbabwe. The key item torpedoed (it seemed) by the 'no' vote, was a plan to redistribute EuroZimbabwean lands without compensation by the Zimbabwean government, an issue that was not close to city dweller's hearts (see Mushonga 2000:14).

Instead of seeking causes for the referendum defeat in the hackneyed myths and unsound policies of government, Mugabe wandered off to the ever more wild side of politics by precipitating the EuroZimbabwean farm invasions and deaths. Less than a month after the referendum, the government formed a working alliance with the very war veterans that had earlier wreaked havoc on government nerves and budget. While the first wave of occupations was taking place, the government introduced a constitutional amendment aimed to acquire land without compensation by the Zimbabwean government. Britain, it was said, should be the compensating party. Forgetting 20 years of public policy – two post-colonial transitions under ZANU (PF) – the ruling party seemingly jumped vigorously on the bandwagon other civil society groups had started in motion with its own back-to-the-future approach to the millennial 'now'. Arguing as though they were still fighting Zimbabwe's war for independence, ZANU (PF) spokesmen on the farms spouted: 'We will not be pushed out from here. We have fought for this land before and, if it means we have to lay our lives for it again, so be it' (Reason Mukapira at Lilyford farm northwest of Harare: Mutsakani 2000:2).[11] Many of the 'veterans' were said to be unemployed non-veterans from areas other than those they invaded, or too young to have fought in the war; they were uniformly unpopular with farm workers. Mugabe, however, publicly thanked the invaders, replaying war themes to the peasantry. There was no need to change the contours of government. The true Zimbabweans – the majority rural keepers of correct ZANU (PF)-guided memories – would ensure that the party retained its place as educator of the nation.

Parliamentary elections were finally set for June 2000 and, as they came closer, the tempo of invasions picked up (900 farms were occupied by April) as did the violence, the anti-MDC rhetoric and ZANU (PF)-led racism. The extent of ZANU (PF) determination to win became evident when Mugabe said that he would fight the whites in order to get their land for blacks, and would fight MDC so that it and its white backers would never be able to let Britain into power in Zimbabwe. To many, the President sounded deluded, even deranged, and rumours circulated during the election period that Mugabe was suffering from various illnesses. He roared: 'Tsvangirai [now the head of the MDC and on leave from the ZCTU], is inviting fire for himself ... and fire burns' (Masamvu 2000:1), and the public mood swung sharply to fear. MDC supporters wearing their black T-shirts and sporting open-hand greetings, were subjected to violence and excluded from official media coverage of the campaign – except when they could be presented as a violent force. Meanwhile, foreign exchange reserves dwindled, an ongoing fuel crisis worsened and additional donor countries backed away from Zimbabwe.

Arguably the worst affected were the workers on invaded farms, especially those seen as backing the MDC by defending any white farmer. On some farms, they were force-marched to all-night *pungwes* (or the farm owner was made to transport them). These were orientation or education meetings that evoked memories of similar meetings called by the ZANLA guerrillas in the 1970s. As in the past, workers were kept awake all night singing old *Chimurenga* (war) songs and listening to speakers denounce whites and sell-outs. Sometime in the night the elders would often be sent away and the young women told to remain behind. The General Agricultural and Plantation Workers Union of Zimbabwe (GAPWUZ) was inundated with complaints of rape and harassment that recalled times during the independence war when young women were told to go with the guerrillas to the *poshito* – 'that meant', recalled one woman, 'you had to sleep with him' (Juliet Makonde in Staunton (ed.) 1990:49).

Farm workers also reported that war veterans had confiscated national identity cards, so that the aggrieved workers could not vote. Sometimes they were made to march to nearby farms against their will, and help the war veterans there to take over (author interview with Phillip Munyanyi, Secretary General of GAPWUZ, 23 June 2000). The 100,000-plus workers affected by the farm invasions were thereby bereft of recourse – they were not allowed to leave the farms – a situation that even the EuroZimbabwean farm owners did not face. GAPWUZ and the Employers Council of Zimbabwe endeavoured to establish a fund for farm workers, arguing that no one seemed to be including them in promises for land redistribution. As earlier, some Zimbabweans were 'the people' (the 'povo') and others were perpetually 'not yet'.

The then GAPWUZ Secretary General explained that, while it was good to share land, especially under-utilised areas of the large farms, people remembered the government record on land.

> In the 1985–6 resettlement period, ZANU (PF) provided no roads to the resettled areas, no transport, and now even some of the "war veterans" suspect the government won't do what it promises. The rest of us, we wonder: Is everyone supposed to become a farmer now? I remember growing up on a commercial farm and now don't want to farm. But what other jobs are there to do? ZANU (PF) has no other plan. (ibid.)

He pointed out that nothing had been planted on the occupied farms for the next season, so 'even if a recovery programme were launched today, there would be no bread at Christmas [2000] and no foreign exchange earnings from tobacco sales to import any food'. Looking tired and stressed, he ended: 'You know, some of the children of farm workers have managed to run away. Look out in the streets and you'll see them with the other homeless kids, killing pigeons for food' (ibid.).

Drawn by the extraordinary actions in Zimbabwe, hundreds of international monitors came in for the elections. Mugabe raged at the veiled opposition to the ZANU (PF) government which this activity represented and stalled accreditation, refusing observers from international NGOs and countenancing war veteran boasts that observers would not be allowed onto the farms. Up to the eve of the polling, the government-controlled media blamed the MDC for the violence that was receiving negative press abroad. However, the Zimbabwe Human Rights NonGovernmental Organisations Forum and others painted a very different picture, one of ZANU (PF) violence.[12] The ruling party had always incited violent provocation in the lead-up to the country's elections. Forgetting none of its old tricks, in 2000 it upped the ante.

ZANU (PF)'s party platform in 2000 contained a litany of difficulties forced on it by the IMF and World Bank during the 1990s. Vowing to extricate itself from these institutions, it claimed it would then eradicate poverty and corruption through a Zimbabwe Millennium Recovery Programme for 2000 to 2005, with unspecified funding. Mostly it emphasised the land issue as an anti-colonial symbol of the party. 'Land is the Economy and the Economy is Land', it proclaimed, thereby writing off concerns of urban dwellers. It would acquire land through a revolution (its word) that would be implicitly less socialist than authoritarian in nature (see Gwarinda 2000:1–4; 2000a:10–12).

The MDC's manifesto emphasised the need to restore prosperity and economic growth to the country. It wanted an immediate end to Zimbabwe's involvement in the Congo war, a reduced Cabinet size and more foreign investment. It proposed to root out corruption across Zimbabwean society and bring all, rather than selected, stakeholders into the process of constitutional reform. The party platform combined aspects of racial reconciliation from the 1980s with the neo-liberal thinking of the earlier 1990s. A key difference lay in its orientation to land: while ZANU (PF) repeatedly promised to 'acquire', 'seize', 'confiscate', 'fight white farmers' and 'resettle white farms', MDC spoke of introducing 'freehold title in communal and resettlement areas, to enable land to be used as security to attract much needed investment', and a tax on underused commercial land – a new approach entirely (MDC 2000:5).

When the polling days arrived, more than 3 million of Zimbabwe's 5 million registered voters turned out. As in the lower turn-out referendum vote, views tended to split between rural constituencies, which mostly returned ZANU (PF) candidates, often by wide margins, and the main two cities that turned away from ZANU (PF). Zimbabwe entered the new millennium with the old guard at the helm and the Young Turks breathing heavily down their necks. Multi-partyism was no longer simply a legal stipulation. Oppositional politics was the order of the 'now' and the instrument of ushering in a rectifying politics of multi-memories of Zimbabwe past and present. So it has continued into 2002, with the ZANU (PF) government taking extraordinary steps around the presidential elections to maintain Robert Mugabe as the only maker of a Zimbabwean 'now'.

INAPPROPRIATING THE 'NOW'

Up to 2000, national elections in Zimbabwe conformed to the mould that Ruth Collier (1982) found across Africa in the 1970s and 1980s: 'mobilised output participation, which is associated not with demand-making or even with the seeking of political office, but with the generation of support' (18n). ZANU (PF) had run against known but weaker regionally based parties, such as PF-ZAPU and ZANU-Ndonga, as well as new parties that had quickly fizzled out – ZUM (1990) and Forum (1995). The point in all the national elections up to 2000 was not who would win – it was always clear that ZANU (PF) would prevail – but how much popular support the ruling party could demonstrate via voter turnout, irrespective of the policies of the government at the time. Suddenly the mobilised output participation changed as a new party articulated a series of demands that were widespread across the beleaguered Zimbabwean population. Throughout all the elections ZANU (PF) repeatedly invented a life-or-death struggle between the 'true' memories of Zimbabwe's 'not yet', 'now' and 'will be', which it alone held in trust, and those of various hooligans and Antichrists.

As one effort at transition from colonial rule to a definitive post-colonial political economy spilled messily into another – not seamlessly, more like oil and water running together – ZANU (PF) strove more determinedly and desperately to ground its actions in the claim to have won Zimbabwe for the people. Because its eyes were on itself and its preferred past, by 2000 the ruling party had to struggle to shape and control counter-memories that threatened to sink it. In its recourse both to some invented ideal time of itself during an abhorrent order of colonisation, and to colonial-style violence whenever an opposition organised against it, the party's actions were colonial-mimicking. Bhabha (1994a) writes that colonialism contains uneasily within one schema the dream of itself as uplifter and the tones of repression. 'Mimicry is ... the sign of a double articulation; a complex strategy of reform, regulation, and discipline, which "appropriates" the Other as it visualizes power' (86). In order for ZANU (PF) to praise-sing to itself, it had to appropriate all late colonial plus post-colonial pasts and presents, disciplining the recalcitrant 'povo' in order to reform and uplift it.

As ZANU (PF) more desperately mimicked the colonial overlord it fought to overthrow – it was 'not yet' time for formal opposition in Zimbabwe – it neglected the political economy and, in effect, invited various forms of opposition. Realisation came during the third transitional moment that ZANU (PF)'s myths were breachable, that alternative claims to memory were not only possible, they could (nearly) prevail in bringing elements of a new 'will be' onto the national agenda. Suffice it to say that the outcome of elections 2000 and 2002 let ZANU (PF) stay in charge, but with MDC rattling the party's cage, mostly by reminding it of the 'now' the noble party could have brought to life had it not chosen to mimic colonial technologies of power.

Bhabha reminds us that '[t]he success of colonial appropriation depends on a proliferation of inappropriate objects that ensure its strategic failure ...' (ibid.). MDC must proliferate strategically inappropriate practices which can prevent it from falling into colonial mimicry itself. One 'inappropriate' move would be to undermine the masculinist politics of war and omnipotence that lie at the heart of ZANU (PF)'s efforts to appropriate Zimbabwe to itself. ZANU (PF)'s 'women' seem to be war commanders from the past and women at the *poshito*, family backbones, praises-singers to Mugabe, and, most recently, 'the custodians of unity, peace and development ... [and] the land' (ZANU (PF) Manifesto quoted in *Moto* 2000:7). There are many left out of this picture, such as women farm workers, the swelling members of the country's informal sector and domestic workers. A broad coalitional politics is a step in the direction of bringing such heretofore 'inappropriate' people into debates about Zimbabwe.

It is noteworthy that the MDC did partially disrupt the masculinism of campaign 2000. While the ruling party threatened and killed, sneered and warred – and yet insisted it was the party of all the people – the opposition showed open hands, organised quietly house to house and shook their heads at ZANU (PF) blusterings. This is not to say that it had no warriors; one young organiser boasted during the election period that 'we have taken out quite a few of the ZANU (PF) boys' (author interview with MDC supporter in Harare, 23 June 2000). The MDC, however, for the most part conducted an exercise in forgetting the wild-men histories of the ruling party and remembering many other components of 'Zimbabwe'. This is the type of inappropriate memory politics that, if carried forward, could disrupt ZANU (PF) colonial myth mimicry in the next post-colonial era.

The main focus need not be uplifting certain persons *per se*, which has a colonial ring to it, but on changing scriptualisations in which some are ordained to rule consistently over others. In the gender arena, 'to be inappropriate' the worker-based leadership of the MDC must not forget to remember politics beyond men talking to or about other men. This is a detail easily forgotten, it seems: for despite a softer organisational style, the MDC fell down in the basic task of recruiting sufficient ('inappropriate') women's bodies for the 2000 elections. A more robust gender politics would entail *enacting* political culture and its memories differently in a society where men have historically dominated women (Sylvester 2000).

As for ZANU (PF), it has clearly lost the thin hegemony of the 1990s. The narrow identity formulas that gave rise to magical myths of national unity, rather than of diversity, now ring hollow. Pretences that were once persuasive to many lie exposed as jejune colonial re-runs. This party will fight on, but there is menace to its tired acts of colonial mimicry and a social urgency to re-member 'Zimbabwe' in more open-ended ways. If the problematic of 1995 was whither opposition (Sylvester 1995:423), today it is a memory politics being driven in part by formal opposition to more of the same forgetfulness. The MDC has already remembered some reconciliatory methods and brought them to the fore. Ahead is the challenge of working through the tensions that its mostly urban middle-class reconciliators might forget to remember (such as the differing interests of middle-class urban women and women farm workers, for example), so that the new transitioning can enable multivalent rather than singular senses of the 'now'.[13] Ahead as well is the challenge of surviving an increasingly cornered and snarling ZANU (PF) long enough to hold memories of oppressor and oppressed in some abeyance so that the pained, the triumphant and the reconciliatory can together ponder multiple ways that Zimbabwe 'is' and 'will be'.

NOTES

1. Moyo, however, saw his efforts to restore voter support for ZANU (PF) pay off. He became Minister of State for Information and Publicity in the new cabinet line-up – without having to run for office and thus without a single vote cast for him by the Zimbabwean population.
2. A ZANU (PF) slogan appearing on posters and in the print media during the election campaign.
3. For example, Ranger (1985) writes of rural Zimbabweans who may have seemed the victims of Rhodesian policy but who selected the peasant option in the 1920s and 1930s as a way of avoiding mine work. Barnes and Win (1992) report that women sometimes found the urban areas reserved for male migrant workers liberating for themselves.
4. Lest the politics of memory seem cynical, it is important to recall that the sheer survival of a society can be at stake in forgetting 'truth' and building

an alternative myth (for example, as in Biafra after the war). In other cases, selective memory can be integral to reconciliation processes that prise apart the myths of state from the actions of state that ruin people's lives (as in South Africa). See Harneit-Sievers and Emezue 2000.

5. 'The Election Manifesto of ZANU/Patriotic Front, 1980' in Goswin Baumhogger et al. (eds) 1984:1308.

6. For discussions of *Gukurahundi*, see Brickhill 1995:163–73, Werbner 1995 and Alexander, McGregor and Ranger 2000.

7. I thank Peter Garlake for raising this point with me during a conversation on 24 June 2000 in Harare.

8. There were signs of creeping change in that direction as early as 1985, when the government introduced several export financing and promotion schemes. The *Five Year Development Plan, 1986–1990*, however, gave the impression, as Peter Gibbon (1995) has argued, of a 'general governmental indifference to the interests of capital, white and foreign, and a vague aspiration toward further state-led social engineering' (Gibbon 1995:8). The confusion was put to rest in 1990 and 1991. In the language of *Zimbabwe Human Development Report, 1999*, whereas the state humanised poverty in the 1980s through a state-paternalist welfare approach, after 1990 poverty was handled 'through "safety nets" incorporated in the Economic Structural Adjustment Programme (ESAP)' (Tandon 1999:22).

9. *Zimbabwe Human Development Report*:23. Rudo Gaidzanwa (1999) shows that in the health sector alone, the structural adjustment programme made work conditions so much more onerous for doctors and nurses, and more expensive for consumers (through the levying of user fees), that the 1980s health safety net frayed and then unravelled. She says: 'The rural and urban poor have suffered in this situation since they cannot access the private health system while the public health system is so run down that in some cases, it can be dangerous to patients' (Gaidzanwa 1999:77).

10. As many as 55 of the 120 parliamentary seats at issue had already been decided for ZANU (PF) because the six opposition parties of the moment had not run candidates for them. With its appointable seats, ZANU (PF) was sure of obtaining 85 of the 150 seats in the House of Assembly before a single ballot was cast.

11. Morgan Tsvangirai accused members of ZANU (PF) of behaving as though they lost the colonial struggle and are in opposition to some other governing force. Conversation with Morgan Tsvangirai, Leiden Netherlands, 24 January 2001.

12. They told of ZANU (PF) supporters being trucked around to terrorise the opposition, with government intelligence agents (CIO) supplying lists of targets and 'high-ranking party members directly involved. There is reason to believe that the perpetrators of violence have been given some basic education in torture techniques.' Zimbabwe Human Rights NonGovernmental Organisations Forum, 'Human Rights Report', 21 June 2000, cited in *The Australian* 22 June 2000:12.

13. These ideas piggyback onto some general comments on reconciliation that Dipesh Chakrabarty offered at a seminar at the Australian National University on 26 July 2000 called 'Reconciliation and Its Historiography'.

REFERENCES

Alexander, Jocelyn, Joann McGregor and Terence Ranger. 2000. *Violence and Memory: One Hundred Years in the Dark Forests of Matabeleland.* Portsmouth: Heinemann.

Barnes, Teresa and Everjoyce Win. 1992. *To Live a Better Life: An Oral History of Women in the City of Harare, 1930–70.* Harare: Baobab Books.

Baumhoegger, Goswin, Telse Diedrichsen and Ulf Engel (eds). 1984. *The Struggle for Independence: Documents on the Recent Development of Zimbabwe Vol. 7.* Hamburg: Institute of African Studies, African Documentation Center.

Bayart, Jean-Francois. 1993. *The State in Africa: The Politics of the Belly.* New York: Longman.

Bhabha, Homi. 1994. 'Interrogating Identity: Frantz Fanon and the Postcolonial Prerogative', in H. Bhabha (ed.) *The Location of Culture.* London: Routledge.

——. 1994a. 'Of Mimicry and Man', in H. Bhabha (ed.) *The Location of Culture.* London: Routledge.

Brickhill, Jeremy. 1995. 'Making Peace with the Past: War Victims and the Work of the Mafela Trust', in Ngwabi Bhebe and Terence Ranger (eds) *Soldiers in Zimbabwe's Liberation War.* Harare: University of Zimbabwe Publications:

Chakaodza, Austin. 1993. *Structural Adjustment in Zambia and Zimbabwe.* Harare: Third World Publishing House.

Chakrabarty, Dipesh. 2000. *Provincializing Europe.* Princeton: Princeton University Press.

Collier, Ruth. 1982. *Regimes in Africa.* Berkeley: University of California Press.

Darnolf, Staffan. 1997. *Democratic Electioneering in Southern Africa: The Contrasting Cases of Botswana and Zimbabwe.* Goteborg Studies in Politics, No. 45.

Financial Gazette. 1998. 'Cabinet in Crisis Talks Over Riots', 22 January. <www.cyberplexaafrica.com/fingaz/stage/archive/980122/national12714.html>.

Gaidzanwa, Rudo. 1999. *Voting With Their Feet: Migrant Zimbabwean Nurses and Doctors in the Era of Structural Adjustment.* Research Report No. 11. Uppsala: Nordiska Afrikainstitutet.

Gibbon, Peter. 1995. 'Introduction: Structural Adjustment and the Working Poor in Zimbabwe', in Peter Gibbon (ed.) *Structural Adjustment and the Working Poor in Zimbabwe.* Uppsala: Nordiska Afrikainstitutet.

Government of Zimbabwe. 1982. *The Transitional National Development Plan: 1982/83–1984/85.* Harare: Government Printer.

Gwarinda, Takawira. 2000. 'A Tale of Two Manifestos', *Moto* No. 209.

——. 2000a. 'Looking at Party Manifestos: A Preview of the Zimbabwean Elections in the Year 2000', Supplement to *Journal on Social Change* No. 50, June 2000: 1–4.

Harneit-Sievers, Axel and Sydney Emezue. 2000. 'Towards a Social History of Warfare and Reconstruction: The Nigerian Case', in Ifi Amadiume and Abdullahi An-Na'im (eds) *The Politics of Memory: Truth, Healing and Social Justice.* London: Zed Press:110–26.

Kriger, Norma. 1992. *Zimbabwe's Guerrilla War: Peasant Voices*. Cambridge: Cambridge University Press.

——. 1995. 'The Politics of Creating National Heroes: The Search for Political Legitimacy and National Identity', in Ngwabi Bhebe and Terence Ranger (eds) *Soldiers in Zimbabwe's Liberation War Vol. 1*. Harare: University of Zimbabwe Publications.

Makumbe, John. 1994. 'Democracy in Zimbabwe', *Human Rights Bulletin* 1(1) August.

——. 1996. *Participatory Development: The Case of Zimbabwe*. Harare: University of Zimbabwe Publications.

Masamvu, Sydney. 2000. 'ZANU PF Declares War on Whites, MDC', *Financial Gazette* 13 April. <www.cyberplexafrica.com/fingaz/99/stage/archive/000412/national3708.html>.

Moto. 2000. 'Election 2000: Where are the Women', No. 209, June.

Movement for Democratic Change. 2000. *Programme for Change, Summary*. Harare.

Moyo, Jonathan 1992. *Voting for Democracy: Electoral Politics in Zimbabwe*. Harare: University of Zimbabwe Publications.

Moyo, Sam. 1999. *Land and Democracy in Zimbabwe*. Monograph Series No. 7. Harare: SAPES Trust.

Mugabe, Robert. 1989. 'The Unity Accord: Its Promise for the Future', in Canaan S. Banana (ed.) *Turmoil and Tenacity: Zimbabwe, 1890–1990*. Harare: College Press.

Mushonga, Allen. 2000. 'Rural-Urban Constituencies, The Born-Free and the Election', *The Zimbabwe Mirror* 23–9 June.

Mutsakani, Abel. 2000. 'War Vets Seize Over 300 Farms', *Financial Gazette* 9 March. <www.cyberplexafrica.com/fingaz/99/stage/archive/000308/national/7645.html>.

Raftopoulos, Brian. 2000. 'Reflections on the Referendum on the Draft Constitution: 2000', *Journal on Social Change* No. 50.

Raftopoulos, Brian and Tsuneo Yoshikuni (eds) 1999. *Sites of Struggle: Essays in Zimbabwe's Urban History*. Harare: Weaver Press.

Ranger, Terence. 1985. *Peasant Consciousness and Guerrilla War in Zimbabwe*. Berkeley: University of California Press.

Schiphorst, Freek. 2001. *Strength and Weakness: The Rise of the Zimbabwe Congress of Trade Unions (ZCTU) and the Development of Labour Relations 1980–1995*. Ph.D. dissertation, Leiden University.

Schmidt, Elizabeth. 1992. *Peasants, Traders, and Wives: Shona Women in the History of Zimbabwe, 1870–1939*. London: James Currey.

Scott, James. 1990. *Domination and the Arts of Resistance: Hidden Transcripts*. New Haven: Yale University Press.

Sithole, Masipula. 1997. 'The Elusive Promised Land', *Zimbabwe's Public Eye* 6 November.

——. 1997a. 'The Fight for Freedom Has No Price', *Zimbabwe's Public Eye* 26 November.

——. 1998. 'War Vets Have Abandoned the People', *Zimbabwe's Public Eye: Political Essays (October 1997 – October 1998)* 4 December 1997. Harare: Rujeko Publishers.

——. 1999. 'What if Referendum Rejects Commission?' *Financial Gazette* 16 September 1999. <www.cyberplexafrica.com/fingaz/99/stage/archive/990916/public-index.html>.

Soyinka, Wole. 2000. 'Memory, Truth and Healing', in Ifi Amadiume and Abdullahi An-Na'im (eds) *The Politics of Memory: Truth, Healing and Social Justice*. London: Zed Books.

Staunton, Irene (ed.) 1990. *Mothers of the Revolution*. Harare: Baobab Books.

Sylvester, Christine. 1985. 'Continuity and Discontinuity in Zimbabwe's Development History', *African Studies Review* 28(1):19–44.

——. 1986. 'Zimbabwe's 1985 Elections: A Search for National Mythology', *Journal of Modern African Studies* 24(1):229–55.

——. 1990. 'Unities and Disunities in Zimbabwe's 1990 Election', *Journal of Modern African Studies* 28(3).

——. 1991. *Zimbabwe: The Terrain of Contradictory Development*. Boulder: Westview Press.

——. 1995. 'Whither Opposition in Zimbabwe?' *Journal of Modern African Studies* 33 (3):403–24.

——. 2000. *Producing Women and Progress in Zimbabwe: Narratives of Identity and Work from the 1980s*. Portsmouth: Heinemann.

Tandon, Yash (principal author). 1999. *Zimbabwe Human Development Report 1999*. For UNDP, Poverty Reduction Forum, and IDS. Harare: no publisher mentioned.

Thompson, Leonard. 1985. *The Political Mythology of Apartheid*. New Haven: Yale University Press.

Werbner, Richard. 1995. 'In Memory: A Heritage of War in South-Western Zimbabwe', in Ngawbi Bhebe and Terence Ranger (eds) *Society in Zimbabwe's Liberation War Vol. 2*. Harare: University of Zimbabwe Publications:192–205.

Werbner, Richard (ed.). 1998. *Memory and the Postcolony: African Anthropology and the Critique of Power*. London: Zed Books.

ZANU (PF). 1984. *Draft Constitution*. Harare: Government Printer.

——. 1990. *ZANU PF Election Manifesto 1990: ZANU PF and the 1990 General Election*. Harare.

3 Contested Memories of Repression in the Southern Cone: Commemorations in a Comparative Perspective[1]

Elizabeth Jelin

The five neighbouring countries of the Southern Cone of South America – Argentina, Brazil, Chile, Paraguay and Uruguay – have shared a similar political path of dictatorship and transition to constitutional governments during the last decades.[2] In fact, these countries have five distinct and specific histories, as well as different social and political structures. Yet, besides the shared history of colonialism and independence, there are several traits that link them into a stronger notion of political 'region' than one based simply on territorial proximity, showing a long history of a transnational social life.

First, there is a long history of highly porous borders, including continuous movements of political exiles across borders from the early nineteenth century onwards. Exiles actively participated in the organisation of opposition movements for political change in their countries of origin, while keeping close and long-lasting contacts in alliance and solidarity with political forces in their host countries. Second, during the recent dictatorships, repression was coordinated at the regional scale. The unearthing of the documentation of the *Operativo Cóndor* began with the discovery of the *Archivos del terror* (Archives of Terror) of the Paraguayan secret police in 1991 and continues with new discoveries since then. These written documents bring to the public sphere the evidence of that which many victims knew because they had experienced international terror 'under their own skins'.[3] Third, as a counterpoint, there was a highly communicated and integrated network of solidarity against human rights violations, which continued its interconnected work after transitions. The human rights network is global; it is very *actively* regional (Keck and Sikkink 1998).

In the 1980s and 1990s, transitions in the different countries were also interrelated, with constant dialogues and exchanges among political strategists, analysts and activists, and much learning from experiences 'across the border'. Yet the processes were clearly different in each of them.[4]

One shared trait is that, in all countries, the recent dictatorial past is still very much part of the present. Accounts with the dictatorial past are not settled, neither in institutional nor in symbolic terms. For many of the victims and their advocates, *NUNCA MÁS* ('never again') implies a complete accounting of what took place under dictatorship and the corresponding punishment for the perpetrators of abuses. Yet efforts to secure justice for violators of human rights have enjoyed little success. In this scenario international and third-country justice systems are becoming key players, as different types of amnesty and impunity laws have been put in place in all countries. At the same time some major political and social actors are concerned above all with the functioning of democratic institutions, and emphasise the need to focus on the future rather than on the past. They are less inclined to revisit the painful experiences of the author-itarian repression, fostering policies of oblivion or of 'reconciliation'. Finally, there are those who are ready to look at the past to glorify the 'order and progress' that dictatorship secured.

Thus, there are competing and conflicting memories of the past in societies that are emerging from periods of violence and trauma. In addition, there are social, cultural and political struggles about the location of these understandings and memories in the democratisa-tion process. In all cases, as time passes and it becomes possible to conceive a temporal distance between past and present, alternative and even rival interpretations of the recent past and its memories take the centre stage of cultural and political debate. They become an unavoidable public issue.

At any time and place, it is unthinkable to find One memory, a single vision and interpretation of the past shared by a whole society (whatever its scope and size). There may be historical times when agreement is higher, when a single script of the past is more pervasive or dominant. That script will usually be the story of the winners in historical conflicts and battles. But there will always be other stories, other interpretations and other memories. After periods of high political conflict and of repression or state terrorism, there is an active political struggle about meaning, about the meaning of what went on and also about the meaning of memory itself. In this arena, the struggle is not one of 'memory against oblivion' or silence, but rather between opposing memories, each of them with its own silences and voids (Jelin 2002).

ON COMMEMORATIONS AND DATES

Where to study processes of construction of memories? Which scenarios display the struggles and conflicts about different interpretations of the past? One entry point to approach the elusive core of memory and oblivion is to study disputes about the meaning of certain dates and the commemorative practices.

Social memories become established through practices and 'markers'. These are social practices that gradually become rituals, markers in material public places and in symbolic inscriptions such as calendars. The yearly rhythm – repetitive yet with shifts from one year to the next – offers the occasions, dates and anniversaries for remembrance and commemorative events. Yet markers are not crystallised once installed. Different social actors will appropriate for themselves specific meanings of these markers, depending on the circumstances and the political scenarios in which their strategies and projects unfold over time. Also, insofar as there are different societal interpretations of the past, public dates themselves may be the object of dispute or conflict. Which dates are to be commemorated? Or, in other words, who wants to commemorate what? How do meanings of dates change over time? The same date may have different meanings for the social actors and forces that frame their *current* struggles in relation to these dates.

Remembrance and oblivion take place at one point in time, governed by a subjective temporality that refers to past events and processes, which in turn get their meaning in connection with projects and plans in the future. This location of memories in the circumstances and contexts of current struggles implies the need to 'historise memories', in other words, to analyse changes and transformations of the actors, of the meanings and the cultural and political scenarios where the practices of commemoration take place.

Let me go over some of the commemorative practices related to dictatorship in the various countries.

CHILE[5]

Since 1973, 11 September has been a highly contested date in Chile. The antagonism between an image of the military coup as a liberating experience to be celebrated, and as a disgraceful aberration, has been established in Chilean society. The initial period after the coup (1974–7) set the basic discourses about the 11th: triumph on one hand, silence and suffering on the other. Massive official public commemoration of the 11th involved the government and an ample spectrum of supporters of the new regime. Celebrations were geared to show the 'recuperation of internal peace' and of the 'liberties' that were presumably lost during the Socialist Allende government. There were marches and festive shows in public places, with many allusions to the 'chaos' of the period 1970–3.

For the opposition these were very dark years. Fear, mistrust and repression dominated. It was a commemoration full of mourning and sorrow, always in private. A few years later, some public expressions of that sorrow started to emerge: women dressed in black, visits to the cemetery where some emblematic figures rested.

In 1981, the regime declared 11 September as a national holiday.[6] Soon, however, the national 'tranquillity' and the institutional-isation of the regime were increasingly questioned. During the 1980s, the struggles around the 11th were open, violent and fought in the streets, as opposition forces organised and expressed in mass protests their antagonism to the regime. These were 'bloody Septembers', with much repression and deaths in popular neighbourhoods.

In March 1990 the new democratically elected government took office. Transition was very complex, and the 11th was directly affected by that complexity (Drake and Jaksic 1999). The map of political actors changed. Three clearly defined positions can be seen since that time: political elites that want to distance themselves from the date and would like to abolish it as a commemoration; the left and various social movements expressing their will to continue remembering the horror of the date and their continuing search for justice; and the defence of the 11th as an heroic date on the part of Pinochet supporters.

In sum, a decade after transition, 11 September is still a contested date in Chilean society, as if the controversies of 30 years ago were still open,[7] and the cleavages that marked the positions of social actors at the time of transition persist.[8] The democratic forces and the left are committed to a message that the victims of dictatorship and dictatorship itself not be forgotten. On the other side, the *Pinochetistas* continue the rallies in front of Pinochet's home, and the military circles fight to ensure that their children and grandchildren will never see them as shameful assassins. At the same time the date offers a space for new actors, including those who confront or reject the political system as it exists – including diverse marginal groups who identify themselves as *mapuches*, young anarchists, or the extra-parliamentary left. All these confrontations take place mostly outside the political system itself. In fact, since transition, Chilean presidents chose to be absent from the capital city on that date.[9]

Everything was in place to re-enact the date and its diverse meanings in 2001: marches took place a couple of days earlier, during the weekend, there was a dinner of Pinochet's supporters, activities in army headquarters. Yet, as radio stations were ready for the first commemorative interviews on the morning of 11 September, the programming was interrupted by the news of the attacks in New York and Washington. Another event was occupying the centre stage. Seen from the centre (the US), 11 September became its 'own' date. Coincidences were visible, and were mentioned by Chilean analysts and observers: a Tuesday morning, airplanes, smoke and destruction, and then, the reiterated images of people with the photos of the missing – an iconography well developed in the Southern Cone. Such references were totally absent in observers and analysts in the United States; 11 September became a date 'owned' by the US. The open question is how this coincidence – and the memories of the role of the United States in the military coup of 11 September 1973 in Chile – will affect future commemorations of the date, and future struggles about its meaning in Chile.

ARGENTINA[10]

On 24 March 1976 a military junta deposed the elected government and began what it itself defined as the *Proceso de Reorganización Nacional*. The military coup took place at a time when the open political conflict in the country had strengthened the instances of paramilitary violence and the activity of armed guerrilla movements was in decline. A systematic plan was designed to eliminate political opponents: kidnapping, torture and forced disappearances were the core of the chosen strategy. Since that date, the '24th' turned into a meaningful date that evokes different meanings for various actors.

During dictatorship, the public scene of commemorations was occupied totally by the military discourse. The military commemoration was a 'closed' event, with no civilian participation.

The only point of contact of the military with civil society was a 'Message to the Argentine People', delivered each year, justifying the coup in terms of a salvational mission of the armed forces, 'forced' to occupy the state to save the nation from chaos, lack of governance and the terrorist threat. Although the military presented themselves as the leaders of this struggle, increasingly they made reference to the fact that the tasks of the *Proceso* were 'tasks for everybody'. The speeches referred to the enemy, 'subversion'; yet, there was no public confrontation of any sort. Repression was too harsh to voice publicly any kind of opposition in commemorative events. There was only private suffering and silent resistance. Abroad, increasing activity was taking place: campaigns to denounce repression in Argentina and express solidarity with the victims were on the rise.

A few years later the solid wall of dictatorship started to crack. Beginning in 1980, the military discourse could not avoid references to their action in response to claims regarding human rights violations. The wear and tear of the regime reached such a climax that during the last commemoration before transition (1983) there was no public message.

The human rights organisations were the main antagonists to the military interpretation of the events of the 24th. This fact coloured the commemorative activities since transition in December 1983, when the human rights organisations occupied the public space of commemoration while political parties and the government kept silent and were absent, as were the military.[11] During the first years after transition, commemorations included a wide variety of aesthetic expressions related to images of dictatorship and its consequences: there were silhouettes, murals and theatre performances accompanying the marches and the white scarves of the *Madres de Plaza de Mayo* (Mothers of the Disappeared). The initial strong impulse of the movement was followed by a gradual decline in public commemorations, coinciding with the political defeats of the human rights cause. One has to remember that after the high point of the trials of the military (1985), there were significant steps back – the *Ley de Punto Final*, the *Ley de Obediencia Debida*, and later on the presidential pardons of 1990 that freed the condemned and jailed generals.

The mood changed in 1995, when the confession of one of the repressors was aired, opening wide media coverage of issues related to the dictatorship. The next year was to be the twentieth anniversary of the military coup. Commemorative activities multiplied, with a variety of daily events during the month of March, and many others during the rest of the year. There was a rally and musical festival that attracted 100,000 people in Plaza de Mayo, and activities in most cities of the country. It was also a time of high participation of youth, including the creation of *HIJOS*, a new human rights organisation, with its new ways of commemorating and denouncing past violations.[12] Also, the scope of denunciations of human rights violations broadened, to include the rights of sexual and ethnic minorities, as well as economic rights – the unemployed, the homeless. There is a growing range of social organisations actively participating in the commemorations. The presence of such a diverse range of actors (around 200 labour unions, NGOs, political groups and grassroots associations, besides the human rights movement in Buenos Aires, for the organisation of the activities linked to the twenty-fifth anniversary of the coup in 2001) in the organisation of the commemorative activities implies the emergence of power disputes around 'ownership' of the 24th (Jelin 2002).[13]

In sum, Argentine history of the past 25 years does not show open confrontations at any time. Rather, what is evident is the alternation of the dominant voice, from the military to the human rights movement. The significant absence is the voice of the constitutional government. Furthermore, although the divergence and disputes within the human rights movement express themselves in each commemoration, it is quite clear that since transition the only voices present in the public sphere on the 24th are voices condemning the coup of 1976 and the dictatorship that ensued.

URUGUAY[14]

In the Uruguayan case, there is no unique and clear date of commemoration linked to dictatorship. There are several candidates, all of them linked to institutional changes during 1973: the setting-up of the *Consejo de Seguridad Nacional* in February, or the date of the military coup, 27 June. However, commemorations of this period and of these events take place on two dates linked to acts of political violence: 14 April (1972) and 20 May (1976). Over time, these dates became the reference points for two clearly opposite visions of the past.

On 14 April 1972 the opposition forces of the *Movimiento de Liberación Nacional Tupamaros* killed four political figures, three military and one civilian. That same afternoon, eight Tupamaros were killed. From that day on, the military took on a much more active role in repressive activities vis-à-vis the guerrilla movement, and political violence increased substantially up to the military coup of 1973.

The commemorative enterprise began the next day, in the burial ceremonies of the four so-called 'martyrs'. The military interpretation of what happened on that day shows up clearly in the first name given to the date: *Día de homenaje a las víctimas de la insanía* (Homage to the victims of insanity). In 1975, the military transformed the date in an official commemorative date, the *Día de los caídos en la lucha contra la sedición* (Day of the fallen in the struggle against sedition). The objective was to transcend the military space and transform it into a national date. In this way, the dictatorial government linked its foundational crusade for a new Uruguay with the remembrance of the 'martyrs' that made it possible.

At the time of transition the date became a source of conflicts. In 1985 the democratically elected President Sanguinetti attempted to change the meaning of the date, altering its name to *Día de los caídos en defensa de las instituciones democráticas* (Day of those fallen in defence of democratic institutions). This change was opposed by the right and by the military, which claimed that the struggle against 'sedition' was being lost in the change. Significantly, the military retreated into their barracks for their own commemorations, using the occasion to express their demands and their critical views about the democratisation process. Governmental authorities maintained the public ceremony on that date, but from 1987 they eliminated discourses and speeches.

The other date, 20 May, is linked to the assassination, in Buenos Aires in 1976, of four political exiles: two major democratic political figures, Senator Michelini, and the ex-President of the House, Gutiérrez Ruiz, and two leaders of the *Movimiento de Liberación Nacional Tupamaros,* W. Whitelaw and R. Barredo. During the dictatorship this date became an emblem for the Uruguayan political opposition, most of it in exile by that time. The date drew considerable consensus among the various opposition groups and democratic forces. After transition, the date became a wider space of commemoration for all victims of political repression of the state. It was never integrated into the official calendar of the state, remaining as a 'societal' date.

14 April constructs a representation of a 'war'. Although different political actors participate in the event, ranging from liberal

democratic sectors to the anti-liberal right, they share an interpretation of the past. The narrative is that in the 1960s the state was in danger of being destroyed by 'subversion'. It was then mandatory to struggle against it forcefully, and in the process, some 'excesses' may have been committed (discrepancies have to do with the degree and need of such 'excesses'). But in the end, victory came, subversion was destroyed and the state survived.

20 May constructs a narrative that denounces state terrorism. In this case, the narrative of the recent past begins in 1973, when the military took power by force. Centre stage is taken by the military coup and its consequences. What went on before 1973 is less important, since it is also the realm of disagreement among the various groups that participate in the commemorations – especially in the acceptance or condemnation of armed struggle.

Both narratives exist side by side in contemporary Uruguay. There is no dialogue between them. Those who attend one rally clearly avoid the other. Both are entrenched in their positions, and there seems to be little room to overcome the duality of visions. However, the new government installed in 2000 brought with it some signs of change. The new president, Jorge Batlle, has for the first time officially recognised that the state has committed violations during dictatorship, and a *Comisión para la Paz* (Peace Commission) has been named, with a mandate to investigate the whereabouts of the disappeared, in spite of the fact that no punishment is possible because of the amnesty laws.

BRAZIL[15]

During the dawn hours of 1 April 1964, a military coup took place in Brazil, a 'Revolution' in the wording chosen by the new regime. However, the military opted to date the coup as taking place on 31 March, and not 1 April. The reason was very simple: they needed a 'serious' date, and 1 April is not: it is April Fool's Day, called in Brazil *'dia da mentira'*. They tried to establish a 'Revolution' that took place on 31 March, as the foundational date for a national project of 'freedom and progress'.

In the following years, there were few public acts or special events to commemorate that date. There were always military commemorations geared to the inner circles of the armed forces. The regime also used the educational system as a strong institutional tool for commemoration. In 1974, for the tenth anniversary of the

'Revolution', schools had to work with the students on projects under the rubric, 'Ten years constructing Brazil'. What they were supposed to do was to praise the accomplishments of the regime in a climate of optimism and progress. There was a 'Week of Commemorations', with ministerial speeches broadcast daily on the national radio system. In these speeches, the progress brought about by the regime, as well as the modernisation process of the armed forces, was praised continuously. The 'radiant dawn of civic faith and democratic fervour' brought about by the military uprising of 1964, facing chaos and the communist threat, was also celebrated.

During the dictatorship, there was little room for dissident voices, silenced not so much by the relatively mild initial repression of 1964 but by the deepening of dictatorship after the announcement of the Institutional Act No. 5, in late 1968. This Act limited freedom of expression, incorporated censorship in daily activities of the media and implied in general a substantial increase in direct repression. To the ambiguity of the exact date of the coup one could add the ambiguity of the dates – either 1964 or 1968 – when life conditions were directly affected by the change in political regime.

In 1984, the commemorative mood was totally different. The Armed Forces were reiterating the historical significance of the 'Revolution' as the utmost expression of the identification between the Armed Forces and Brazilian society. They were also paying attention to the similarity of the dangers in 1964 and in 1984, when social demands for direct elections and for transition were dominant in the public sphere. There were many voices in the public space, with a core confrontation between the *'Brasil, ame-o o deije-o'* (Brazil, love it or leave it) voiced by the hardest defenders of the dictatorial government, and the *'Diretas, ya'* (Direct elections, now), the demand for democratisation that led to the election of the first civilian president in 1985.

The military commemoration of 1994 (30 years) was the last one. The three military ministers made one joint statement, in which they once again explained that the military intervention of 1964 was necessary to protect the basic values of nationality and the survival of the national institutions. They reiterated their view of the ample popular support of the 'Revolution'. For the media and academic institutions, on the contrary, this was an occasion to voice critical perspectives on the dictatorship.

The erasure of the date from official calendars, however, does not imply silence or oblivion. On each anniversary, the press concentrates on the date, carrying interviews with political leaders or with ordinary citizens. It is also an occasion for round tables, seminars and meetings. Finally, since 1987 the organisation *Tortura Nunca Mais* has announced on this date the recipients of their award, the medal 'Chico Mendes', an award granted to recognise people who suffered human rights violations or who act in their defence, all over the world.

PARAGUAY[16]

The question regarding commemoration of dictatorship-related dates in Paraguay leads in a very different direction. There is no public memory or commemoration of anniversaries of the military coup of 1954, nor of the date of the 'election' of Alfredo Stroessner as president that same year. There is no major public commemoration of the date of the coup that ousted Stroessner in 1989 (the night of 2–3 February). Rather, the most important date during the long dictatorship, that has continued being a popular *fiesta* since, is 3 November, Stroessner's birthday.

The celebration of the dictator's birthday was initiated soon after he took office. There were early-morning salutes to the president, and a popular festivity in the evening, held in *Barrio Stroessner*, where the leader would always inaugurate some public work.[17] During the day, radio stations and other media would broadcast special messages of thanks and songs as a salute to the General.

In the first year of the transition (1989) there were no celebrations. The previous night, there was a *Vigilia contra la impunidad* (a vigil against impunity) in the centre of Asuncion. On 3 November, there was a rally in repudiation of the date, calling for justice and punishment of those responsible for repression during the dictatorship. At the same time, in the *barrio* Stroessner's supporters gathered to remember his birthday, making long-distance phone calls to Brazil (Stroessner's place of exile) to wish him happiness and a prompt return. The next year there were no expressions repudiating the dictatorship, and the celebrations in the *barrio* were subject to repression.

Gradually through the 1990s, the popular celebration in the neighbourhood returned as the centre of commemoration, with no further expression of anti-dictatorial feelings. The neighbourhood had a change in name, and Stroessner's statue was removed from the plaza. Without the personal markers of the dictator, the ritual changed: the morning salute is replaced by long-distance phone calls to the exiled dictator, people dress in festive clothes (red, the colour of the party), there are dances, fireworks, banners and decorations of houses and streets. The fiesta combines political patronage of important Stroessner supporters and local initiatives that extend the celebration beyond its political meaning.

At the same time, those who suffered repression at the hands of the regime do not find a specific date to commemorate and express their demands or feelings. Their memories did not find a way to express themselves in rituals and public commemorations, where a shared identity and a sense of community could be expressed. Their demands are expressed publicly at critical moments in the experience of the country in the last decade (such as an attempted coup in 1996, or the popular protests in March 1999). In such moments, democratic forces, that include the older generation – those who have personal memories of the Stroessner regime's repression – and the young to whom these memories were conveyed, become visible actors in the public sphere, struggling to contain the danger of a return to dictatorship. Yet, in such moments, present-day struggles take centre stage, and issues of memory of repression fade.

Perhaps past and present are too close to each other in contemporary Paraguay. In a scenario of disillusionment with the present and some idealisation of the past, the risk exists that the memories of the 'good old days' become the 'historical truth' for the younger generation.

COMMEMORATIONS IN PERSPECTIVE

Dates and anniversaries are conjunctures in which memories are produced and activated. They are public occasions, open spaces, to express and act out the diverse meanings given to the past – reinforcing some, widening and changing others. There are some regularities across countries, linked to the institutional frames and the ways in which different social actors appropriate those meanings in terms of their own identities and their own expectations and projects for the future.

In all cases, when taking power, the military emphasised their 'salvational' role, as bastions defending the nation in continuity with the founding heroes. The threat was always seen as external, as 'subversion' or 'communist infiltration'. In fact, the event – the military coup – installs its own determination to be commemorated.

The present projects itself towards the future, trying to determine and fix the meaning of what should be remembered. However, success can never be assured. The discourse, with its foundational narrative, will be revised in later periods, according to the different scenarios where disputes take place.

At the same moment that the winners attempt to install their narrative, controversy about the event begins. The alternative views and explanations may be censored, forbidden, repressed, kept in private and family circles, silenced and hidden. Yet, channels of expression start to develop, gradually. Performative acts are crucial in this period, as signals and hints helping to construct destroyed and threatened communities of belonging: black clothes, silenced trajectories in city streets. The protagonists are the human rights movement, with a very limited role for political parties and – after transition – for the democratic state itself in the commemorations. They are clearly not the central forces in the elaboration of social memories or in the attempt to build the 'legacies'. It is rather social actors – organised in the human rights movement or dispersed in popular expressions of protest, heterogeneous and diverse – who attempt to produce alternative memories to the military narrative, claiming an interpretation of the past that emphasises repression and suffering. They are also the actors who demand justice and denounce impunity.

Three issues can be presented as final comments. First, memory refers to the way people construct a sense or meaning of the past, and how they relate that past to their present position and future expectations in the act of remembering. There are, however, different visions and interpretations, and different ways to convey meaning. Insofar as we are talking of traumatic circumstances, there are voids, holes and fractures in the possibility of expressing and conveying meanings of that past. At the limit, trauma implies the absence of words, and therefore the absence of narrative memories, the impossibility of communicating and transmitting: only repetition of symptoms and silences are possible. What cannot be said in words is then expressed in fragments and broken messages.

How then, can meaning be conveyed? How can these affect the views and the participation of younger cohorts, those who did not live personally the events being commemorated? There are times when the young show a complete lack of interest regarding the political past. At other times some young people may become involved and express highly militant attitudes towards those events.

Inter-cohort differences – among those who lived through repression at different times in their personal lives, between them and the very young who do not have personal memories of repression – and the relationships and dialogues between generations produce a distinct societal dynamics vis-à-vis the memory issue. Information and knowledge, silences, feelings, ideas and ideologies – these are the symbolic goods to be conveyed. However, there is always a question mark as to which new interpretations and meanings will be given, both at the individual and group levels.

Second, dates of commemoration, as part of memory itself, suffer transformations with time, visible especially in public manifestations around the date and in the political discourses, when compared year after year. Can past and present be separated? Is it possible then that the meaning of a date can change so profoundly that the original reason becomes only a 'pre-text' for political and social struggles that are *always* anchored in the present? Are the events and activities that are carried out 'really' commemorations of past events? Or are they rather vehicles of a conjunctural political struggle, as could be the case with electoral propaganda, public works inaugurations or corruption denunciations? If this is the case, what is the place for social memory of historical subjects?

Third, the relationship between societal processes and the state – or rather processes of legitimation and recognition of responsibilities – is also an open question. The absence of the state in public commemorations has already been mentioned. If the state was the main repressor, how can it be brought back to the public scenario? Under which circumstances will the state assume responsibility for the past? The equilibrium between legitimacy, responsibility and state action is always unstable, and the post-dictatorial states of the region have not yet found a legitimate way to address the conflicts of the past. Notably, they have not been able to respond to societal demands for justice. In fact, justice is the most solid block of memory, and its absence is felt in the space where struggles for commemoration are taking place.

NOTES

1. This chapter is based on research carried out by fellows within the framework of the program on 'Collective Memories and Repression: Comparative Perspectives on the Process of Democratization of the Southern Cone of Latin America', sponsored by the Social Science

Research Council (New York). Results have been published in Jelin (ed.) 2002.

2. On 11 September 1973 the military took over the government in Chile. President Allende resisted at first, then, as aeroplanes were bombing the Presidential Palace, he died inside *La Moneda*. There followed 17 years of military dictatorship, until a negotiated transition led to elections and the installing of President Awlyin in 1990. In Uruguay, the violent political confrontations of the early 1970s led to the suspension of civil liberties and constitutional guarantees in 1973, with a dictatorial state that lasted until 1985. In Argentina, on 24 March 1976, in the midst of high levels of violent political confrontation, a military coup displaced President Isabel Peron and installed a military government that lasted until December 1983. Brazil and Paraguay started their long dictatorial experiences earlier – Paraguay through a coup in 1954, followed by innumerable 're-elections' of President Stroessner until he was ousted in 1989. Brazil had a military coup in 1964 and experienced a slow, almost unending transition that led to the election of the first civilian president in 1985, 21 years later.

3. For instance, Celiberti and Garrido (1989) narrate Celiberti´s kidnapping in Porto Alegre, Brazil, by Uruguayan security forces, and her transfer to Uruguayan detention centres and prisons, where she spent several years afterwards.

4. I am not going to deal with the challenges that the weak democracies have faced since transition. There are widespread difficulties in honouring social and economic rights, economic and social inequalities are growing, and some countries are facing deep economic crisis. There are also continuous instances of police brutality, weak judiciaries and obstacles of all sorts in attaining the 'rule of law'. Yet, for the most part, citizens need no longer live fearful of systematic repression by state agencies, such as forced disappearances and widespread political torture.

5. This section is based on Candina Palomer 2002.

6. After transition 11 September continued to be a national holiday. There was no political will and probably not enough political power to change that. In 1998, when Pinochet became a Life Senator, he himself proposed to eliminate the holiday and replace it by a day of 'National Reconciliation'. Only in 2002 was this alternative official date abolished.

7. Undoubtedly, the comings and goings of the Pinochet case since October 1998 have had an impact on this 'past present'.

8. In September 2001 a Chilean newspaper web site conducted a survey asking for opinions regarding reinstating the 11th in the official calendar. The options offered reiterated the three societally established interpretations of the date: 'yes, it is a historic date when Chile liberated itself from the Marxist yoke' (24.2 per cent); 'yes, to commemorate a date of mourning for Chile' (19.5 per cent); 'no, it is a date that divides Chileans. Commemoration only provokes death and destruction' (56.3 per cent).

9. This tradition was broken in 2000 by President Lagos, who participated in some of the commemorative events of the day.

10. This section is based on Lorenz 2002. Acuña and Smulovitz (1995) and Jelin (1995) analyse the process of transition in Argentina and the role of the trial of the members of the military juntas and of the human rights movement.
11. As a clear indication of governmental silence, it is worth showing that in 1984, on the eve of the anniversary of the coup, President Alfonsín delivered a special '100 days in office' message to the nation. In that message, which was published in all newspapers on 24 March, there was not a single reference to the date and the anniversary.
12. HIJOS (meaning children or offspring) is an organisation of sons and daughters of the victims of state terrorism in Argentina. The organisation came into being in the mid-1990s. Its full name is *Hijos por la Identidad y la Justicia, contra el Olvido y el Silencio* (Children Fighting for Identity and Justice, Against Oblivion and Silence). These new youthful activities included dance and music, colourful costumes and a variety of expressive performances, which broadened participation.
13. In 2002, in the midst of a major economic and financial crisis, the commemorative rally of 24 March was especially significant. Besides the historical core of the human rights movement and the variety of social groups claiming rights, there were two new messages: one clearly rejecting the threat of military intervention in politics (a strong reaffirmation of *Nunca Más*); the other linking the policies of dictatorship with current poverty, unemployment and economic crisis.
14. This section is based on Aldo Marchesi 2002. For a historical account of Uruguay, see Caetano and Rilla 1998.
15. This section is based on Alessandra Carvalho and Ludmila da Silva Catela 2002.
16. This section is based on Myrian González Vera 2002.
17. The neighbourhood was inaugurated on 3 November 1957, three years after his coming to power. Since then, it has expressed its gratitude to the regime with a *fiesta popular*.

REFERENCES

Acuña, Carlos and Catalina Smulovitz. 1995. 'Militares en la transición argentina: del gobierno a la subordinación constitucional', in *Juicio, castigos y memorias: derechos humanos y justicia en la política argentina*. Buenos Aires: Nueva Visión.

Caetano, Gerardo and José Rilla. 1998. *Historia contemporánea del Uruguay. De la colonia al MERCOSUR*. Montevideo: Colección CLAEH / Editorial Fin de Siglo.

Candina Palomer, Azun. 2002. 'El día interminable. Memoria e instalación del 11 de septiembre de 1973 en Chile', in Elizabeth Jelin (ed.) *Las conmemoraciones: Las disputas en las fechas 'in-felices'*. Madrid and Buenos Aires: Siglo XXI.

Carvalho, Alessandra and Ludmila Da Silva Catela. 2002. '31 de marzo de 1964 en Brasil: memorias deshilachadas', in Elizabeth Jelin (ed.) *Las conmemoraciones: Las disputas en las fechas 'in-felices'*. Madrid and Buenos Aires: Siglo XXI.

Celiberti, Lilian and Lucy Garrido. 1989. *Mi habitación, mi celda*. Montevideo: ARCA.

Drake, Paul and Iván Jaksic (eds). 1999. *El modelo chileno. Democracia y desarrollo en los noventa*. Santiago, Lom.

González Vera, Myrian. 2002. '"Fecha feliz" en Paraguay. Las memorias del 3 de noviembre, cumpleaños de Alfredo Stroessner' in Elizabeth Jelin (ed.) *Las conmemoraciones: Las disputas en las fechas 'in-felices'*. Madrid and Buenos Aires: Siglo XXI.

Jelin, Elizabeth. 1995. 'La política de la memoria: el movimiento de derechos humanos y la construcción democrática en Argentina', in *Juicio, castigos y memorias: derechos humanos y justicia en la política argentina*. Buenos Aires: Nueva Visión.

——. 2002. *Los trabajos de la memoria*. Madrid and Buenos Aires: Siglo XXI.

—— (ed.). 2002. *Las conmemoraciones: Las disputas en las fechas 'in-felices'*. Madrid and Buenos Aires: Siglo XXI.

Keck, Margaret and Kathryn Sikkink. 1998. *Activists Beyond Borders. Advocacy Networks in International Politics*. Ithaca: Cornell University Press.

Lorenz, Federico. 2002. '¿De quién es el 24 de marzo? Las luchas por la memoria del golpe del '76', in Elizabeth Jelin (ed.) *Las conmemoraciones: Las disputas en las fechas 'in-felices'*. Madrid and Buenos Aires: Siglo XXI.

Marchesi, Aldo. 2002. '¿"Guerra" o "Terrorismo de Estado"? Recuerdos enfrentados sobre el pasado reciente uruguayo', in Elizabeth Jelin (ed.) *Las conmemoraciones: Las disputas en las fechas 'in-felices'*. Madrid and Buenos Aires: Siglo XXI.

4 'What is Written in Our Hearts': Memory, Justice and the Healing of Fragmented Communities[1]

Victoria Sanford

We are often criminals in the eyes of the earth, not only for having committed crimes, but because we know that crimes have been committed.

Alexandre Dumas, *The Man in the Iron Mask*

To forget our past is to risk our future.

Bishop Juan Gerardi, *Nunca Más*

INTRODUCTION

In 1984 Pablo's community was occupied by the army. After being told by a Guatemalan army officer to forget the massacre in his village, Pablo responded,

You can forget, but we are the ones in pain. We will never forget. What happened is written in our hearts. What would you do if they killed your whole family? Would you be capable of forgetting it? Look sir, the truth is that I am not afraid to declare and speak the truth.

Ten years later, in 1994, Pablo and his neighbours told me this story in Plan de Sánchez when I was working with the Guatemalan Forensic Anthropology Foundation (FAFG) on the excavation of a clandestine cemetery there.[2] This was the forensic team's sixth exhumation of a clandestine cemetery, the third in the municipality of Rabinal.

In Plan de Sánchez, there were 18 mass graves containing the remains of 168 known victims of the 1982 army massacre. The quantity of graves and skeletons meant we were unearthing a tremendous number of artifacts and clothing associated with each skeleton. On one occasion, local villagers sorted through artifacts found in a grave of burned skeletons. The bones were so badly burned and contorted from the fire that although we could count that there had been at least 16 victims, we had no complete skeletons and were unable to associate any of the artifacts with individual skeletons. Survivors asked us if they could examine the artifacts. We laid them out above the grave in an orderly and respectful manner on top of flattened paper bags. Then the survivors surrounded the artifacts spread out before them. With great tenderness, they began to look through burned bits of clothing, necklace beads and half-melted plastic shoes trying to recognise something of their relatives who had been killed in the massacre. A few of the men recognised their wives' wedding necklaces and asked us if it might be possible for them to have the necklaces after the investigation was completed. There was no dissension in the community about which necklaces had belonged to which wives. Those who couldn't find the necklaces of their wives, sisters and daughters asked if they might be able to have some of the stray beads because 'surely some of those beads must have fallen from our relatives' necklaces'. Then, they said something I was to hear repeated in every other exhumation in which I have participated, 'Si no tiene dueño, entonces es mío' ('if it doesn't have an owner, then it is mine').

This chapter is an ethnographic study of the forensic exhumation of clandestine cemeteries, individual and community memory of genocide, and local mobilisations for truth, healing and justice. I focus on the exhumation of a clandestine cemetery in Plan de Sánchez, the reburial of Panzós massacre victims and the trial of some of the perpetrators of the Río Negro massacre. Plan de Sánchez and Río Negro are Achí-Maya villages located in the municipality of Rabinal in the department of Baja Verapaz and Panzós is a Q'eqchi-Maya town in the department of Alta Verapaz.[3] The massacres in these communities are but three in the army's scorched-earth campaign which ultimately razed 626 Maya villages and left more than 200,000 people dead or disappeared (CEH 1999a). Though most of the massacres took place between 1980 and 1982, the massacres were preceded by selective assassinations and many rural Maya continued to live in ambient violence after the 1985 elections and into the 1990s – some even up until the signing of the Peace Accords in December 1996 (Arias 1990, Carmack 1988, Falla 1992, Manz 1988, Warren 1993). The Commission for Historical Clarification

(CEH) identified 83 per cent of the victims as Maya and attributed blame for 93 per cent of the human rights violations to the Guatemalan army (CEH 1999a, 1999b). Significantly, the CEH concluded that the army had carried out genocidal acts against rural Maya with the intention of destroying in whole, or in part, the Maya culture. This genocide is remembered as *La Violencia*.

TRUTH, WITNESSING AND THE RESHAPING OF HISTORY

On 28 May 1998, 20 years after the Panzós massacre, I had the privilege of accompanying the Guatemalan Forensic Anthropology Foundation to return the boxed skeletal remains of the victims to their wives, mothers, fathers, daughters, sons and grandchildren. This concluded the investigation we began in July of 1997 for the Guatemalan Historical Clarification Commission to document the Guatemalan army massacre of Q'eqchí Maya peasants in the Panzós plaza.[4]

In Panzós, in the late evening after the church mass and public gathering, we moved the boxed skeletal remains to the community centre. We placed the bones in small coffins and the artifacts on top of the closed coffins. We had only been able to identify two of the 35 skeletons exhumed scientifically. Because the greatest desire of family members is to carry the remains of their loved ones in the burial procession, we give them an opportunity to look at the artifacts to fulfil their desire to identify their lost loved one – 'para sentir bien en el corazón', to feel good in the heart (what we might call closure). Although not considered 'scientific' identifications, when a survivor recognises artifacts, we mark the coffin so that they may carry it in the burial procession. Sometimes there is nothing concrete in the identification, but at other times it is emotionally overwhelming.

One elderly man had passed nearly half of the coffins. He passed those with women's clothing and stopped at each that had men's boots. He would pick up the boots and swiftly review the instep. In front of one of the coffins, as those in line pushed forward to look at the next set of artifacts, he remained frozen in place, gripping the heel of a plastic boot. I walked over to him. He said, 'This is my son. These are his boots. Look here. See that stitching? That is my stitching. I sewed his boot together the morning before he was killed. This is my son.' As other survivors reached the end of the row of coffins without immediately recognising anything, they would return and start over again. During the second round, they began to stand by different coffins. When I approached them to find out what they had identified, each said, 'Si no tiene dueño, entonces es mío.'

Witnessing is necessary not simply to reconstruct the past, but as an active part of community recovery, the regeneration of agency and a political project of seeking redress through the accretion of truth. The very issues that had met with such violent repression when first brought up were not silenced by the violence. Rather, they were held in suspension until the community could reconstruct memory in a public space. Reburial following the exhumation did not draw a process to an end; it reinvigorated community mobilisation for social justice – mobilisation which had been suspended by fear. Just as institutionalised forgetting could not end community desires for justice, forgetting could not end fear. As Veena Das (2000) writes, 'if one's way of being-with-others was brutally injured, then the past enters the present not necessarily as traumatic memory but as poisonous knowledge' (221). Das' theorising of 'poisonous knowledge' advances work on trauma and memory. Pierre Janet wrote that memory 'is an action', but that when an individual is unable to liquidate an experience through the action of recounting it, the experience is retained as a 'fixed idea' lacking incorporation into 'the chapters of our personal history' (cf. Herman 1992:37). The experience, then, 'cannot be said to have a "memory"... it is only for convenience that we speak of it as "traumatic memory"' (37). Further, Janet believed that the successful assimilation or liquidation of traumatic experience produces a 'feeling of triumph' (41).

My research indicates that collective recovery of community memory of experiences of extreme violence can begin to break through fear and create new public spaces for community mobilisation – perhaps by recasting this individual 'poisonous knowledge', when collectively enacted and remembered, as a discourse of empowerment. Further, I suggest that these discourses are often local appropriations and reformulations of global human rights discourse (Sanford 2000, 2001).

'YOU ARE SEEING THE TRUTH'

After all the graves had been exhumed in Plan de Sánchez, there were 18 large holes in the earth. The sizes of the graves ranged from 8 x 10 feet to 15 x 20 feet. Each was about four to five feet deep. Because July falls in the rainy season, the holes quickly filled with water. As I looked at the gaping holes in the earth, they seemed to be many things. They looked like miniature versions of the wounds left in the earth by nickel mines or gravel pits. They also looked like muddy ponds. The area, which had always been filled with people, was deserted, and the holes heightened the empty feeling of absence. My thoughts were broken by the laughter of children who trailed Juan Manuel, Erazmo, Pablo and José. We sat on a grassy knoll and looked at the empty spaces, the valley below and the mountain range beyond.

'It looks sad here', said Don Erazmo.[5] 'But when we have a proper burial, everyone will live with tranquillity.' He said this with the knowledge that it was unlikely he would receive the remains of his family members because it appeared that they had been among those who were burned beyond recognition. As he spoke, the children played with each other and climbed on their fathers seeking embraces.

By the end of the exhumation, I had interviewed all massacre survivors still living in Plan de Sánchez. I asked them why they wanted the exhumation. In addition to not wanting their relatives buried 'como perros' – like dogs, each person gave me several reasons beyond the proper burial.

The first and most stark reason is that survivors want concrete, real, hard evidence. You can touch the bones of the victims we pulled out of the earth. As Dr Clyde Snow always says, 'The bones don't lie.' The army claimed there had been a battle with the guerrillas in Plan de Sánchez. The exhumation clearly showed that the vast majority of victims were women, children and the elderly. Moreover, the forensic evidence unquestionably demonstrated that the skeletons in the grave were victims of a massacre, not casualties of an armed confrontation and not civilians caught in crossfire as the state had claimed (FAFG 1997: Case 319–93, 5TO).

Don Pablo asked me, 'How could they say these were *guerrilleros*? How can an infant of six months or a child of five, six or seven years be a *guerrillero*? How can a pregnant woman carrying her basket to market be a *guerrillero*?'[6] About the exhumation, Don Erazmo told me, 'Allí, no hay mentira. Allí, estan veyendo la verdad' ('There, there is no lie. There, you are seeing the truth').

In 1994, surrounded by the muddy ponds of the empty graves, I asked them why an already vulnerable community would put itself at greater risk by supporting and actively collaborating with the exhumation. Don Juan Manuel told me that the community supported the exhumation because they wanted the truth to come out that the victims were natives of the area. Our children who knew nothing, who owed debts to no one. They killed women and the elderly who did not even understand what they were accused of by the army. *Campesinos*, poor people. People who work the fields for the corn we eat.

The community wanted the truth to be known. Don Erazmo said, 'We have worked in the exhumation. We have worked for truth.' I asked what importance truth could have twelve years after the massacre. This is what I was told:

We want peace. We want people to know what happened here so that it does not happen here again, or in some other village in Guatemala, or in some other department, or in some other country.

We strongly support this exhumation and that everything is completely investigated because we do not want this to happen again.

We do this for our children and our children's children.

We want no more massacres of the Maya.

We want justice. We want justice because if there is no justice, the massacres will never end. God willing, we will have peace.

Some said they wanted revenge. All said they wanted justice. There was great hope that someone involved in the massacre would be tried in court and prosecuted.[7] Just as army threats had sent tremors of fear through Plan de Sánchez, and indeed throughout Rabinal, the process of the exhumation restored community beliefs in the right to truth and justice. Rural Maya have a strong community tradition of publicly voicing their objections and seeking redress within the local hierarchy. Moreover, in rural Maya culture the ancestors help the living move into the future and continue to play a role in the life of the community by defining place and its significance as social space, as living space (Personal Communication, Patricia Macanany, 12 April 2000). In this sense the exhumations not only pushed the state and legal system to respond, thereby activating the rule of law, but also resuscitated local Maya cultural practices.

THE BURIAL

On 4 July 1994, Juan Manuel, Pablo, Erazmo and José asked several of us from the FAFG if we had time to meet with them. They appeared concerned. They explained to us that the mayor of Rabinal was scheduled to visit the site that same day. They asked us if we would help them present a petition to the mayor because they felt our presence would affect the mayor's response. The community had decided that when the remains of their loved ones were returned, they did not want them buried in the cemetery in Rabinal. They wanted the location of the clandestine cemetery declared a legal cemetery. They wanted the proper religious burial in Plan de Sánchez. Juan Manuel explained, 'We want them to rest here because this is where their blood spilled, this is where they suffered, so their spirits are here. We don't want to leave them abandoned. We can't bury them anywhere else. We are prepared to sacrifice this land.' The owner of the land was in agreement with this plan and was willing to sign a document releasing his property rights.

We agreed to assist the community in whatever way we could. We said that we imagined the mayor would have no problem with their plan because there was no dispute regarding land ownership and everyone was in agreement. 'Everyone except the mayor', they responded. They had been to the Rabinal cemetery, the mayor, the health centre and the public ministry. 'They always meet with us', explained Juan Manuel, 'and they always listen to us. But then they say, "It's not possible to have a cemetery there. It will affect the health of everyone in the community. It isn't sanitary. There are microbes that can kill people."' Incredulously, Juan Manuel said, 'How is that going to affect our health? They were buried here for twelve years. No one ever died from microbes.'[8]

So when the mayor arrived with two armed guards, we all stopped our work to greet him. Then Juan Manuel gave a speech for the community. He thanked the mayor for his support and for coming to visit. Then he explained to the mayor that the community wanted to bury their loved ones in Plan de Sánchez and that the owner of the land was in agreement. He publicly requested the mayor's support for their petition. The mayor glanced around at the community members and then at each of us. He said, 'Of course I will help you in any way I can.' Juan Manuel thanked him and said, 'Then, we have your word here before the public that we can have a legal cemetery here in Plan de Sánchez?' 'I give my word', the mayor firmly responded.

Of course, his word was less steady when Juan Manuel returned to the mayor's office for the paperwork. Again, he was sent from the mayor's office to the cemetery, to the public ministry and to the health centre. Again, they all discussed microbes and claimed a cemetery in the community would be a health hazard. 'I told them we had worked in the exhumation and no one died from microbes. In twelve years, no one died with the clandestine cemetery there', recounted Juan Manuel.

> Finally, I told them, and this is the truth, I told them that if they didn't stop sending me from one office to the other and if no one had the courage to sign the legal documents, then we were just going to do it anyway. I told them that we were prepared to carry out the idea we had which was a legal cemetery in Plan de Sánchez.

With satisfaction, he told me:

> In the end, they signed the papers and everyone who had watched me being pushed from office to office saw that really, if we stand together, there are possibilities. And, thanks to all the international brothers and sisters who came here to take our declarations, everyone saw that it is possible to speak the truth.

In October 1994, the plaza of Rabinal filled with thousands of Achí from outlying villages and Rabinal to witness the burial procession. After a mass inside the church, the crowd in the plaza listened to the words of the survivors from Plan de Sánchez which were amplified throughout the community. Juan Manuel remembered that moment:

> After the exhumation, people had been congratulating me. They would say, 'Congratulations Juan. You really have balls to declare the truth.' But then they would tell me to be careful because everyone knew who I was and there were people who didn't like what I did. I was thinking about this as we carried the coffins to the church. After mass, when I was standing there in front of everyone, I just wasn't afraid. I told the whole truth. I said that the army should be ashamed. 'How shameful for them to say that my wife with a baby on her back was a guerrilla. They dragged her out of my house and killed her. Shameful! They opened the

abdomens of pregnant women. And then they said that they killed guerrillas. Shameful!' I said. I talked about the people in Rabinal who had collaborated with the army and how they walked through the streets with no shame for the killings they had done. In this moment, I had no fear. I declared the truth.

Afterwards, a *licenciado*[9] told me, 'What a shame that you are a poor peasant and not a professional. If you were a professional, there would really be change here.' I thought to myself, 'I may be a sad peasant who can only half-speak, but I wasn't afraid and I spoke the truth.' The entire pueblo was there. The park was completely full. Everyone was listening to what I was saying and I didn't feel embarrassed. I knew that afterwards maybe they would be waiting for me in the street somewhere and that that might be my luck. I said, 'Believe me, the guilty think that with just one finger they can cover the sun. But with what they have done here, they simply can't.'

I suggest that this public speaking of truth is a transformation of 'poisonous knowledge' into a collective discourse of empowerment. And truth, as Agamben (1993) suggests, 'cannot be shown except by showing the false, which is not, however, cut off and cast aside somewhere else' (13). Indeed, for Agamben, truth can only be revealed by 'giving space or giving a place to non-truth – that is as a taking-place of the false, as an exposure of its innermost impropriety' (13). Moreover, this transformation is possible because 'truth is a thing of the world: it is produced only by virtue of multiple forms of constraint. And it has regular effects of power' (Foucault 1980:131). In this way, these public events of exhumations, burial, processions and reburials, like the legal cases against perpetrators, represent a public performance of accretion of truth, and thus, the accretion of power. The effects of this power are experienced in the everyday life of the community and directly challenge the spectral presence of the state (the state's production of truth) by establishing a new domain in which Foucault found 'the practice of true and false' to be transformed (Foucault 1980:131–2). These new domains represent the constitution of safe collective spaces for individuals to speak and be heard that enables them, and their communities, to recuperate and redefine collective identity in the aftermath of violence. It is this nascent collective identity which offers hope for the recovery of human dignity and the reconstruction of the social fabric so damaged by political violence. This process of collective recovery of identity also establishes the community as the conduit from the individual to the nation. It is through this connection that projects of memory also form a bridge between recovery from past violence to future-oriented action.

Following Juan Manuel's speech, the survivors of Plan de Sánchez carried the decorated coffins of their loved ones in a procession throughout Rabinal, then three and a half hours up the mountain to Plan de Sánchez where they reburied the remains of their loved ones at the site of the massacre and clandestine cemetery. Later, a Maya Death House (or *capilla*) was built on the site with marble plaques chronicling the Plan de Sánchez massacre. Residents of Plan de Sánchez regularly visit the *capilla* to pray with their ancestors. Each year a public commemoration with a Catholic mass and Maya *costumbre* mark the anniversary of the massacre. Also following the exhumation, many new community projects were started in Rabinal, including a community healing project and widows' organisation.

In Plan de Sánchez, the local development of these political and social practices began with the community organising and 'standing up' to request an exhumation and ultimately succeeding not only in the exhumation, but also in the retaking of public spaces – the municipal plaza, the church and the clandestine cemetery. As a community, survivors challenged these public spaces as mere reminders of Maya loss and re-made them into sites of popular memory contesting official state stories. Far from eroding agency, these appropriations, re-workings and enactments of global rights discourses created 'a framework within which people [were able to] develop and exercise agency' (Nussbaum 2001:407). Further, these same survivors, widowers and widows seized the space they had created not only to publicly adjudicate collective memory, but also to move forward with legal proceedings against intellectual and material authors of the massacre. I now turn to the Río Negro trial.

THE RÍO NEGRO TRIAL

Since 1994 the forensic team has conducted more than 120 exhumations and was a major contributor to the report of the Commission for Historical Clarification. Each exhumation has provided forensic evidence to local prosecutors for court proceedings against perpetrators. To date, only the Río Negro case has come to trial, resulting in the conviction of three civil patrollers who were sentenced to death by lethal injection for their participation in a

Guatemalan-army orchestrated massacre in 1982. At first glance, this conviction might suggest that Guatemala's newly reconstructed legal system is finally functioning. However, the conviction raises more questions than it answers. Among them, the chilling effect this conviction will have on the collection of evidence for future prosecutions of military officials; the propensity of the Guatemalan state to exterminate Maya peasants for political expediency; and, the meaning of this prosecution for Maya survivors.

On March 13, 1982, as the army and civil patrol approached Río Negro, the men fled because just a few months earlier 70 men from Río Negro had been massacred by the same army and civil patrol from Xococ. The women and children remained in the village because the army had only ever looked for men, not women and not children. These 70 women and 107 children were gathered into one large group and ordered to climb on foot up a nearby mountain with the armed men. The women were ordered to dance with the soldiers 'like you dance with the guerrilla'. Forensic analysis of the remains showed that the women had been strangled, stabbed, slashed with machetes and shot in the head. Forensic analysis also revealed that many of the women had received severe beatings to the genital area as evidenced by numerous fractured pelvises including that of Marta Julia Chen OsoRío who was nine months pregnant at the time of her death. All the women, including the little girls were buried naked from the waist down.

Fourteen adolescent girls were separated from the group and set aside for mass rape following the killings of their mothers, brothers and sisters. After the mass rape, the girls were stabbed and macheted to death. The majority of children died from having their heads smashed against rocks and tree trunks.

Eighteen children survived because the patrollers from Xococ who had killed their families decided to take these children home in slave-like conditions. The patrollers never imagined that 17 years later these same survivors would testify against them in a court of law. At the time of the massacre, Jesus Tec was ten years old and carrying his two-year-old brother in his arms. During the massacre, one of the defendants in the 1999 court case grabbed the baby by the ankles and pulled him from Jesus. 'I begged him not to kill my brother', Jesus testified during the court proceeding, 'but he broke his head on a rock'. Jesus was one of the survivors of the massacre because the civil patroller who killed his baby brother decided to take him home as a slave.

The Río Negro case was initiated in 1993 when massacre survivors, including Jesus, denounced the massacre to authorities in Salama, the departmental capital of Baja Verapaz. The survivors asked for an investigation of the civil patrollers from Xococ, the platoon of 40 soldiers from the Rabinal army base, and the intellectual authors.

During the 1999 court proceeding prosecutors called military officers to the witness stand. One witness was General Benedicto Lucas Garcia who served as army chief of staff during the reign of his brother General Romeo Lucas Garcia who ushered in the epoch known as *La Violencia*. Trained by the US Army School of the Americas in combat intelligence and high military command and credited with designing the 'scorched earth' campaign, Benedicto testified that the civil patrols were his idea and that he had personally reviewed the patrols in Salama in 1981. (This would be the same year that a US State Department document classified as secret stated that General Romeo Lucas Garcia believed that 'the policy of repression' was 'working' – a conclusion based on a definition of a 'successful' policy of repression as one that led to the 'extermination of the guerrillas, their supporters and sympathizers'.) Entering the courtroom as the grand populist, Benedicto waved and shook hands with everyone including the prosecutors, the defence, the judges and the defendants. When asked about the Río Negro massacre, he pleaded ignorance. When asked if he had ordered it, he gasped as if in shock and said, 'That, that ... would be ... a crime against humanity.'

Another witness was General Otto Erick Ponce, previously a commander of the Rabinal army base and vice-minister of defence in 1994 – the same year that, as we entered our fourth month of the exhumation in Plan de Sánchez, the army gathered 2,000 local Achí peasants from 19 villages in a meeting at the Rabinal army base and declared: 'The anthropologists, journalists and internationals are all guerrilla. You know what happens when you collaborate with the subversives. The violence of the past will return. Leave the dead in peace.' 'Deja los muertos en pas hijo de puta [*sic*]', ('Leave the dead in peace son of a whore'), was a threat received that same week at the Office of the Human Rights Ombudsman. General Ponce refused to provide the court with names of ranking officers at the base and indeed denied that the civil patrols had ever existed.

Witnesses for the defence argued that the defendants 'were not military commissioners', had 'never been in the civil patrol', that 'there had never been a civil patrol in Xococ' and that the defendants 'did not even know what a civil patrol was'. Further, they argued that the day of the massacre, the defendants 'had been planting trees in a reforestation project'. As for the Río Negro children, they had 'gone voluntarily to Xococ to live'. Amongst the extensive evidence against the defendants were official documents with signatures of the military commissioners with their titles and photographs of the same with other Xococ patrollers carrying army-issue weapons.

During the trial, relatives of the Río Negro victims held marches demanding justice, placing banners in front of the tribunal. These relatives filled the courtroom throughout the trial. Achí from other Rabinal communities (including Plan de Sánchez) also attended the trial – hoping that their massacre case would be the next to be heard in court. Civil patrollers from Xococ demonstrated for the release of the military commissioners.

The criminal court proceeding in Salama was marked by death threats to survivors and witnesses; a military officer defiantly raising his right hand in a salute reminiscent of Nazi Germany as he was sworn in; the relocation of defendants to prevent the possibility of a mob 'liberating' them from jail; and the clearing of the courtroom on several occasions due to threats of violence.

The ambient violence which marked this trial is not unique to legal attempts to prosecute perpetrators of human rights violations in Guatemala. On 7 October 1999, as the trial in Salama proceeded, Celvin Galindo, the prosecutor investigating the murder of Bishop Juan Gerardi, resigned and fled to the United States following numerous death threats. Indeed, in the first six months of 2000 a second judge assigned to the Gerardi case and two key witnesses had also fled the country after receiving death threats.

In 1994 when I first interviewed massacre survivors in Plan de Sánchez and asked them what they wanted from the exhumation, I was told collectively by 24 widowers that they wanted 'revenge'. In 1998, after much community reflection on collective trauma, healing and truth, the same Achí told me they wanted the intellectual authors to be punished, but not their neighbours who participated in the massacres. They did not want their neighbours to go to jail because 'jailing my neighbour will only create more widows and orphans. More widows and orphans will not help anyone.'

As the 1999 court proceedings dragged on with the intellectual authors mocking the legal process and local perpetrators threatening survivors and witnesses, Río Negro survivors did not express the generosity of forgiveness. They demanded the dismantling of the impunity in which the local perpetrators had lived and requested the application of the death penalty. Taking account of the violent behaviour of the accused, the magnitude of the crime and the feelings of the survivors, the prosecutor, who is personally opposed to the death penalty, requested this maximum sentence. Despite the volatile and tense atmosphere in Salama and elsewhere, the three judges in the Río Negro trial distinguished the court proceeding by demonstrating objectivity and equanimity in their efforts to discover the truth about the massacre. This alone has given many Guatemalans the hope that justice, which has generally been a privilege of the powerful, may now be within the reach of the poor and the indigenous.

THE CIVIL PATROLS, IMPUNITY AND THE 'GREY ZONE' OF JUSTICE

Nevertheless, the image of justice emerging from this verdict is skewed, regardless of one's moral position on the death penalty. The massacre was committed by civil patrollers from the neighbouring village of Xococ under army order. The civil patrols themselves constituted an integral part of the army's counter-insurgency campaign. Forced participation in the civil patrols often took the form of torturing, assassinating and massacring innocent people under army orders. Those civil patrollers who refused to comply were always tortured and often killed. It is within this context that civil patrollers from Xococ committed the Río Negro massacre – which was only one of the 626 known massacres committed by the Guatemalan army in the early 1980s. Indeed, the victims of the Xococ civil patrol were not limited to Río Negro, just as Xococ was not the only civil patrol to commit crimes against humanity.

In its comprehensive investigation, the Commission for Historical Clarification (CEH) found that 18 per cent of human rights violations were committed by civil patrols. Further, it noted that 85 per cent of those violations committed by patrollers were carried out under army order (CEH T-II:226–7). It is not insignificant that the CEH found that one in every ten human rights violations was carried out by a military commissioner and that while these commissioners often led patrollers in acts of violence, 87 per cent of the violations committed by commissioners were done in collusion with the army (181).

In 1995, there were 2,643 civil patrols organised and led by the army. In August 1996 when the demobilisation of civil patrols was begun, there were some 270,906, mostly Maya peasants, registered in civil patrols (234). This is significantly fewer than the 1 million men who were organised into civil patrols in 1981 – one year before the Río Negro massacre. Taking into account the population at the time and adjusting for gender and excluding children and the elderly, this means that in 1981, one in every two adult men in Guatemala was militarised into the army-led civil patrols (226–7).

Like recent genocides in other parts of the world, the systematic incorporation of civilians in murderous army operations complicates the prosecution of perpetrators in many ways because it shifts a seemingly black-and-white crime into what Primo Levi (1988) called the 'grey zone'. One lesson of the recent conviction and sentencing of the patrollers in Guatemala is that if civilians evade certain death under military regimes by acquiescing to army orders to commit acts of violence, the democratic state that follows will kill them, albeit through a civilian court, for following the orders of the previous regime.

This is not to suggest that civilians who participated in crimes against humanity should not be tried for their crimes. The point here is that to focus on the least powerful perpetrators in the military regime ultimately protects the intellectual authors. What civil patroller will now come forward as a material witness to identify army perpetrators in the knowledge of the Río Negro precedent?

As previously mentioned, the desire for local justice appeared to increase as the trial proceeded. Having explored issues of truth, memory, justice and healing in Rabinal communities (including Plan de Sánchez, Río Negro and Xococ) since 1994, I believe this publicly expressed desire for local justice is located in collective and individual memory of experiences during *La Violencia* which reflected the vulnerability of communities to the violence of both the army and the civil patrols. At the local level, during and after *La Violencia*, inter- and intra-community problems and injustices were as often traced to the impunity of military commissioners as they were to army orders. Massacres and other gross violations of human rights in Maya communities were systematically carried out by the army and civil patrollers under order from the army high command. Many of the daily injustices suffered by massacre survivors were, however, enacted by civil patrollers (and especially by military commissioners) who acted with impunity at the local level, confident in the real or perceived support of the army officials who appointed them. I call this 'lateral' impunity – that is, the local expression of structures of impunity, both formal and informal, born out of the national vertical structure of impunity. This local structure of impunity can take on a life of its own with lateral impunity continuing long after the vertical structure of state repression and the impunity it fomented withdraws from the area, falls into remission, or crumbles.

It was within this lateral impunity that military commissioners used their ill-gotten power to steal the lands of neighbours, plunder livestock, extort money, rape women and commit other crimes – even after their military commissions had officially ended. Though the prosecution of the patrollers might act as a deterrent at the national level to other patrollers coming forward to name army officials who gave them orders, from a local perspective this prosecution may also serve to decrease lateral impunity in other communities where military commissioners fearing prosecution may now think twice before threatening or abusing their neighbours.

CONCLUSION

An Achí woman who survived an attack by the Xococ civil patrol in her village of Santo Domingo told me 'I complain to god and pray that one day the guilty will pay for what they did.' An Achí man from another village who accompanied me, later commented, 'She isn't demanding that they ask forgiveness. *Perdon* (forgiveness) is not in our linguistica. This idea of forgiveness comes from the NGOs.' He went on, 'The guilty can say, "We did these bad things under someone else's order, forgive me." But this *perdon* has no meaning for me because there is no *perdon* in Achí.'

Where we might use 'forgive' in English or 'perdon' or 'disculpe' in Spanish, the Achí say 'Cu-yu la lu-mac' which in Spanish is translated as 'Aguantame un poco', and in English roughly as 'tolerate me a little'. From ongoing communication with survivors, it is my sense that if the intellectual authors of massacres and other crimes against humanity (as well as those who perpetuated lateral impunity in local communities) are brought to justice, the survivors will again find the generosity and strength to tolerate the guilty among them.

Although I wish I could close this chapter by writing that the intellectual authors have been brought to justice, I cannot. Indeed, General Efrain Ríos Montt (who came to power by military coup in March 1982 and ruled Guatemala for 18 months of genocidal massacres in rural Maya) is now the President of the Guatemalan Congress of Deputies in which his party holds a majority of seats. His party also holds the actual presidency. The other 120-plus massacre cases sit in courthouses throughout the country awaiting trial. As one forensic anthropologist commented, 'they used to try to stop the exhumations with threats. Now they are more sophisticated, they hold up the proceedings in court.' Several massacre cases have been filed at the Inter-American Court and also await hearings. As I write this in 2002, eleven current and former FAFG forensic anthropologists are under 24-hour protection due to ongoing death threats. On 21 February 2002 they received individually typewritten letters: 'We will finish you off ... you are not the ones to judge us ... your families will be burying your bones and those of your children.' These written threats have been followed up by regular telephone threats to offices, homes and cell phones. After more than 190 exhumations, these continuing threats are intended to intimidate these eleven anthropologists who will be called as expert witnesses in forthcoming cases against current and former high-ranking army officials.

Despite this, Maya survivors, forensic anthropologists and human rights organisations continue to push for justice and the rule of law. As the recent international legal proceedings and debates about General Agosto Pinochet demonstrate, the desire for truth and justice does not end with the dictatorship. I do believe that one day the forensic evidence that has been gathered will be used in Guatemalan courts or the Inter-American Court to prosecute the intellectual and material authors of genocide. In the meantime, these generals no longer travel in Europe and most avoid the United States as well for fear of civil suits by survivors residing in the US.

The ethnography of exhumations in Guatemala demonstrates that: (1) the development and voicing of community memories of surviving genocide can break through fear and create new space for community mobilisation; (2) each testimony creates a new political space for another survivor to come forward and share 'poisonous knowledge', thus incorporating trauma into memory; and that the collection of testimonies gives this memory a community space that is no longer poisonous; (3) individual testimony represents the expansion of potential and real agency which in the collectivity of testimonies creates new space for political action; (4) the exhumation represents a physical re-taking of public spaces which transforms these spaces from symbols of pain and loss to sites of popular memory and action; (5) the exhumation can lead to legal proceedings and even prosecution; (6) Maya appropriation, re-working and enactments of global rights discourses develop new frameworks for the expansion and exercise of agency; and, (7) the exhumations and collective testimonies create what Foucault called new domains of truth with real power effects.

Some of these power effects have to do with the exhumations, public burials and legal proceedings while others have to do with consequent community mobilisation for land rights, cultural rights, bilingual education, rural health clinics, beneficiary participation in NGO decision making on local projects and the creation of new local Maya political parties which have won office at the local level. Each of these projects builds on political space garnered through the exhumations. Hannah Arendt (1969) asserted that power cannot be equated with violence because, while violence can destroy power, it is unable to create it. These myriad community projects resulting from local mobilisation are the real power effects of truth as well as the hope for the future.

NOTES

1. I thank Asale Angel-Ajani, Fernando Moscoso, Erika Bliss, Michael Bosia, Kathleen Dill, Julia Lieblich, Phyllis Beech, Ramiro Avila Santamaria, Scott Appleby, Philippe Bourgois, Anna Haughton, Yazir Henri, Ivan Jaksic, Terry Karl, Purnima Mankekar and Shannon Speed for many thoughtful conversations about community healing, testimony and agency. I especially thank Paul Gready for inviting me to present this paper at the 'Cultures of Political Transition' Conference at the University of London and for his commitment to bringing the conference papers together in this volume. Thanks also to Veena Das, Deborah Poole, Elizabeth Jelin, Rosemary Jane Jolly, Carolyn Nordstrom, Rachel Seider and Billie Jean Isbell for comments on my presentation and earlier drafts of this chapter. The Virginia Foundation for the Humanities and the Department of Anthropology at Cornell University also provided venues for excellent feedback from colleagues. A Faculty Fellowship at the Kellogg Institute for International Studies gave me the opportunity to write for a semester; fieldwork in Guatemala was supported by the Inter-American Foundation, the Fulbright-Hays Fellowship Program, Stanford Anthropology Department and Latin American Studies Center awards, Shaler Adams Foundation, Peace and Life Institute and the Guatemalan Forensic Anthropology Foundation. Any errors are mine alone.
2. The FAFG was founded in 1993 with support from Dr Clyde Snow and the American Association for the Advancement of Science to conduct forensic investigations of clandestine cemeteries in Guatemala.
3. On 28 May 1978 the Guatemalan army opened fire on a peaceful land rights protest in the plaza of Panzós. Thirty-five men and women were killed in the plaza and several hundred men were killed in the selective violence of death squads in the months that followed (Sanford 1998, 2000, 2001 and FAFG 2000). My work in Panzós is based on testimonies from

some 200 widows. Under order of the Guatemalan army, the Xococ Civil Patrol massacred 70 women and 107 children in Río Negro on March 13, 1982. In Plan de Sánchez, the army massacred 168 women, children and elderly in July of 1982 (FAFG 1997). Narratives from Plan de Sánchez are based on testimonies from each of the 24 widowers whose lives were spared because they were working in the valley below when the soldiers destroyed their village. Río Negro is based on testimonies from child survivors and two Xococ perpetrators of the massacre as well as other local observers.

4. At the request of the FAFG, I developed a research methodology and led the investigation for the historical reconstruction of massacres in Panzós, Alta Verapaz and Acul, Nebaj, El Quiche. The methodology was then replicated in two additional investigations for the CEH in Chel, Chajul, El Quiche and Belen, Sacatepequez. In May and June 1998 I wrote the historical reconstruction of the massacres in Panzós and Acul, and supervised the writing of the reconstructions for Chel and Belen for the FAFG Report to the CEH.

5. All names used in this chapter are pseudonyms except for those of public figures.

6. Rabinal Testimony No. 7–3, 18 July 1994.

7. Rabinal Testimony Nos 7–3, 27 July 1994; 7–5, 20 July 1994; 7–3, 18 July 1994; 7–2, 27 July 1994; 7–1, 18 July 1994; 7–1, 27 July 1994; Plan de Sánchez, collective interview, 25 July 1994.

8. Plan de Sánchez, collective meeting, 4 July 1994.

9. A *licenciado* is someone with a university bachelor's degree.

REFERENCES

Agamben, Giorgio. 1993. *The Coming Community* (trans. Michael Hardt). Minneapolis: University of Minnesota.
——. 1998. *Homo Sacer – Sovereign Power and Bare Life*. Stanford: Stanford University Press.
Angel-Ajani, Asale. Forthcoming. 'Negotiating Small Truths', in Victoria Sanford and Asale Angel-Ajani (eds) *Engaged Observer: Activism, Advocacy and Anthropology*. Tucson: University of Arizona Press.
Arendt, Hannah. 1969. *On Violence*. New York: Harcourt Brace.
Arias, Arturo. 1990. 'Changing Indian Identity: Guatemala's Violent Transition to Modernity', in Carol Smith (ed.) *Guatemalan Indians and the State: 1540–1988*. Austin: University of Texas.
Benjamin, Walter. 1968. *Illuminations*. New York: Schocken Books.
Carmack, Robert. 1988. *Harvest of Violence: The Maya Indians and the Guatemalan Crisis*. Norman: University of Oklahoma Press.
Commission for Historical Clarification (CEH). 1999a. *Guatemala Memory of Silence – Conclusions and Recommendations*. Guatemala City: CEH.
——. 1999b. *Guatemala Memoria del Silencio, vols 1–12*. Guatemala City: CEH.
Das, Veena. 1989. 'Subaltern as Perspective', in Ranajit Guha (ed.) *Subaltern Studies VI – Writings on South Asian History and Society*. Delhi: Oxford University Press.
——. 2000. 'The Act of Witnessing-Violence, Poisonous Knowledge, and Subjectivity', in Veena Das, Arthur Kleinman, Mamphela Ramphele and

Pamela Reynolds (eds) *Violence and Subjectivity*. Berkeley: University of California.

FAFG (Fundación de Antropología Forense de Guatemala). Formerly EAFG (Equipo de Antropología Forense de Guatemala).

1995. *Nada Podrá contra la Vida!* Guatemala City: EAFG.

1996. *EAFG Anuario No.3: 1994–1995*. Guatemala City: EAFG.

1997. *Las Masacres de Rabinal*. Guatemala City: EAFG.

2000. *Informe de la Fundación de Antropología Forense de Guatemala: Cuatro Casos Paradigmaticos Solicitados por La Comisión para el Escalrecimiento Historico de Guatemala Realizadas en las Comunidades de Panzós, Belén, Acul y Chel*. Guatemala City: FAFG.

Falla, Ricardo. 1992. *Masacres de la Selva*. Guatemala City: Editorial Universitario.

Foucault, Michel. 1979. *Discipline and Punish – The Birth of the Prison*. New York: Vintage Books.

——. 1980. *Power and Knowledge: Selected Writings and Interviews*. New York: Pantheon.

——. 1988. 'The Dangerous Individual', in L. Kritzman (ed.) *Politics, Philosophy, Culture: Interviews and Other Writings, 1977–1984*. New York: Routledge.

——. 1994. 'The Punitive Society', in P. Rabinow (ed.) *Michel Foucault: Ethics, Subjectivity, and Truth, the Essential Works of Foucault 1954–1984, vol. 1*. New York: New Press

Herman, Judith. 1992. *Trauma and Recovery*. New York: Basic Books.

Levi, Primo. 1988. *The Drowned and the Saved*. New York: Vintage.

Manz, Beatriz. 1988. *Refugees of a Hidden War – The Aftermath of Counterinsurgency in Guatemala*. Albany: State University of New York Press.

Moussa, Mario and Ron Scapp. 1996. 'The Practical Theorizing of Michel Foucault: Politics and Counter-Discourse', *Cultural Critique* 33:87–112.

Nussbaum, Martha. 2001. *Upheavals of Thought – The Intelligence of Emotions*. Cambridge: Cambridge University Press.

Sanford, Victoria. 1997. *Mothers, Widows and Guerrilleras: Anonymous Conversations with Survivors of State Terror*. Uppsala: Life and Peace Institute.

——. 1998. *Strengthening the Guatemalan Peace Process – A Proposal of the Guatemalan Forensic Anthropology Foundation to the Open Society Institute*. Guatemala City: FAFG.

——. 2000. *Buried Secrets: Truth and Human Rights in Guatemala*. Ph.D. dissertation, Stanford University.

——. 2001. 'From *I, Rigoberta* to the Commissioning of Truth: Maya Women and the Reshaping of Guatemalan History', *Cultural Critique* (47).

United States Department of State. 1981. Secret Memorandum Reference: Guatemala 6366. October 5. Declassified January 1998.

Warren, Kay. 1993. *The Violence Within: Cultural and Political Opposition in Divided Nations*. Boulder: Westview Press.

5 Memory and Forgetting: The Roma Holocaust

István Pogány

INTRODUCTION

Although the Nazis' hatred or contempt for certain races was focused pre-eminently on the Jews, Germany and some of her wartime allies were also engaged in a murderous campaign against Europe's Gypsies. However, that is a topic about which comparatively little is known, even today. Only recently have scholars and Roma organisations begun to draw attention to the *Porajmos*, literally 'devouring' in Romani (Kenrick and Puxon 1995; Fings, Heuss and Sparing 1997; Kenrick 1999; Lewy 2000; Karsai 1992). However, to date, far less research has been conducted on this topic and far less written or broadcast than about the *Shoah* in which up to 6 million Jews were slaughtered.

Why has the persecution of the Roma during World War II received so much less attention than the carnage of Europe's Jews? Why has there been such a massive disparity in the number of narratives, both fictional and scholarly, that have been constructed about these parallel crimes? Is the apparent lack of concern with the *Porajmos*, until recently, evidence of a pervasive racism? Has that racism, albeit unconscious, tainted even liberal intellectuals, writers and artists who have struggled to comprehend and communicate the evils of the Nazi era? If so, I am as guilty as anyone. In a book that I published a few years ago, analysing patterns of human rights abuses in East Central Europe during the twentieth century, I devoted a footnote to the treatment of the Roma (Pogány 1997:219, n.12).

There are many reasons why the *Porajmos* have received comparatively little attention. They tell us much about attitudes towards the Roma but also something about the Roma themselves. But, before considering these explanations, we should pause and ask ourselves an uncomfortable question. In some respects, at least, was the general neglect of the wartime persecution of the Gypsies justifiable? In strictly objective terms, were Nazi policies towards the Roma far less stringent than those pursued against the Jews? However randomly terrible, did the treatment of the Roma during World War II fall short of outright genocide, as some reputable historians have argued (Lewy 2000:222–4)? In virtually ignoring the persecution of the Gypsies during the War, have many writers and scholars simply chosen to focus on the central and most terrible crime committed by the Nazis and their allies – the destruction of Europe's Jews?[1]

THE ROMA HOLOCAUST: AN HISTORICAL OUTLINE

Although accurate statistics are notoriously difficult to come by, it seems clear that far fewer Gypsies than Jews were killed during the war. The number of Roma who perished in the Nazi death camps, or who were murdered elsewhere during World War II, has been variously estimated at between 200,000 and 500,000 persons (Brearley 1996:9). Donald Kenrick and Grattan Puxon, authors of one of the best-known texts on the Roma Holocaust, estimate that around 200,000 Gypsies were deliberately killed by the Nazis and their allies (Kenrick and Puxon 1995:150). By contrast, Jewish deaths in the *Shoah* are thought to be close to 6 million.[2] However, it is not simply, or even primarily, a question of numbers. If it were, the former Soviet Union would easily win such a grisly and pointless competition. During World War II, civilian deaths in the USSR were, at a minimum, 16 million, while the number of Soviet soldiers, sailors and airmen who died accounted for 8 or 9 million more (Davies 1996:1328).

The principal reason why the Jewish Holocaust has attracted so much and such enduring attention is not simply because of the numbers killed but because of the ruthless and cold-blooded policy that lay behind the statistics. Nazi Germany instituted a methodical programme for killing all the Jews in Europe. *Every* Jew, irrespective of age, sex, occupation, nationality, or even religion, was to be conscientiously slaughtered. The resources of a highly industrialised modern state, including its bureaucracy, armed forces, scientists, engineers, architects and transport workers, were harnessed to this end (Dawidowicz 1990: Chapters 6–8; Hilberg 1985).

Nazi policies towards the Roma are much harder to unravel. In the East, beginning in the spring of 1941, German *Einsatzgruppen,* augmented by thousands of locally recruited auxiliaries, followed in the wake of the *Wehrmacht* as it advanced across the Soviet Union. Although the *Einsatzgruppen* concentrated their energies on killing Jews and Bolsheviks (categories which were seen as largely interchangeable by the Nazis),[3] Gypsies were also routinely targeted as they were suspected of espionage and of aiding Soviet partisans (Overy 1999:140; Lewy 2000:117–22; Kenrick and Puxon 1995:90–8). The *Einsatzgruppen* generally machine-gunned their hapless victims, including women, children and the elderly, disposing of the corpses in nearby ditches.

In January 1942, Reinhard Heydrich, a high-ranking Nazi official, convened the Wannsee Conference to coordinate 'the total solution of the Jewish question in Europe' (Dawidowicz 1999:176–9). The object of the Conference was to consider ways of collecting Europe's Jews in transit ghettos as a prelude to transporting them 'farther to the East' for use as slave labour (Dawidowicz 1990:177). As Heydrich explained to the assembled delegates, mostly second-level functionaries, including representatives from the German Ministries of Justice, the Interior and Foreign Affairs, a large proportion of the Jews would 'fall away through natural reduction'. Those who survived would 'be dealt with appropriately' (Gilbert 1987:282). Despite the careful use of euphemisms, Heydrich's intentions were perfectly clear to those present. There is no evidence that the Conference even considered the fate of the Gypsies.

Whether Nazi leaders subsequently took the decision to annihilate all of Europe's Gypsies, along with the Jews, remains controversial. Some scholars continue to argue for the uniqueness of the Jewish Holocaust. The Oxford-based historian, Martin Gilbert, while acknowledging the terrible sufferings of the Roma during the war, has written that, '[i]t was the Jews alone who were marked out to be destroyed in their entirety' (Gilbert 1987:824). More recently, the American historian, Guenter Lewy, contended that, 'no overall plan for the extermination of the Gypsy people was ever formulated, and … the evidence shows that none was implemented' (Lewy 2000:225). Others, such as Donald Kenrick and Grattan Puxon, insist that 'a decision had been taken in 1942 to wipe out the Gypsies throughout Europe', although they offer little by way of proof (Kenrick and Puxon 1995:41).

Such scholarly arguments, though sincere and well intentioned, can all too easily degenerate into an unseemly scramble for 'first prize', or even 'equal first prize', amongst Hitler's victims. The persecution of Roma and Jews in the Holocaust was, in many important respects, comparable and it was carried out for comparable reasons. In viewing Jews and Gypsies as *innately* corrupt and corrupting, these two ethnic groups were gradually singled out by the Nazis from every other people in Europe.[4] One of the Nuremberg Laws, hastily adopted by the Reichstag in September 1935 under the watchful eye of the *Führer*, aptly illustrates this thinking. The Law for the Defence of German Blood and Honour, whose passage had been advocated by influential groups of German doctors, prohibited marriage or sexual relations between Jews and Germans to ensure 'the purity of German blood'.[5] Within a couple of months, the prohibition was extended to forbid Germans from marrying or engaging in sexual relations with Gypsies, or with others of 'alien blood' such as 'Negroes'.[6] In a subsequent decree, forbidding marriage between Germans and persons with even one Gypsy grandparent, Germany's Minister of the Interior declared, 'Gypsy blood endangered the purity of ... German blood to a marked degree' (Lewy 2000:97).

Historians may be correct in holding that 'Nazi policy towards the Gypsies lacked the kind of single-minded fanaticism that characterized the murderous assault upon the Jews' (Lewy 2000:225). They may be right in concluding that, unlike the Jews, '[t]he Gypsies were considered a "nuisance" and a "plague" but not a major threat to the German people' (Lewy 2000:225). After all, as a recent book points out, Gypsies were a numerically insignificant minority in Germany when Hitler became Chancellor in 1933, accounting for only 26,000 persons. Frequently itinerant, mostly poor, these Roma were 'a strictly marginal element' in German society (Lewy 2000:43). Yet, if Gypsies were despised rather than hated, they, like Jews, came to be regarded by the Nazis as less than human. Nazi ideology transmuted Jews *and* Gypsies into virulent microbes capable of infecting the Aryan race.[7]

Even if the alleged intention of the Nazis – to kill every single Gypsy in Europe – remains unproven, the scale of the atrocities committed against the Roma during the War and the classification of the entire race as a potential source of biological pollution places Gypsies in close proximity to Jews as fellow victims of the Holocaust. History, it seems, does not provide us with grounds for dismissing the *Porajmos* as a sideshow.

The severity of the persecution of the Roma during the Holocaust varied, depending on local factors. In Hungary, anti-Roma policies were introduced later and applied more selectively, sometimes even arbitrarily, than the battery of legislative and other measures constricting the country's Jews (Crowe 1996:88–91). Estimates of the numbers of Hungarian Roma killed in the *Porajmos* vary from as little as a few hundred to as many as 32,000, although the true figure cannot be calculated with any degree of accuracy (Karsai 1992:144). By contrast, over 400,000 Hungarian Jews perished at Auschwitz-Birkenau alone (Cesarani 1997:5).

Nevertheless, at its worst, the persecution of the Roma was indistinguishable from that of the Jews. In the German Protectorate of Bohemia and Moravia, itinerant Gypsies were interned in labour camps, such as Lety and Hodonin, where the guards were Czechs, not Germans (Lewy 2000:150–1; Necas 1999:49–151). In overcrowded and insanitary conditions, weakened by lack of food, hundreds of internees died of contagious diseases such as typhus. Survivors, along with the bulk of all the Gypsies remaining in Bohemia and Moravia, were deported to Auschwitz where all but a few hundred died (Kenrick and Puxon 1995:55–9). In Jasenovac, a notorious death camp in the wartime Fascist state of Croatia, *Ustasa* guards killed Gypsies, Jews and Serbs indiscriminately in what was widely seen as a 'holy war' against the country's ethnic and religious minorities (Fraser 1995:267). Reportedly, even German military personnel who visited the camp were appalled. Out of an estimated 28,500 Roma in Croatia, in 1941, between 26,000 and 28,000 are thought to have died in the *Porajmos* (Crowe 1996:219–20). In Romania, a close ally of Nazi Germany for part of World War II, over 13,000 sedentary Gypsies were rounded up and deported, by train, to Transnistria during September 1942. Transnistria, formerly Soviet territory, had been occupied by Axis forces and placed under a Romanian administration. Thirteen thousand nomadic Gypsies from Romania had already been forcibly resettled in the region by the end of August, while Transnistria had also become a dumping ground for Romania's Jews. A total of 180,000 Romanian Jews were deported to Transnistria between 1941 and 1944 (Kelso 1999:95–130). Amidst terrible conditions, which resulted from a combination of malice and incompetence on the part of the Romanian authorities, Gypsies and Jews succumbed to typhus, starvation and to random persecution by gendarmes. According to an official report compiled by Romanian officials in December 1942, in the Oceacov region of Transnistria Gypsies were 'insufficiently fed being given only 400 grams of bread for those capable of working and just 200 grams for the old people and children' (Kelso 1999:114). This meagre diet was supplemented with 'a few potatoes and very rarely salted fish … in extremely small quantities'. The report went on to note that, in the Oceacov area, '[i]n recent days … as many as ten or fifteen [Gypsies] have died daily' and that the corpses were 'full of parasites' (Kelso 1999:114). Despite the severe cold in winter, the Gypsies were 'naked without any clothes, and clothing and heating materials are completely lacking' (Kelso 1999:114). Of the 26,000 Romanian Gypsies deported to Transnistria in 1942, only 6,000 survived (Kelso 1999:130). Even in the Netherlands, long a byword for liberalism and tolerance, the Dutch police and gendarmerie diligently rounded up Gypsies in the spring of 1944, screening out Dutch nationals who were not ethnically Romani and handing over the 'real' Gypsies for deportation to Auschwitz (Fraser 1995:266). Of these, less than 10 per cent remained alive at the end of the war.

In Germany, tens of thousands of Gypsies, chronically sick and others deemed 'unworthy of life' were gassed in euthanasia programmes between the beginning of 1940 and August 1941 (Gilbert 1987:239). By the end of the war, more than half of Germany's former Gypsy population had perished (Lewy 2000:221). At the village of Chelmno, in a zone of Poland which had been annexed by the Reich in 1939, almost 5,000 German Roma were gassed in the back of specially constructed trucks, in January 1942, as a 'precautionary' measure (Lewy 2000:113–15). Typhus had broken out at the camp where the Gypsies had been interned. The same trucks had been used to gas Jews for at least a month. Approximately half of Germany's Roma population, over 13,000 Gypsies, were sent to Auschwitz during 1943, in accordance with a decree issued by Himmler which nominally exempted 'pure Sinti and Lalleri Gypsies' (Lewy 2000:140–9). As a leading historian of the period notes, '[m]any of those exempt from deportation were made subject to compulsory sterilization' (Lewy 2000:148). Inside Auschwitz, where the Roma were kept in a specially constructed family camp, Gypsy children, along with Jews, were subjected to bizarre and medically worthless experiments by Josef Mengele, in a brutal parody of scientific inquiry (Fings 1997:104–6, Lewy 2000:158–62). Gypsies were also experimented on at Natzweiler, Dachau, Sachsenhausen and Ravensbrück. At the beginning of 1945, within the space of four months, 15,000 Gypsies died of starvation and disease at the German concentration camp of Mauthausen (Gilbert 1987:807). Apart from Mauthausen, Gypsies were interned in various concentration camps, including Dachau, Sachsenhausen, Buchenwald, Bergen-Belsen and Ravensbrück, while others were sent to specially constructed extermination camps – Birkenau (Auschwitz II), Belzec, Chelmno, Maidanek, Sobibór and Treblinka. If fewer Gypsies than Jews died in the Holocaust, the persecution and prolonged torment of a large proportion of Europe's Gypsies was real enough.

Overall, the treatment of the Gypsies by the Nazis and their allies was not merely 'persecution', as some historians contend. In many parts of Europe, the Gypsy experience in World War II would, in all probability, satisfy the definition of genocide or of complicity in genocide found in the Genocide Convention of 1948.[8] At the very least, the persecution of the Roma constituted 'Crimes Against Humanity' and 'War Crimes' as understood by the Charter of the Nuremberg Tribunal.[9]

THE FORGOTTEN HOLOCAUST: TOWARDS AN EXPLANATION

A number of explanations have been offered for the neglect of the Roma Holocaust until comparatively recently. Some of these explanations centre on the perceived nature of Roma culture, particularly the Gypsies' apparent lack of interest in their own past. On this view, the failure of Europe to acknowledge the enormity of the *Porajmos* has been due, in no small measure, to the absence, until lately, of concerted Gypsy protests about their treatment during the war. This silence has been compounded by the dearth of attempts by Roma artists, writers and intellectuals, during much of the second half of the twentieth century, to convey these experiences through theatre, books, articles, or the visual arts. In other words, a people who live overwhelmingly in the present (a commonly held perception of the Roma) are not preoccupied with their often tragic history and do not assert it in their dealings with others.

A related explanation might focus on the Gypsies' alleged view of themselves as lucky. Although this carefully constructed self-image rests on a great deal of wishful thinking, it would allow the Roma to reinterpret the *Porajmos* as proof of their good fortune rather than as a tragedy in which the Roma (like the Jews) were mostly helpless victims. Survival in the face of overwhelming odds, cheating death in incredible ways, is the underlying theme of the testimonies I recorded from elderly Romani (Gypsy women) who lived through the war. Those who consider themselves lucky are less likely to demand redress or to appeal for recognition of the injustices done to them.

Other explanations for the neglect of the Roma Holocaust are more prosaic, centring on the socioeconomic status of the Roma, particularly in Central and Eastern Europe where their conditions have worsened dramatically in the decade or so since the collapse of communism. On this view, a people who are overwhelmingly poor, illiterate and marginalised lack the means or even the will to protest or to draw attention to past wrongs that were done to them. Their thoughts are taken up with more immediate concerns such as paying the rent and feeding and clothing themselves and their families. Dwelling on events that occurred almost sixty years ago is an unaffordable luxury.

LIVING IN THE PRESENT

Usually, it is the victims of any major human rights abuse who are the first, and the loudest, in articulating their anger and sense of injustice. For a long time, the silence of *Gadzos* (non-Roma) about the Nazi persecution of the Gypsies was very nearly matched by the silence of the Roma themselves. For years, the Roma seemed almost to collude with the tacit consensus not to draw too much attention to this neglected aspect of the war. As Isabel Fonseca remarks, Gypsies have 'no tradition of commemoration, or even of discussion' of the *Porajmos*, '[i]t is a story that remains almost unknown – even to many Gypsies who survived it' (Fonseca 1996:243).

To speak of a Roma culture of silence, or forgetting, would be misleading. In other contexts, the Roma are often highly vocal in their denunciation of injustices. Until recently, however, the *Porajmos* has mostly elicited silence. Michael Stewart, a British anthropologist who lived in a Romani settlement in Hungary in the 1980s, wrote *The Time of the Gypsies* about his experiences. Tellingly, the wartime persecution of Gypsies is not mentioned in Stewart's narrative, except for a couple of sentences in a historical introduction (Stewart 1997:5). The almost total absence of any reference to the *Porajmos* in Stewart's book reflects the fact that the Roma whom Stewart befriended rarely if ever mentioned the wartime persecution of the Gypsies.

In interviews with Roma in Hungary and Romania, I have never recorded a single spontaneous comment about the *Porajmos*. Invariably, I have had to coax some recollection out of my elderly interviewees. It was not fear or innate reserve that prevented these Roma from volunteering their memories of that period. The same people complained readily enough about the prejudice or obstruction they encountered in their dealings with local officials, policemen or relief agencies. They spoke at length about the hardships of their daily lives.

If many Roma do not talk unprompted about the war, perhaps it is because so many of them live overwhelmingly in the present rather than in the past or in the future. As I was told repeatedly by social workers and officials of aid agencies, chronically poor Roma – which means most Roma in post-communist Central and Eastern Europe – are preoccupied with *immediate* needs and concerns. The past, including the war years when many Roma faced persecution, or the imminent threat of persecution, has somehow lost its importance.[10] It could be recalled, in order to satisfy the curiosity of a *Gadzo* questioner, but the exercise was artificial.

A LUCKY PEOPLE

Bangyi is a *Vlach* Romani woman and the oldest of the Roma I have come to know in Kétegyháza, a village in south-eastern Hungary close to the border with Romania. At the end of the war she was eight years of age. When I asked her about the Holocaust, her first and most vivid memories were not of the German *Sonderkommando* responsible for rounding up Hungary's Jews (Braham 1981:394–6), or of the Hungarian *csendőrök*, or gendarmes, who had assisted them so energetically, but of the Russian troops who had briefly occupied the village towards the end of the war.

'The Russians came', said Bangyi, 'They did horrible things to the women, they raped them.' 'Rape' is a word I had suggested, although Bangyi adopted it. She was coy in her references to sexual behaviour, like other elderly Roma. 'Almost fifty of them did it to Zsófi, one of the women in the neighbouring house', Bangyi continued. She recalled that Zsófi's elderly mother, who was approaching 70 at the time, had hurried over to their house for help. But Bangyi's family were powerless to intervene; the Russian soldiers were armed and determined. Some of the Russian troops even pursued the old woman to Bangyi's home, prompting Bangyi's elder sister to hide in the unlit oven. Bangyi's mother, who was around 40 at the time and still handsome, grew alarmed that she too would be raped. In her despair, she cried out in Romani, 'My God, what will happen to us?'

As Bangyi tells it, when her mother cried out in Romani one of the Russian soldiers who had entered her house pricked up his ears; he was a Russian Gypsy. He replied to her in Romani saying, 'Don't be afraid, I am your brother. I will speak to the other soldiers and make sure you come to no harm.' He was true to his word. For as long as the Russian troops remained in the village, the Gypsy soldier watched over Bangyi's home. Bangyi's family were spared further molestation by their Russian liberators.

However, Bangyi began to grumble about something else that the Russians had done. She recalled that they had positioned a big field gun in the yard of her house. The soldiers busied themselves, preparing the gun for use. Bangyi's parents grew alarmed thinking that, if the gun were fired, this would only prompt German and Hungarian troops to rain shells on the Russians, almost certainly destroying the family's home in the process.

Again there was a near miraculous intervention. A small Soviet spotter plane appeared, swooping low over the field gun. The pilot, a woman, motioned impatiently to the artillerymen to pack up and move further west, towards the receding front line. Bangyi's family and their home were spared; there was to be no more fighting in the village.

Bangyi fell silent. I had to ask her again if German or Hungarian forces had mistreated any of the Roma in the village during the war. She said that the Russian troops had arrived in Kétegyháza before the gendarmes could round up the Gypsies, although that was already in preparation. Bangi told me, however, that the gendarmes had killed the Gypsies in a neighbouring village, throwing the corpses into pits where they were covered with quicklime.

Bangyi reserved her most memorable, if incredible, story for this part of her reminiscences. As Bangyi tells it, a heavily pregnant Gypsy woman was taken before the most high-ranking gendarme in a village just a few miles from Kétegyháza. The officer was sitting behind his desk when she was brought to him. He rose from his chair and, without any preliminaries, shot her in the head with his pistol, killing the woman instantly.

Somehow, and *this* is the incredible part – not the fact that a police officer in wartime Europe should have shot a pregnant Gypsy – the woman's husband heard of what had happened and reached his wife's body within minutes of her death. Miraculously, the corpse had been left unattended. According to Bangyi, the husband had brought his cut-throat razor with him. Without a moment's hesitation, the Rom sliced open his wife's belly and carefully removed the living foetus from her womb. Bangyi assured me that the baby had thrived and that it had grown up into a strapping woman who was alive to this day, with a large family of her own.

For a long time I wondered how to treat Bangyi's 'recollections' of the war. Even if her reminiscences are not literally true – although for all I know they might be – the stories serve as striking metaphors for Roma resilience and good fortune, sometimes in the face of overwhelming odds. In that sense, the narrative has a truthfulness that transcends mere factuality. The Roma survived, so their stories suggest, even overcoming such monumental tragedies as the *Porajmos*.

POVERTY, MARGINALISATION, LIMITED EDUCATION

Most Roma have remained silent about their sufferings during the war. In part, as suggested above, this may represent a conscious decision to put the past behind them. In part, though, the Roma have been silent because they lacked a voice with which to command the attention of politicians, the media, or the public at large. Low levels of literacy amongst a people with a vibrant but predominantly oral culture has meant that most ordinary Roma lack the skills needed to communicate effectively with non-Roma society.[11] When I asked Bangyi how to spell the name of the street on which she lives in the village of Kétegyháza – I had promised to send her some photographs – she became flustered and could not tell me. Bubi, a Rom almost 60 years of age and living in the same village, was unable to write his name when I asked him to sign something. He had to call in his son, János, to sign it for him. Even János, more than a generation younger than Bangyi or his father, asked me to write out the word 'Anglia', which is Hungarian for 'England', so that he could send me a letter after my return to Britain. The letter never arrived.

There have been too few Roma, until recently, able to write articles for highbrow newspapers, or Romani scholars who could produce books on Roma history. Even now there are very few Romani lawyers who can take up claims on behalf of their people; I know of only one Romani film-maker, Tony Gatlif. Although his art-house films on Roma themes are much admired by the critics, they lack the wide commercial appeal and popular impact of Steven Spielberg. Poverty, social marginalisation, lack of formal education and, frequently, even of respect for education, as well as a widely held suspicion of bureaucracies and officials have kept the Roma mute. As János confided to me, the first time we met, '[education] isn't very popular with Gypsies, that's the problem'.

Gypsies, whether in Central and Eastern Europe or beyond, are overwhelmingly poor. There are few, if any, Roma investors whom governments in Prague, Bucharest or Bratislava would wish to court. Politically, the Roma have made little impact, although fledgling

Roma political parties have been established in a number of countries including Romania. While there is a large Roma Diaspora, it lacks political influence, extensive intellectual resources or economic 'muscle'. There is no Roma state to represent Roma interests in the way that Israel, somewhat erratically, has championed the cause of vulnerable Jewish minorities in various continents. Apart from occasional and limited help from India, the Roma stand alone.[12]

CONCLUSION

In recent years, Roma NGOs and interest groups have begun to draw attention to the *Porajmos*. In Hungary, a powerful collection of testimonies by Roma survivors was published with an introduction by the British anthropologist, Michael Stewart (Bernáth 2000). For anyone with access to the internet a wealth of material, albeit of rather variable quality, is available on the Roma Holocaust.[13] Demands from Roma organisations for enhanced public recognition of the *Porajmos* and for appropriate compensation for survivors and for Roma communities in general have become increasingly insistent.[14] Many Roma born since the end of World War II now know something about their collective past during the war, however sketchy and imperfect, aside from what they have heard from family or community members with direct experience of these tragic events. The dangers of the Roma losing any sense of their own history during World War II (or that Europe will be able to take refuge in collective amnesia), is receding.

There are, however, also causes for concern. Authentic memories of the *Porajmos*, encompassing startling variations of treatment of Roma across wartime Europe – ranging from indifference and even occasional humanity to brute sadism and orchestrated mass murder – are being challenged by a cruder, less nuanced representation. A struggle is taking place over the collective memory of the *Porajmos* in which some Roma interest groups are waging a campaign for recognition of the Roma as fully equal victims of the Nazis along with the Jews. No doubt, the object of such campaigning is to elicit greater sympathy for the Roma. It also stems from a desire to correct the persistent under-recognition of the abuses inflicted on the Roma people during the Nazi era.[15] However, tinkering with history is never justified. The Roma do not need an invented or exaggerated history to negotiate civilised and humane treatment from European governments, or to have a proper sense of their own identity. The true record of the wartime persecution of many of Europe's Gypsies should suffice.

NOTES

1. Tellingly, a recent – and widely lauded – history of the Third Reich, by Michael Burleigh (2001), contains only a few, passing references to the treatment of Gypsies during World War II, while entire chapters (4, 8) deal with the treatment of Europe's Jews.
2. According to the historian, Norman Davies, the average of various estimates of the numbers of Jews who died in the Holocaust is 5,571,300. The minimum estimate is 4,871,000, while the maximum is 6,271,500 (Davies 1996:1328).
3. On the conflation of Jews and communists in Nazi thinking see, for example, Dawidowicz 1990:163–5.
4. Gradually, the Nazis began to formulate racial theories about the Gypsies, classifying them as alien and inferior (Lewy 2000:15–16).
5. The quotation, which is from the Preamble of the 1935 Law, is reproduced at Friedländer 1998:142.
6. The additional restrictions on sexual relations were effected by means of a Decree of 14 November 1935, which extended the scope of the 1935 Law, and a subsequent circular from the German Ministry of the Interior which explicitly refers to Gypsies (Friedländer 1998:153).
7. Professor Lewy places considerable emphasis on the fact that 'pure' Jews were considered by the Nazis to represent much more of a threat to Germans than persons with mixed Jewish and Gentile ancestry, whereas 'pure' Gypsies were viewed more favourably than *Zigeunermischlinge* (Gypsies of mixed ancestry) (Lewy 2000:55). While true, it is doubtful whether this quirk of Nazi ideology is of especial importance. Even 'pure' Gypsies were seen as sufficiently corrupting to require sexual segregation from Germans, while at least 90 per cent of all Gypsies in Germany were thought to be *Mischlinge* and, thus, deemed particularly dangerous (Lewy 2000:49).
8. The legal construction of 'genocide' and of 'complicity in genocide' is far from straightforward. Following the establishment of the International Criminal Tribunals for the former Yugoslavia and Rwanda, both of which have considered allegations of genocide, there is now an expanding jurisprudence (Ratner and Abrams 2001:26–45).
9. For an analysis of the Nuremberg Tribunal's consideration of the persecution of the Roma, see Rooker 2002:38–46. Dr Rooker concludes that, although the 'Romany people were not explicitly named in the judgment', the Nuremberg Tribunal implicitly recognised that the treatment of the Roma amounted to 'Crimes against Humanity' and 'War Crimes' (45–6).
10. There is, however, a small but growing body of published testimonies by Roma survivors of the *Porajmos*. See, for example, Bernáth 2000.

11. A study conducted in 1971, in Hungary, found that 73–4 per cent of *young* Roma were almost entirely illiterate. Levels of illiteracy amongst older Roma was, of course, significantly higher (Kemény 1999:229).
12. India helped to finance the First World Romany Congress, convened in London in 1971. Subsequently, Indian governments have offered limited diplomatic and material support to the Roma (Hancock 1997).
13. See e.g. the unattributed materials on 'Roma History' at <http://www.romnews.com/>, and the articles on 'The Holocaust', by Ian Hancock and others, at <http://www.geocities.com/~patrin/holcaust.htm>.
14. Details of some of these demands can be found using the search engine at <http://www.romnews.com/>.
15. Of course, the reverse view is put forward by some Roma scholars and activists, such as Ian Hancock, who argue that Jewish historians have sought to exaggerate the uniqueness of the Jewish Holocaust. See, for example, Hancock's review of Guenter Lewy's book ('Downplaying the Porrajmos: The Trend to Minimize the Romani Holocaust'), at <http://www.geocities.com/~patrin/holcaust.htm>.

REFERENCES

Bernáth, G. 2000. *Porrajmos*. Budapest: Roma Sajtó Központ.

Braham, R. 1981. *The Politics of Genocide*, Vols I–II. New York: Columbia University Press.

Brearley, M. 1996. *The Roma/Gypsies of Europe: A Persecuted People*. London: Institute for Jewish Policy Research.

Burleigh, M. 2001. *The Third Reich: A New History*. London: Pan Books.

Cesarani, D. (ed.). 1997. *Genocide and Rescue: The Holocaust in Hungary 1944*. Oxford and New York: Berg.

Crowe, D. 1996. *A History of the Gypsies of Eastern Europe and Russia*. New York: St Martin's Griffin.

Davies, N. 1996. *Europe*. Oxford University Press: Oxford.

Dawidowicz, L. 1990. *The War Against the Jews 1933–45*. Middlesex: Penguin Books, 10th Anniversary edition.

Fings, K. 1997. 'Romanies and Sinti in the Concentration Camps', in K. Fings, H. Heuss and F. Sparing (eds) *From 'Race Science' to the Camps*. Hertfordshire: University of Hertfordshire Press.

Fonseca, I. 1996. *Bury Me Standing*. Vintage: London.

Fraser, A. 1995. *The Gypsies*. Oxford: Blackwell, 2nd edn.

Friedländer, S. 1998. *Nazi Germany and the Jews*, Vol. 1 London: Phoenix.

Gilbert, M. 1987. *The Holocaust*. London: Fontana Paperbacks.

Glatz, F. (ed.). 1999. *A cigányok Magyarországon [The Gypsies in Hungary]*. Budapest: Magyar Tudományos Akadémia.

Hancock, I. 1997. 'The Struggle for the Control of Identity', *Transitions* September 1997, at <http://www.ijt.cz/transitions>.

——. 'Downplaying the Porrajmos: The Trend to Minimize the Romani Holocaust', at <http://www.geocities.com/~patrin/holcaust.htm>.

——. 'The Holocaust', at <http://www.geocities.com/~patrin/holcaust.htm>.

Hilberg, R. 1985. *The Destruction of the European Jews*, Vols 1–3. New York: Holmes and Meier, rev. edn.

Karsai, L. 1992. *A cigánykérdés Magyarországon 1919–1945 [The Gypsy Question in Hungary 1919–1945]*. Budapest: Cserépfalvi Kiadás.

Kelso, M. 1999. 'Gypsy Deportations from Romania to Transnistria 1942–44', in D. Kenrick (ed.) *In the Shadow of the Swastika*. Hertfordshire: University of Hertfordshire Press.

Kemény, I. 1999. 'Tennivalók a cigányok/romák ügyében' ['Things to Be Done in the Affairs of the Gypsies/Roma'], in F. Glatz (ed.) *A cigányok Magyarországon*. Budapest: Magyar Tudományos Akadémia.

Kenrick, D. and G. Puxon. 1995. *Gypsies Under the Swastika*. Hertfordshire: University of Hertfordshire Press, 2nd edn.

Kenrick, D. (ed.) 1999. *In the Shadow of the Swastika*. Hertfordshire: University of Hertfordshire Press.

Lewy, G. 2000. *The Nazi Persecution of the Gypsies*. Oxford: Oxford University Press.

Marrus, M. 2000. *The Holocaust in History*. Toronto: Key Porter Books, 2nd edn.

Necas, C. 1999. *The Holocaust of Czech Roma* (trans. S. Pellar). Prague: Prostor.

Overy, R. 1999. *Russia's War*. Middlesex: Penguin Books.

Pogány, I. 1997. *Righting Wrongs in Eastern Europe*. Manchester: Manchester University Press.

Ratner, S. and J. Abrams. 2001. *Accountability for Human Rights Atrocities in International Law*. Oxford: Oxford University Press, 2nd edn.

Rooker, M. 2002. *The International Supervision of Protection of Romany People in Europe*. Nijmegen: Nijmegen University Press.

Stewart, M. 1997. *The Time of the Gypsies*. Boulder, Colorado: Westview Press.

Part II
Identities

6 Continuity and Discontinuity of East German Identity Following the Fall of the Berlin Wall: A Case Study

Molly Andrews

Nietzsche once commented that it is typically German to ask what it is to be German (McFalls 1995:143). Interest in German identity, or 'the German identity problem' has endured for more than a century (Gilliar 1996:20), and indeed the project of forming a German identity is said to have begun in the eighteenth century, with the campaign to establish a 'cultural nation' (Jarausch, Seeba and Conradt 1997:42). However long ago this fascination began, it is clear that the events of the autumn of 1989 have given it new life. In the ten years since the unification of the two Germanies, questions about German identity have increasingly permeated national consciousness. Despite the early optimism of many – epitomised by Willy Brandt's now famous statement of November 1989, 'Now grows together what belongs together' (quoted in Minkenberg 1993:53) – the challenges of unification (economic, political, social and political) persist.[1] Even former Chancellor Helmut Kohl has commented: 'inner unity ... will admittedly take longer and cost more than most, including myself, had originally assumed' (quoted in Steininger 2001:27).

Significantly, the passage of time has not simplified the question of national identity. Rather, it has prompted many, as Nietsche might have predicted, to think more deeply not only about what it means to be a German, but to be a German from a particular part of Germany. In this chapter, I will examine the effect of the changes of 1989 on East Germans' sense of their national identity. The picture I will paint is one of apparent contradictions as East Germans continue to probe, explore and struggle with who they are and where they belong.

IDENTITIES

Pickel (1997) comments upon the 'essentially contested' (203) nature of identity, and describes three distinct meanings of the term. First, and 'politically by far the most successful' (203), is national collective identity, which is based on the assumption of 'the nation as a natural and homogeneous whole with essential and unchanging characteristics, a common past and common future' (203). Second is the 'more "social scientific" conception of identity' which quantifies 'measurable individual attitudes and value orientations' (203). Finally, there is the post-modern perspective which regards identity as 'a great diversity of constantly changing meaning structures embodied in and mediated by discourse practices and codified in a variety of texts' (203).

Clearly, how one conceptualises East German identity is influenced by how one understands the meaning of identity more broadly. East German national collective identity is, in Pickel's description, roughly equivalent to the 'official' East German identity, that is, the concept of citizenship rights and duties as propagated by the East German state. The project of national-identity-building was high on the agenda of the socialist state, and there were a wide variety of programmes – for instance the Free German Youth (FDY) and the Young Pioneers – in which individuals were virtually required to participate, whose explicit purpose was to instil and promote a very particular concept of the duties of citizenship amongst its populace. Perhaps because of this, rather than despite it, many East Germans appeared to have 'a fundamental ambivalence towards the manifest successes and failures of the East German state' (Jarausch et al. 1997:41).[2] It was precisely this aspect of identity which had been in crisis long before the revolutionary changes of 1989. At no time was this more clear than when East Germans went to the polls in March 1990, to participate in the first and only democratic elections their country would know; the resounding message was a rejection not only of communism, but of the East German state. Offe (1996) comments upon 'the total lack of GDR loyalty towards its own political existence' (22), and writes,

> It turned out that the GDR had not been solidly recognized internally, that is, by its own people ... How far the GDR had been from becoming a 'nation' through its own collective self-

confidence and identity became apparent in the lack of a voice of its own during the process of unification. (23)

If the 'official' East German national identity can be said to have been in a critical condition before, surely this was the time of its death.

Paradoxically, however, this new situation created an opportunity for the revival, even rediscovery, of other less tangible and perhaps therefore more powerful aspects of East German identification. Jarausch et al. (1997) comment: 'History plays a central role in the creation of national identity ... Groups represent their fate in stories which create a feeling of community by recounting their trials and tribulations' (25). The fall of the wall opened up new spaces for East Germans to experience their common history, both that which they had lived through and that which they were making. Times of political upheaval are particularly ripe conditions for collective narrative reconstruction (Roßteutscher 2000:62) and this in turn has high potential for the renewal of collective identity. If, from a postmodern perspective, identity is fragmented, multilayered, and in constant flux, then the quality and the complexity of the psychological challenges posed by the transformation of East Germany can perhaps be best captured by a framework which problematises homogeneity and internal consistency, and rather emphasises the dynamic tension inherent in identity work.

For those interested in the quantifiable aspects of identity – Pickel's second meaning – statistics abound. As a result of unification, there was massive reorganisation of East German social structures. Kolinksy (1995b) comments 'the collapse of state socialism and the integration of East Germany into the western polity had the hallmarks of a transformation: nothing remained unchanged, unquestioned or predictable' (13). Nowhere can the effects of the changes be seen more clearly than in the alteration in the rates of birth, marriage and divorce.

The incorporation of the GDR into the political, social and economic system of the old Federal Republic has been accompanied by a series of dramatic changes to the pattern of family life in the five new Länder. These changes have found vivid expression in the precipitous fall in the marriage, divorce and birth rates of around 66 per cent, 80 per cent and 60 per cent respectively between 1988 and 1992. (Dennis 1998:83)

Employment – 'the core of ... life and the yardstick to measure all the value of all things and of all people' (*Bauernmoral* 1908, cited in Knabe 1995:71) – was severely affected by the changes of 1989. In 1988, the workforce was 9.7 million (out of a population of 16 million); within five years, it had fallen by 5 million (Knabe 1995:73). In all areas of life the changes were most dramatic for East German women: under state socialism, women were 'as numerous in the labour force as men, enjoyed equal access to education, and were as likely as men to obtain vocational qualifications, although less likely to reach advanced levels anywhere' (Kolinksy 1995c:177). For a variety of reasons, most of this has changed in the decade since unification, and as a result, East German women have proved to be particularly vulnerable to the previously unknown phenomenon of poverty.

Judging from these statistics, one might assume, along with Kolinsky (1995b), that 'nothing has remained unchanged' (13), including that elusive phenomenon, East German identity. However, while the scale of structural change is well documented, the underlying meanings which East Germans attribute to these changes are less understood. Initial research into 'shifts in the collective attitudes towards key policy issues that were triggered by the process of unification ... suggest[s] both major changes and astounding continuities' (Jarausch 1997b:8). Indeed, the deeper one probes into the effects of unification on East German identity, the less uniform is the picture.

In the first half of 1992 I was in Berlin collecting life stories from 40 women and men who had been leaders in the citizens' movements which spearheaded the revolutionary changes of East Germany in 1989, or what one of my respondents, documentary film-maker and later parliamentarian Konrad Weiß, refers to as 'the German Autumn'. I arrived only weeks after the Stasi files had been opened to the public, and the general atmosphere in those grey winter months was of a very raw society. Conversations about identity were commonplace – where to get one, how to lose one, how to find one which had been lost. Wolfgang Herzberg, East Germany's first oral historian, told me that identity had become 'a fashionable word'. People of East Germany, he said, had 'lost their old identity, which has always been a bit unstable. Now they are looking for a new identity.' Major social changes had occurred in East Germany between the opening of the Berlin Wall in 1989 and when I collected my data in 1992; writing in 1994, German historian Jurgen Kocka observed: 'Germany has changed more in the last four years than it has in the last four decades' (173). What I witnessed in the months I spent there was a revolution of memory and identity. In this chapter, I will explore the complex interplay between the continuity and discontinuity of identity as articulated in my interviews with these 40 East Germans.

'MAUER IN KOPF' – THE WALL IN THE MIND

Reinhard Weißhuhn is an East German who had been part of the small underground opposition in his country for more than twenty years when, on 9 November 1989, the Berlin Wall was opened. Here he describes his reaction to this momentous event:

> This was such a ... a very elementary transformation of one's existence, of the ... well, the total ... world in a way. I'll try to explain. I have lived ... [For 20 years] I have always lived 200 metres from the wall. And this wall, to me, has become a symbol of captivity in every respect, also in a metaphoric, symbolic sense. And this is what I have been ramming my head against for the last 20 years. And I had ... as a way of survival, I had resolved to ignore this wall as far as I could, you know by reason. You see, in other words, I have suppressed the problem of 'the wall', tried to suppress it. I tried to do the same throughout the week when the wall had gone. I did not only try to suppress the fact that the wall had been there previously, but I also tried to suppress the fact that it had gone. And it didn't work.

The conversations I had with East Germans were full of descriptions of the wall, and its function as an organising principle in their lives. Clearly, the wall was both physical – 45 miles long, and, at places, ten foot thick, concrete reinforced with steel rods – and metaphorical. For many years the wall was a prominent feature in the dreams of East Germans. Although the wall took more than two years to dismantle, its psychological hold is even more enduring.

Wolfgang Templin, once identified by Eric Honecker as 'the number one enemy of the state', tells a very different story from that of Weißhuhn above. Although both men, as co-founders of the Initiative for Peace and Human Rights, were well-established figures in East Germany's underground opposition, on the night the wall opened they found themselves living on opposite sides of the wall, owing to Templin's forced exile to the west in 1988.

Well, my sentiments of this night were different from those of other people, because I was on the wrong side of the wall … I immediately rang friends and said 'if the wall comes down then my route back into the GDR is free', and I was ecstatic … The fall of the wall for me meant that I could go back into the GDR rather than get out of it. And purely physically I experienced this – everybody pushing past me in the opposite direction and me pushing against the stream the other way. Well, I was overjoyed and it was in that mood that I re-entered the GDR … Two, three weeks later, we all, that is my children, my family, moved back here.

The wall had always been something which structured one's very existence, physically and psychologically. Wolfgang Ullmann, senior churchman and member of the Bundestag, explains: 'If you live beside the wall, it's strange, untenable, and so unnatural. When I took a little walk with my wife in the churchyard … you always had the soldiers watching you from the towers.' Even now, the long-term psychological consequences of the presence of the wall for more than a quarter of a century are difficult to ascertain. The phrase 'the Wall in our minds', attributed to West Berlin author Peter Schneider (1983), 'assumes that 45 years of communist rule have had a profound cultural and political impact' (Klingermann and Hofferbert 1994:38). The phrase is now commonplace in discussions of the transition to post-communism, and its updated version 'rests on the assumption that the trend of current developments is toward the heightening of barriers between eastern and western Germany, especially as regards attitudes and behaviour' (Klingermann and Hofferbert 1994:38).

Jens Reich, a senior East German biologist and key leader of the citizen's movement, compares himself to his children, who, at the time of our interview – less than three years after the opening of the wall – were already living, working and studying in the west.

[they live] without looking any longer at that inner wall. But for me the inner wall is still present … You always pass a border when you go through Wollenstraße, [you] feel people are different, the unspoken. Conventions are different … you don't feel depressed in any way, but it's different.

Ironically, as the Berlin Wall came down, the inner wall – the wall which marked the psychological distance between eastern and western Germany – was for many strengthened. Prior to 1989 East Germans had had ample exposure to West German culture particularly through the medium of television; however, actual contact between the two parts of Germany only served to highlight differences.

Ruth Reinecke is an actress at the Maxim Gorki Repertoire Theatre in Berlin, and was one of the organisers of the November 4th demonstration in Alexanderplatz, which precipitated the opening of the wall five days later. She describes that time in her life as 'difficult to analyse, because the events took place so rapidly, one was chasing the next. Not only the events in the street, but the events inside the self.' As the Berlin Wall was opened, Reinecke was immediately aware that this would have vast implications, not only for the political situation in the GDR, but for her very personal sense of self.

> When the wall was opened, suddenly another world existed, which I did not know, which I would have to live in, whether I wanted it or not. There was of course a great curiosity to explore the world, this still exists. On the other hand I had the fear somehow whether I would be capable of making this new world ... my own ... Maybe there was also some fear that I could not stay any more the same person I had been so far.

For Reinecke, as for Weißhuhn, the opening of the wall had an immediate and profound impact on 'the events inside the self'. For her, deep personal reflection and change are inevitable, and this is both frightening and exciting.

One of the most intriguing aspects of the many conversations I had with East Germans was the extent to which they intimately experienced the dynamic relationship between their own biography and the forces of history. Many felt that they had helped to make history and that history was most definitely changing not only their life circumstances, but their very selves.[3]

NATIONAL IDENTITY: IMAGINED COMMUNITY VERSUS REAL BOUNDARIES

The events of and subsequent to that autumn caused many East Germans to re-evaluate their relationship to their country. Ruth Reinecke explains to me:

I believe for myself the GDR has left behind a very decisive influence on my life which cannot be extinguished. On the other hand I believe that I am still at an age in which I can actively cope with the new things which have come. Certain things I cannot lose, nor do I want to lose. I do not want to extinguish my life, my former life as a citizen of the GDR.

Reinecke's phrase 'my life, my former life as a citizen of the GDR' reveals an ambivalence towards this aspect of her identity which is also evident in other interviews. Is she still East German, or is she not?

One of the questions I asked in my interviews was, 'When you are asked where are you from, what do you say?' Most interview participants paused over their response, but eventually gave some form of the answer 'the GDR' – in the present tense, with comments such as 'throughout my life I will remain a citizen of the GDR' (variations on this included one respondent describing himself as 'coming from the east of Germany' and another saying she was from 'the other Germany'). Several respondents said they did not feel German at all, but rather European. Virtually no one responded that they felt they were from 'Germany'.[4] This question provoked a strong response from Jens Reich:

I am from the GDR. I've lived in the GDR, I was brought up in the GDR. I've no misgivings of any sort in saying it. I never use the word *ehemalig* [former, as in the former GDR] ... I find it ridiculous. The GDR is a fact, an historical fact. You don't say the *ehemalig* German Reich; it [simply] doesn't exist any longer ... This emphasis on *ehemalig* and on the disassociation of yourself from it ... is a sign of psychic instability in those people [who use this word].

Later in the interview, Reich elaborates further on this point:

I've no inner drive to deny the GDR ... [which] has proven its right of historical existence in '89. By our own activity we freed ourselves and made it a decent society, for some weeks and some months. We did it at least, so ... without any feeling of shame you can say '[I am from the] GDR.'

Sebastian Pflugbeil is a physicist and leading environmentalist who, along with Reich and 28 others, was a founder member of Neus Forum, the first and most significant of the citizen's groups to form in autumn 1989. While he shares with Reich a deep sense of national pride surrounding the events of the bloodless revolution, his overall outlook is far more pessimistic.

> Compared to Poland, Hungary or Czechoslovakia, our national consciousness was very underdeveloped or non-existent ... [we] were not at all proud of our history or ... proud of being a GDR citizen. Then, in the autumn of '89, within a few days, [we developed] a very strong, extremely strong, extremely pronounced national identity ... But that lasted exactly until the night the wall came down. In the autumn of '89 this was a positive identity, a constructive, national identity. Now it has more the appearance of a hospital community.

Michael Passauer is a pastor, and served a vital role providing a safe harbour for dissident East Germans during the 1980s. He is very interested in the problem of identity, and notes marked changes which have occurred as a result of political events. Like Pflugbeil, he explains that citizens of the GDR had always had 'problems with identity'.

> He [the East German citizen] had a hard time to say 'I am German' – it is associated with, for instance, the Third Reich ... but he also didn't say 'I am a GDR citizen.' That's not a possible thing to identify with. So he was permanently in search for an identity. In Autumn '89 ... the GDR citizen for the first time identified himself very closely ('skinclose') with the GDR ... 'We are the people.' This we had for about half a year, and this we, I experienced ... we had this strong self-confidence, we were able to break down totalitarian systems. And with October 3rd [the day unification took effect], there is a new identity crisis.

Passauer outlines a collective psychological journey which resonates with the descriptions offered by other respondents. Until 1989, the historical moment of self-determination, East Germans were 'vague' about their *heimat*, where they belonged and what was their home. Both Pflugbeil and Passauer note the lack of identification between East Germans and their state. This was 'not something they felt proud of'; for reasons of history and circumstance, the German Democratic Republic was 'not possible to identify with', as discussed earlier. All this changed with the bloodless revolution, when the citizens of the GDR 'proved [their country's] right of historical existence'. Yet that sense of national identity, so heightened by these political events, would take different forms following unification.

RESISTING IDENTITY APPROPRIATION

Initially, many East Germans reacted to the changes of 1989 by moving to the west, seeking to become as fully integrated into that society as possible. Andre Brie, Deputy Chairperson of the Party of Democratic Socialism (the remake of the old Communist Party), told me he felt that East Germans had been 'forced into the West German identity' whereas he 'would have preferred to come to a new identity ... I think millions of East Germans are living at the moment as if they have no past'.[5] Henning Shaller, set designer for the Maxim Gorki Theatre in Berlin and one of the key organisers of the 4 November demonstration in Alexanderplatz, echoes some of these sentiments. For him, there is a critical connection between national identity and a consciousness of history, and he too expresses concern about living as if one had no past. 'This process of rapid unification', he explains,

> led to a loss of identity, because everything which still reminds us of the old structures of the GDR is destroyed. It is difficult for people now to have their own identity. Identity in a way I believe is related to the consciousness of history. But if I ignore history, or deal with history in a selective way saying 'well I will not bear in mind this and this here', then I won't have an identity. It cannot be denied that a great part of my life developed in this somewhat rotten state. But I can't say that everything I have done was bad, and I observe this great fear that people who are living here in this part of Germany within the shortest time have been taken over by a new identity which may be fatal in its consequences.

Bärbel Bohley, the so-called 'mother of the revolution',[6] shares Brie's assessment. She explains 'some people do not want to profess their identity, they feel second class citizens compared to the West Germans, so they say they are German' (Bohley's description does not apply to most of the respondents in my study who had always been and continued to be unusual East German citizens).[7] She expands on this:

I think that there is an East German identity, and there are those that accept it and those that reject it. But it does exist. And even this rejection is a way of distancing oneself from it, of saying 'farewell'. We have lived here for forty years, and you cannot deny that. One can say ten times one is German, but Germany did not exist. There was the Federal Republic and there was the GDR and this formed the West Germans and the East Germans.

One example of trying to say 'farewell', of living as if one had no past, is reported by Naimark (1992), who tells of an interview with a 22-year-old *punkfrau* from the GDR. Six months after having moved to West Germany, she was asked 'Why did you leave the GDR?' 'The GDR? Never heard of it' (87).[8]

A one-line comment such as this has clarity and finality which a more in-depth conversation might lack. In Naimark's account the reader is not given any information about the context in which the exchange occurred, who the young woman perceived herself as speaking to, and in whose presence. Moreover, one has no sense of her identity over time. Ten years later, how would she answer the same question? The more researchers probe questions of identity, the more complex the picture which emerges.

In 1994, Jennifer Yoder conducted a study interviewing elite parliamentarians in Brandenburg. When asked whether a particular eastern German identity exists, slightly more than half (ten out of 18) responded positively. Follow-up questions, however, evoked responses that revealed a distinct 'eastern' dimension in terms of elites' self-identification. Typical of the responses she found were the following:

I will remain an East German in this [political rebuilding] process. I have a different political culture. I try to bring a different politics over ... [I]nstead of making people feel indebted [to the West], hesitant to be active, I have to encourage them to assert their own voices. (SPD member, Potsdam, May 1994)

But what exactly is meant by an 'East German identity'? For one of Yoder's respondents, it means simply having had 'a common history, experiences, life relationships, upbringing, schooling, work world ... and these have formed people in a special way' (1999:135), and for another it indicates '[e]xperience under the wall and a particular socialization pattern' (136). Yoder states that 'the most common identification may be summed up as "East Germans in a united Germany"' – an identity which some interviewees referred to as 'the eastern biography' (136).

A REVITALIZED IDENTITY?

However, with the growing realisation of the appreciable differences between eastern and western Germany, noted by Bohley and others, there has been a movement towards a new grassroots post-communist eastern identity (Berdahl 1999, Hogwood 2000). Bohley herself comments upon those East Germans who 'are very conscious of the fact that they have lived under extraordinary conditions and have had very special experiences and they are proud of it'. In 1990, 66 per cent of East Germans identified themselves as more German than East German, whereas by 1995, this figure had dropped to only 34 per cent. Correspondingly, in 1990 28 per cent identified themselves as more East German than German, while in 1995, this figure had climbed to 60 per cent (Yoder 1999:204–5). As Yoder explains, 'a discovery of ... differences [between East and West German societies] led to a rediscovery of separate identities' (205). Yoder (1999) summarises the revitalised appeal to a distinctive eastern identity:

> eastern identity has been rediscovered as a response to the encroachment of west German norms and rules for behaviour and the devaluation of eastern culture and identity. This rediscovery can also be interpreted as a positive/proactive development ... a process of self-assertion, an expression of pride and autonomy, and a recognition that the east was and is different from the west. (209)

Wiesenthal's (1998) analysis of the revival of eastern identity is more wholly reactive than that suggested by Yoder. Widespread post-unification dissatisfaction experienced by many East Germans can be explained, at least partially, by the 'treatment–response thesis'. While, before unification, East Germans may have felt themselves to be very similar in terms of values and cultural patterns,

> the experience of western supremacy gave way to a process of increasing cultural differentiation. Feeling labelled as more naïve, less professional, less competent, and culturally outdated, east Germans would appear to be lining up for a counter-attack. They remind themselves of 'their', up to now, not so deeply held

'socialist' and 'communist' values and confront 'the west' by claiming allegiance to a revived east German collective identity ... [which is seen to embody] 'true' values of egalitarianism, modesty, solidarity, social security and stability. (17)

Ursel Herzberg, in her seventies, expresses views compatible with the 'treatment–response thesis'. Speaking from her own experience and that of others she knows, she comments:

> I think that people have acquired an East German identity after the changes more than they had before. Before that they were very dissatisfied with many things in this part of Germany that was called GDR, but now they feel quite different ... Now they feel that they are East Germans, or ex-GDR citizens, much more than they did before, I think. So do I ... People feel East German, also because a lot of the West Germans treat them with some arrogance, with a lot of arrogance in fact ... therefore, East German people feel they have to emphasise their identity again, sort of regain their self-respect.

As a result of unification some East Germans felt that they had become, as Werner Fischer described it to me 'an alien in my own country'. Bärbel Bohley expresses a similar sentiment: 'we were annexed in a way. We emigrated to the Federal Republic in our entirety ... against my will ... the West came to me.' East German author Christ Wolf (1997) describes 'the manner and the speed with which everything connected with the GDR was liquidated, considered suspect' and views herself and her fellow citizens as being 'housed in a barracks under quarantine, infected with Stasi virus' (241). This context provides a ripe breeding ground for a siege mentality, in which self-identification is primarily reactive, and in this case at least, retrospective, a 'counter-identity' as Roßteutscher describes it (2000:74). However, such an unstable foundation does not augur well for long-term identity maintenance.

Why was it easier for East Germans to embrace an East German identity only after the demise of East Germany? Historically, East German national identity was primarily reactive, existing in relation to the west in general and to West Germany in particular. As Sebastian Pflugbeil commented earlier, in contrast to other Eastern Bloc countries with hundreds of years of history behind them, East Germany was an artificial creation; as such, national identity had never been very strong. Nonetheless, another kind of GDR identity did exist 'within the dominant culture ... [which] developed in at least partial opposition to the official culture' (McFalls 1995:148). It is this aspect of national identity which became revitalised after unification.

Benedict Anderson (1991) has written of the nation as an imagined community.[9] If one applies this definition to the case of East Germany, one can begin to see why the dissolution of the actual country created a new psychological space for national identity. As the parliamentarians in Yoder's study quoted above explained, the new eastern biography is based upon a sense of a shared community, and a common experience of life under the wall. It is not surprising that this could be best appreciated when in comparison to something else, in this case, with West Germany. Hogwood (2000) describes four distinctive expressions of eastern German identity which have developed over the last decade: 1) third-way socialism; 2) the 'Trotzidentität' (identity of contrariness); 3) '(N)Ostalgia' (nostalgia for the East Germany of the past),[10] and 4) 'Ossi' pride. It is the last of these which Hogwood sees as having 'the greatest potential to sustain itself as a live and lasting expression of separate easternness with a united Germany' (45).

Ultimately, how enduring will eastern identity prove to be? Will Germans living in the new Länder continue to experience, if indeed they still do, a 'hospital community' ethos? How long is the life of the 'Stasi virus'? Will Ossi pride subside with increased integration between east and west? If much of the revived sense of eastern biography is founded on 'the memory of shared experiences within the social structures of divided Germany' then will this phenomenon 'be limited to the generations born in the aftermath of the Second World War' (Hogwood 2000:64–5), or will these memories survive in the form of cultural narratives, to be transmitted from one generation to the next? Writing more than a decade after unification, Hogwood warns 'it is not possible to arrive at a definitive conclusion as to whether a distinct eastern identity will prove to be merely transitional, or will become a lasting German subculture' (64).

My own data as well as that of others – especially that which relies upon in-depth exploration of individual lives – suggests that many East Germans living in a unified Germany experience neither a total transformation[11] of their former existence, nor an identity which is unaffected by the profound changes of the context in which they live their lives. Rather, such research reveals a continuity of self coexisting with a profound sense of personal and political change.

Berdahl's (1999) research on the re-emergence of East German commodities offers compelling evidence of this claim. For instance, the popularity of board games testing detailed knowledge of life under the *ancien régime* only makes sense in the context of two facts: 1) that system is no longer in place; and 2) those who lived under state socialism still have memories of it, which function as a form of bonding with others, as well as a bridge between the past and present. Ruth Reinecke comments: 'The GDR citizen inside myself will always accompany the movements which will take place in my life.' I asked writer and activist Freya Klier – who, in 1988, had been expelled to West Germany, where she continued to live at the time of our interview – where she felt she was from. Similarly to Reinecke, she responds:

> From the GDR, of course ... I lived there for 38 years, it was the most important time of my life ... it was a very intensive time, and it is my identity ... Now a new piece of identity has been added [but] the other thing is still existing ... The meaning of my life does not depend on the country I live in. I did not change when I came to this part.

Klier and Reinecke minimise neither the degree nor the importance of the changes around and within themselves, but for them, identity is an additive, not substitutive, phenomenon.

There is an awkward moment in my interview with Bärbel Bohley, in which I ask the rather leading question: 'Has there been a shift in the general consciousness of what it means to be East German?' Bohley clearly bristles, and ultimately responds:

> I think it [your question] is too simple. Probably you now want to hear, 'we have had our experiences with a dictatorship and in the Federal Republic they have had their experiences with democracy', but this is too simple. In my view the experiences under a democracy are not so different from those made under a dictatorship. Personal courage is always difficult, to keep one's chin up, to assert oneself, well ... to stay honest. These are human experiences and it's those that are important for me. I made them against the background of a dictatorship and others made them against the background of democracy. Insofar these human experiences are much more important for me than any psycho-

logical analyses ... Well, this is too complicated for me that I could answer that in a simple way.

Bohley rejects my question as being too simplistic, built upon naïve assumptions regarding all that has changed in her world, both inside and out. For her, the most important human qualities, such as courage and honesty, are transcendent. Concluding our interview, I ask her if there is anything which, in retrospect, she wishes she had done differently. She rejects the 'othering' which she feels is implicit in my question: 'I would do many things differently', she responds, 'wouldn't you?' Answering in this way, Bohley emphasises our common humanity and rejects the bipolarism which she feels is inherent in the questions I ask her.

Undeniably, the events of the German autumn have precipitated profound psychological change for East Germans, but importantly, this change has occurred within a relative constancy of identity. As MP Ingrid Koppe commented to me 'the past ... is not as past as we assume. We are the result of the past and the past is in us.' The more micro the analysis, the less unequivocal the evidence of discontinuity. Human beings are, by our nature, forever in the process of becoming; there is an ongoing relationship between who we have been, who we are, and who we will be. As researchers of identity, our frameworks of analysis must seek to capture this complex interplay between change and consistency which characterises our lives and the lives of others as we and they struggle to meet the challenges of the new societies they are helping to create.

NOTES

1. Less than a year later, on the day of the completion of Germany unity, Brandt moderated his earlier statement: 'Today I would say that what politically belongs together from this 3rd of October onward still has to grow together' (cited in Minkenberg 1993:53).
2. For a thoughtful discussion on the vacillating attitude of the East German government toward its 'Germanness', see McKay 1998:108–20.
3. Because state socialism did not permit public political debate, the arts had a heightened role as a forum for political expression. Performing, and even attending theatre became increasingly political engagements; the shows, often embodying controversial themes, were always followed by discussions between audience and actors. Many theatre people, including Ruth Reinecke, were key in helping to organise the demonstration which took place on 4 November 1989. Reinecke herself had to leave Alexanderplatz at midday, for her afternoon performance. She

describes the atmosphere backstage that day as electric; actors, when they were not on stage, sat huddled by transistor radios following the events at the demonstration. Rarely have life and art more simultaneously mirrored one another.

4. The one exception to this was Wolfgang Ullmann, whose attitude towards the changes was unusual in my study. He commented to me: 'It's not the end of my country, it's the end of this state of despotism and party governorship ... It was an awakening and revival of my country.' Question: So you don't really feel now that you lost your country? 'No, absolutely not, I got it back.' This contrasts directly with the views of many of my respondents, whose views are epitomised by the East German film-maker and dissident Konrad Weiss, who was also in my study: 'I have lost my homeland, this gray, narrow, ugly land. This beautiful land ... the land of my anger' (cited in Cary 2001:617).

5. Interestingly, since the early 1990s the PDS has enjoyed increasing voter popularity. As noted by Kupferberg (1999): 'Ideological loyalty to the previous regime ... has not disappeared. In particular the professionals and young people with higher education tend to support the ... PDS' (145). As Wiesenthal comments (1998), 'many east Germans ... appear to be on their way to becoming what they never were before: true believers in democratic socialism' (17).

6. Bohley herself detests this label, and comments, 'I find the phrase "mother of the revolution" stupid. Only men could have invented such a phrase. They needed it as a media hype, but I find it absolutely idiotic.'

7. Leaders of East Germany's opposition were virtually uniform in their disappointment with the ultimate outcome of the events of 1989. Werner Fischer captures the feelings of many:

> my roots were here [in the GDR] ... I had become firmly rooted to this soil, where was the friction that sparked controversy. I did not want to see the GDR disappear. This is how many opposition members express it today: 'better to have stormy relationships than none at all'.

For an elaboration of this argument, see Andrews 1998.

8. After the demise of the East German state, there were strong incentives for individuals to recast their experiences under state socialism. East German sociologist Marianne Schultz comments ironically that of the East German population of 16 million, there were 16 million who claimed to have been resistance fighters, as well as 16 million who portrayed themselves as victims (Andrews 2000:184).

9. For a very stimulating discussion on the relationship between imagination and national identity, see also Reicher and Hopkins 2001.

10. Berdahl (1999) offers a more complex view of the genesis and implications of (n)ostalgie. She refers to the 'multiple meanings of *Ostalgie*' and comments that

> in all its various forms, [it] does not entail an identification with the former GDR state, but rather an identification with different forms of oppositional solidarity and collective memory. It can evoke feelings

of longing, mourning, resentment, anger, relief, redemption, and satisfaction – often within the same individuals. (203)

Summarising this position, Berdahl states that (n)ostaligia 'is about the production of a present rather than a reproduction of a past' (202) and, paradoxically, it 'both contests and affirms a new order' (193).

11. For a critique of the 'transformation model', see Konopasek and Andrews 2000.

REFERENCES

Anderson, Benedict. 1991. *Imagined Communities: Reflections on the Origin and Spread of Nationalism*. London: Verso Books.

Andrews, Molly. 1995. 'Against Good Advice: Reflections on Conducting Research in a Country Where You Don't Speak the Language', *Oral History Review* 20(1):75–86.

——. 1998. 'Criticism/Self-Criticism in East Germany: Contradictions between Theory and Practice', *Critical Sociology* 24 (1/2):130–53.

——. 2000. 'Text in a Changing Context: Reconstructing Lives in East Germany', in J. Bornat, P. Chamberlayne and T. Wengraf (eds) *The Turn to Biographical Methods in Social Science: Comparative Issues and Examples*. London: Routledge.

Berdahl, Daphne. 1999. '"(N)Ostalgie" for the Present: Memory, Longing, and East German Things', *Ethnos* 64(2):192–211.

——. 2000. 'Text in a changing context: Reconstructing lives in East Germany', in Joanna Bornat, Prue Chamberlayne and Tom Wengraf (eds) *The Turn to Biographical Methods in Social Science: Comparative Issues and Examples*. London: Routledge.

Cary, Noel. 2001. '"Farewell Without Tears": Diplomats, Dissidents, and the Demise of East Germany', *The Journal of Modern History* 73:617–51.

Dennis, Mike. 1998. 'The East German Family: Change and Continuity', *German Politics* 7(3):83–100.

Epstein, Catherine. 1999. 'The Production of "Official Memory" in East Germany: Old Communists and the Dilemmas of Memoir-Writing', *Central European History* 32(2):181–201.

Gilliar, Beate. 1996. *The Rhetoric of (Re)unification: Constructing Identity Through East and West German Newspapers*. New York: Peter Lang.

Hogwood, Patricia. 2000. 'After the GDR: Reconstructing Identity in Post-Communist Germany', *Journal of Communist Studies and Transition Politics* 16(4):45–67.

Jarausch, Konrad (ed.). 1997a. *After Unity: Reconfiguring German Identities*. Oxford: Berghahn Books.

——. 1997b. 'Reshaping German Identities: Reflections on the Post-Unification Debate', in Konrad Jarausch (ed.) *After Unity: Reconfiguring German Identities*. Oxford: Berghahn Books.

Jarausch, Konrad, Heinrich Seeba and David Conradt. 1997. 'The Presence of the Past: Culture, Opinion, and Identity in Germany', in Konrad Jarausch (ed.) *After Unity: Reconfiguring German Identities*. Oxford: Berghahn Books.

Klingermann, Hans-Dieter and Richard I. Hofferbert. 1994. 'Germany: A New "Wall in the Mind"?', *Journal of Democracy* 5(1):30–68.

Knabe, Frithjof. 1995. 'Unemployment: Developments and Experiences', in Eva Kolinsky (ed.) *Between Hope and Fear: Everyday Life in Post-Unification East Germany/A Case Study*. Keele: Keele University Press.

Kocka, Jurgen. 1994. 'Crisis of Unification: How Germany Changes', *Daedalus* 123(1):173–92.

Kolinksy, Eva (ed.). 1995a. *Between Hope and Fear: Everyday Life in Post-Unification East Germany/A Case Study*. Keele: Keele University Press.

——. 1995b. 'Preface', in Eva Kolinksy (ed.) *Between Hope and Fear: Everyday Life in Post-Unification East Germany/A Case Study*. Keele: Keele University Press.

——. 1995c. 'Women after *Muttipolitik*', in Eva Kolinksy (ed.) *Between Hope and Fear: Everyday Life in Post-Unification East Germany/A Case Study*. Keele: Keele University Press.

Konopasek, Zdenek with Molly Andrews. 2000. 'A Cautious Ethnography of Socialism: Autobiographical Narrative in the Czech Republic', in Andrews et al. *Lines of Narrative: Psychosocial Perspectives*. London: Routledge.

Kupferberg, Feiwel. 1999. *The Break-Up of Communism in East Germany and Eastern Europe*. New York: St Martin's Press.

Larres, Klaus (ed.). 2001. *Germany Since Unification: The Development of the Berlin Republic* (2nd edn). London: Palgrave.

McFalls, Laurence. 1995. *Communism's Collapse, Democracy's Demise? The Cultural Context and Consequences of the East German Revolution*. London: Macmillan.

McKay, Joanna. 1998. *The Official Concept of the Nation in the Former GDR*. Aldershot: Ashgate.

Minkenberg, Michael. 1993. 'The Wall after the Wall: On the Continuing Division of Germany and the Remaking of Political Culture', *Comparative Politics* 26: 53–68.

Naimark, Norman. 1992. '"Ich will hier raus": Emigration and the Collapse of the German Democratic Republic', in Ivo Banac (ed.) *Eastern Europe in Revolution*. Ithaca: Cornell University Press.

Offe, Claus. 1996. *Varieties of Transition: The East European and East German Experience*. Cambridge: Polity Press.

Pickel, Andreas. 1997. 'Creative Chaos: Concluding Thoughts on Interdisciplinary Cooperation', in Konrad Jarausch (ed.) *After Unity: Reconfiguring German Identities*. Oxford: Berghahn Books.

Reicher, Stephen and Nick Hopkins. 2001. *Self and Nation*. London: Sage.

Roßteutscher, Sigrid. 2000. 'Competing Narratives and the Social Construction of Reality: The GDR in Transition', *German Politics* 9(1):61–82.

Schneider, Peter. 1983. *The Wall Jumper*. New York: Pantheon Books.

Steininger, Rolf. 2001. 'The German Question, 1945–95', in Klaus Larres (ed.) *Germany Since Unification: The Development of the Berlin Republic* (2nd edn). London: Palgrave.

Wiesenthal, Helmut. 1995. 'East Germany as a Unique Case of Societal Transformation: Main Characteristics and Emergent Misconceptions', *German Politics* 4(3):49–74.

——. 1998. 'Post-Unification Dissatisfaction, or Why Are So Many East Germans Unhappy With the New Political System?' *German Politics* 7(2):1–30.

Wolf, Christa. 1997. *Parting from Phantoms: Selected Writings, 1990–1994*. Chicago: University of Chicago Press.

Yoder, Jennifer. 1999. *From East Germans to Germans? The New Post-Communist Elites*. Durham: Duke University Press.

7 Mobilising Memories: Protestant and Unionist Victims' Groups and the Politics of Victimhood in the Irish Peace Process

Graham Dawson

Since the republican and loyalist ceasefires of August and October 1994, histories and memories of the Irish Troubles have been voiced, debated and fought over in an extraordinary proliferation of cultural activity in Northern Ireland, as individuals and communities attempt to come to terms with the traumatic legacy of the past. Powerful and often contradictory dynamics are at work here, in the interplay between the politics of peace-making and conflict resolution on one hand, and the imperatives of remembrance – psychic and emotional as well as political – on the other (Dawson 1999). These dynamics are evident in attempts to address the needs of the victims and survivors of violence, and the debate (and conflict) surrounding this issue.

This chapter, which forms part of a larger study,[1] explores the memories of violence articulated by grassroots 'victims' groups' which have emerged since the ceasefires. These groups' aims are to give the victims a voice, to tell their stories, and to promote their interests by lobbying for financial, psychological and other kinds of practical support. In the process, they have been involved in organising a particular kind of public voice: one which claims to have been marginalised hitherto, and is now authorised to speak from the newly constructed position of 'victim', about 'silenced' or 'forgotten' memories. My concern here is with those victims' groups that describe themselves, variously, as Protestant, British, loyalist, or Unionist, and whose members have experienced violence mainly at the hands of Republican paramilitaries – the Irish Republican Army (IRA) and the Irish National Liberation Army (INLA). My analysis explores the memories of violence articulated by these groups in the context of the 'politics of victimhood' generated by the unfolding of the Irish peace process. It also reflects upon the complex intertwinings, tensions, paradoxes and contradictions that exist between this politics of victimhood, the political identity of Ulster Unionists and Protestants as shaped by the Troubles, and the psychic and emotional needs of the victims.

From 1966, the year of the first killings in the current Troubles, until July 1999, 3,636 people had lost their lives as a result of the conflict, while a further 40,000–50,000 people had been seriously injured (McKittrick et al. 1999:1477, Bloomfield 1998:13). The vast majority of these – whether civilians, members of the state's security forces, or Republican or loyalist paramilitaries – were killed and injured in Northern Ireland. As the report of the Bloomfield Commission on the victims of the Troubles pointed out: 'If the UK as a whole, with its population of some 58 million people, had experienced death pro rata ... there would have been a total of over 130,000 dead. The trauma of the killing has been protracted, and particular communities have suffered disproportionately from it' (Bloomfield 1998:12).

Despite this, a discourse on 'victimhood', seriously addressing the ongoing traumatic impact of this violence across Northern Irish society, only began to emerge from the late 1980s, and became central to social and political debate only after the initiation of the peace process. Prior to this, a general lack of provision of support services at community level to address the needs of the victims of violence was exacerbated by a culture of silence, in which the existence of ongoing and widespread psychic trauma was neither publicly acknowledged nor discussed (Bolton 2001). The paramilitary ceasefires of 1994 significantly reduced the climate of fear, and as the psychological pressure of coping with the unremitting and compounding impact of violence abated, bereaved people finally found time to mourn losses, often sustained years or even decades earlier, where 'grief was suspended' or suppressed in order to cope (Peake 2000:6–7).[2] The opening of space for reflection and remembrance stimulated widespread telling of personal stories of loss, trauma and survival, and also a new public receptivity to such stories as representations of a collective experience (see, for example, *An Crann*/The Tree 2000, Smyth and Fay 2000, McKittrick et al. 1999). Grassroots initiatives for victims' support at local level were further stimulated by the European Union's Special Support Programme for Peace and Reconciliation, first announced in December 1994, which injected into Northern Ireland and the Border areas of the Republic some £240 million over three years (subsequently extended in 1997 and 2000), and specified the victims of violence as a special target group suffering 'social exclusion' as a result of the Troubles (*Irish News* 1995, European Commission 1998, Black 2001:27–8).

Following the election of the Labour government in the UK in May 1997, the needs of the victims also became incorporated into the framework of All-Party Talks to agree a political settlement to the conflict, culminating in the Belfast 'Good Friday' Agreement of April 1998. In November 1997 the Northern Ireland Victims Commission (headed by Sir Kenneth Bloomfield, the former head of Britain's Civil Service in the North) was established 'to examine the feasibility of providing greater recognition for those who have become victims in the last thirty years as a consequence of events in Northern Ireland' (Bloomfield 1998:8). The Bloomfield Commission's report, *We Will Remember Them* (April 1998), defined the category of 'victim' as including all 'the surviving injured and those who care for them, together with those close relatives who mourn their dead' (14). The Agreement itself, in a section on 'Reconciliation and Victims of Violence', affirmed that 'it is essential to acknowledge and address the suffering of the victims of violence as a necessary element of reconciliation'; and recognised that 'victims have a right to remember as well as to contribute to a changed society' (*The Belfast Agreement* 2000:316). A commitment was made to allocate British government resources to 'community-based initiatives ... that are supportive and sensitive to the needs of victims', and to this end a permanent Victims Liaison Unit was established within the Northern Ireland Office of the British government at Stormont (ibid., *VLU Newsletter* 1999). These developments created a new framework for representation and recognition of victims of the Troubles and the ongoing difficulties they face, and new possibilities for reparation or redress. In response, there has been a flowering 'from below' of victims' groups representing – and usually composed of – victims from a local area.

While the 'victims' issue has been placed centrally within the framework of an inclusive process of conflict resolution, it has also figured within the strategy adopted by the British government for hegemonic leadership of that process 'from above'. Through the Bloomfield Commission and the VLU, the state sought to lead and direct the developing 'victims' movement' by constructing a single, integrated victims' lobby, that would function as a conduit for funding and speak with a consensual voice about the needs of victims, within the overarching political framework of the

Agreement. Within this strategy, the state represents itself as a neutral arbiter (rather than as a participant in the conflict): as holding the ring and encouraging dialogue, reconciliation and consensus-building between the 'two warring factions', in the arena of the victims of violence as also in those of 'community relations' and political conflict itself. Those victims' groups or their members which do not embrace this agenda – whether nationalist or Republican groups mainly addressing the legacy of state violence, or Protestant and Unionist groups concerned primarily with the legacy and continuing threat of Republican paramilitary violence – find themselves engaged in a struggle to make their own voices heard whilst resisting incorporation into the state-sponsored consensus and the particular version of the past (and the future) that it promotes. Through the various victims' groups' support for, or resistance to, the state's strategy for victims, a new politics of victimhood has been generated, in which the emerging discourse on the victims of violence has been appropriated and articulated from a number of different ideological positions.

In examining the politics of the Protestant and Unionist victims' groups, my particular focus is on those which have emerged in the border areas where, along with Belfast and Derry, the Republican campaign has been most intensely concentrated. Between July 1999 and April 2000 I visited three such groups to meet activists and members.[3] FEAR Fermanagh Ltd (FEAR being an acronym for Fear Encouraged Abandoning Roots) was formed in 1995 to campaign on behalf of those Protestants from the border areas of Co. Fermanagh 'who were displaced and forced to abandon roots, their homes [as a result of] direct intimidation or fear' of IRA violence (FEAR Fermanagh Ltd [1997]:2). Families Acting for Innocent Relatives (FAIR), based in Markethill, Co. Armagh, was formed in 1998 to represent the British victims of Republican violence in South Armagh. West Tyrone Voice, based in Newtownstewart, Co. Tyrone, was formed in early 1999 'as a result of needs which were identified amongst those who had been the innocent victims of paramilitary terrorism' in the western border area of County Tyrone (West Tyrone Voice [1998]).

The formation of these groups was a response to the British government's strategy for victims and its conduct of the peace process more generally; both groups were widely considered by Unionists to be biased towards nationalists. In order to represent the practical and emotional needs of their members, these groups assert the memory of a distinctive Protestant and Unionist experience of violence, as a counter to what they perceive as the government's 'appeasement of Republican terrorists' and its responsiveness to nationalist campaigns on behalf of the victims of state violence (particularly by its investment of an estimated £100 million in the Bloody Sunday Inquiry) (FAIR [1999:1], *Guardian* 2002a). Their common aim is 'to tell our side of the story' (Jackson 2000): to break the silence about, and give voice to, the trauma, loss and suffering inflicted on the Protestant and Unionist people of Northern Ireland as a result of the Troubles, primarily by the IRA.

This collective story takes different forms in different areas according to the varying local impacts of the Troubles, described by Fay, Morrissey and Smyth (1999) as 'a mosaic of different types of conflict' (136). The border regions of Armagh, Fermanagh and Tyrone experienced a 'rural war' fought 'directly between the protagonists' and characterised by 'the capacity for surgical strikes on precise targets' (in contrast to the urban war in which car bombs and rioting produced 'a high rate of civilian casualties ... [and] "collateral" damage') (133). Of all rural deaths from 1969–93 53 per cent occurred in the southern border areas of these three counties, and South Armagh experienced the highest intensity of violence outside North and West Belfast and parts of Derry City (76–8,142–3). A particular characteristic of the war along the border was the high concentration of casualties suffered by the locally recruited forces, the Royal Ulster Constabulary (RUC) and the Ulster Defence Regiment (UDR), including part-time, off-duty and former members (McKittrick et al. 1999:1478–9). The campaign by the IRA against members of the security forces who were living with their families within the local border communities, often carried out in or near their homes and civilian workplaces, meant that Protestant and Unionist civilians were exposed to violence – and themselves subject to attack – in a distinctive pattern of violence. This 'is not adequately reflected in death or injury data' (Fay et al. 1999:147), nor does it always feature in standard histories of the Troubles.[4] However, it is a key theme in Protestant and Unionist cultural memory of the conflict, where it is described, controversially, as 'ethnic cleansing'.

Originating in the wars accompanying the break-up of the former Yugoslavia in the early 1990s, the term 'ethnic cleansing' entered popular discourse as a synonym for violent ethnic hatred expressed in a systematic, state-sponsored policy to eliminate from a particular region those who were considered 'ethnically different', by killing or intimidating them, and burning their homes, shops and other centres of communal life (Ahmed 1995). The term was first applied to Northern Ireland in 1992, when its emotional resonance was exploited by the Ulster Unionist leader, Sir James Molyneux, together with the Orange Order. Molyneux claimed that Protestants in the border areas 'had been the victims of "ethnic cleansing" for over twenty years ... Thousands ... have been intimidated from the border regions of Fermanagh and Armagh' (*Orange Standard* 1992; see also, for example, *Orange Standard*, 1993). This narrative of ethnic cleansing provided a potent contemporary frame for longer-standing claims, voiced at funeral services as well as in political arenas since 1972, about the existence of 'an overall republican strategy of genocide against Protestants living in border areas' (McKittrick et al. 1999:255).[5] These claims are fiercely rejected by Republicans, who have always insisted that the IRA's military campaign was politically motivated and 'non-sectarian', being directed against the British state rather than against Northern Irish Protestants (Adams 1986:51–2, 119–21; Harnden 1999:137–8). Thus, the war along the border has long been a site of intense and ongoing conflict over cultural memory of the Troubles.

In the course of the Troubles, border Protestants and Unionists have been subjected to a politics of intimidation and terror, but this has not taken place on a scale, nor with the consistency of pattern, to warrant the description of either 'ethnic cleansing' or 'genocide'.[6] Rather, the Protestant and Unionist narrative of 'ethnic cleansing' is best understood as a form of cultural memory that has articulated aspects of the emotional or psychic reality of the border Protestants, while at the same time constructing a relatively coherent cultural as well as political identity to coalesce the disparate currents within Unionism and loyalism. This cultural memory celebrates the longevity and tenacity of the Protestant and British presence in Ireland since the seventeenth century, but also warns of the dangers it has always faced as a beleaguered culture under repeated threat of annihilation – as symbolised by the massacres of 1641 and 1798, and the displacements during the Independence War of the early 1920s – by the hostile and violent forces of Irish nationalism (Dewar, Brown and Long 1967, Jarman 1997:171–89). In the context of the current Troubles it has provided the Protestant and Unionist people with a means to make sense of recent traumatic events in terms of a meaningful historical pattern; to handle the horrors of the conflict and counter the psychic effects of the Republican armed campaign;

and to respond politically as a community, united in its will to survive and defeat the IRA.

The Protestant and Unionist victims' groups of the Border areas have drawn on the cultural memory of 'ethnic cleansing' as the collective story of their communities' experience of the Troubles. However, its re-articulation in the new context of the peace process also relates to a range of tensions, pressures and needs generated within Protestant and Unionist communities as they have struggled to come to terms with the traumatic aftershocks of the violent past, while also adjusting to – and contesting their own place within – the transformed cultural and political environment.

Furthermore, there is no neat fit between the collective 'we' of Ulster Unionism, loyalism and Protestantism – themselves no simple essences but the sites of fierce internal difference and conflicts – and the 'we' of the 'suffering community' (West Tyrone Voice [1998]) as variously constructed by the victims' groups. The self-designation by FAIR and Voice as 'British' or 'pro-British' represents an 'anti-sectarian' gesture to encourage a more inclusive, cross-community 'we' embracing, for example, Catholic Unionists (Wilson [1999]: 3.2.2 and Constitution [Draft III]; Lynch 2000:4); and in April 2000, both claimed to have 'some Catholics in our group', even if the numbers were negligible (Lynch, 2000:8, Wilson [1999]: 5.5.9). In the work undertaken by all three groups to support and assist the victims whose lives have been damaged as a result of the Troubles, memorywork is necessarily threaded through their activities, in complex ways which produce a number of contradictory and paradoxical ramifications.

First, through their engagement with personal trauma, the groups are involved in the articulation of individual memories that do not always simply reinforce the anti-Republican collective narrative of 'ethnic cleansing'. Since the victims of violence have had to live without adequate support hitherto, the groups have had to alter the 'stiff-upper-lip mentality of, "if we don't discuss it then we're not victims of it"', by helping people to identify their needs (Foster 1999:2). In the process, the telling of, and listening to, personal life stories emerged as powerful and important activities in their own right. This has posed a fundamental challenge to the culture of silence, which requires internal, psychic (as well as external, cultural and political) inhibitions against speaking out; inhibitions which, it emerged, had in many cases been self-maintained as a strategy for survival. Within Protestant and Unionist communities, victims' groups have enabled the telling for the first time of stories of trauma, in some cases going back 30 years. Arlene Foster describes how the FEAR activists spoke to border farmers in their sixties:

> [they] had left their homes and they'd never really spoken about how they felt at the time that they were forced to leave[... A] lot of the emotional hurt is only coming out now[... I]t's almost like post-traumatic stress disorder. Things that happened twenty years ago are still there in the subconscious. (2–3)

Similarly, the FAIR group found that survivors of the Darkley massacre in 1983, when Republican gunmen entered a rural Pentecostal church during a Sunday service and fired automatic weapons into the congregation, killing three and wounding seven, had never spoken about it in 15 years (Wilson, [1999]:2.1.5, FAIR website 2000). Social recognition of these traumatic experiences – even in the restricted private arena of a personal interview – may make it possible for the feelings attached to them to be made conscious and their meanings explored.[7] Besides unlocking emotions associated with the trauma of violent bereavement or loss, and often expressed in terms of the cultural memory of 'ethnic cleansing', the telling of these stories also evokes other memories and emotions. For example, in the case of Leslie Finlay of West Tyrone Voice, and a former UDR soldier, remembering the losses of the Troubles also involves a difficult realisation of official neglect during the time when '*nobody* seemed to be really interested in us' (Finlay 2000b:12); a realisation that may be especially acute for Unionists who have been deeply identified with, and fought to defend, the Northern Ireland state.

Second, in the groups' work to articulate traumatic memories of the Troubles within the public domain, a number of distinct needs and desires come into play, that may involve contradictory goals and effects. Hazlett Lynch (2000), Coordinator of West Tyrone Voice, speaks of the strong local support for the formation of a group that would: 'Be a *voice* for the victims, somebody to articulate our suffering and our pain, seek recognition ... seek justice for our members and for our community' (6–7). One motive for this voicing has been the necessity to remember and represent the experience of victimhood in order to qualify for grants and other support. This requires the framing of personal memories so as to lay claim to the category of 'victim'; and also the narration of a collective history of unacknowledged trauma that seeks social recognition of, and establishes the case for, forms of redress on behalf of a damaged community.

In FEAR's 'Research Document and Development Plan', the identification of various economic, social and cultural needs of the victims was grounded on the claim that border Protestants had been collectively victimised by 'republican terrorist violence'; a claim underpinned by reference to the narrative of 'ethnic cleansing' (FEAR [1997]:4; also see 3, 12–15, 17, 22). Personal life-history interviews were used as evidence to demonstrate the 'traumatic experience of having to move under threat and fear' (18), and as 'verbal testimony that scars remain and that individuals are still living with the social, psycholog[ical] and medical impact of being forced to move' (19, see also 'Personal Stories' section). Thus, Mrs Gillen remembers how: '[W]hen we had to leave Garrison, I was expecting. That child only lived for ten weeks. That was the stress of that time. In the time before we left, I used to have to go round the shed with a gun in my hand' (ibid.).[8]

According to the Wilson Report for FAIR, 'groups like the Enniskillen victims got their own dedicated social welfare officer and recognition of their needs' due to the publicity afforded to major single-event atrocities like the Remembrance Day bomb; whereas the violence suffered by the South Armagh Protestants 'went largely unrecognized' because of the 'incremental' nature of the killings (Wilson [1999]:4.2.2). Wilson argues that this lack of recognition has compounded the traumatic effects of violence (ibid.:1.2.2). The border victims' groups have sought wider social recognition in several ways, not least by 'encourag[ing] our people to tell their story to the media at every opportunity' (West Tyrone Voice [1998]). One successful example of this was the case of FEAR's John McClure, whose personal story received widespread and sympathetic coverage in Northern Ireland's main daily newspapers including the nationalist *Irish News*, as well as in the local Fermanagh press and national papers in the Irish Republic and Britain (*Impartial Reporter* 1997, *Irish Times* 1997, *News Letter* 1997, *Irish News* 1997a, *Daily Telegraph* 1997, *Observer* 1997, *Irish News* 1997b). Formerly a part-time UDR soldier who abandoned his farm and home on the border near Garrison and moved to a safer area 'inland' in 1972, McClure spoke in 1997 of how 'I'd love to come back' (*Irish News* 1997b). His memories of trauma and loss were tempered by hope about the possibility of return buttressed by memories of life along the border before the Troubles, when, he recalled, his family enjoyed good-neighbourly relations: 'All my old Catholic neighbours would like me to return. It was never them I was worried about but the fear of people from across the border' (*Daily Telegraph* 1997). The idea of his return was indeed welcomed publicly by some local nationalists (*Observer* 1997, *Irish News* 1997b), demonstrating the potential of the personal life story to generate understanding and dialogue across the communal divide.

However, the endeavour 'to articulate our suffering and our pain' has also given rise to less reconciliatory narratives, motivated by the rather different desire for (as the Wilson report puts it) 'the cathartic relief of telling the story' (Wilson [1999]:5.5.26). This points to a psychic dimension to the victims' demand for recognition,[9] driven by powerful impulses to express and discharge the feelings associated with the experience of victimhood. These are not necessarily restricted to pain, hurt and loss, but may embrace a gamut of intractable emotions, including horror, fear, anger, bitterness, revulsion and hatred. Unsurprisingly, such feelings are likely to be directed primarily at those held responsible for causing the suffering: the 'perpetrators' of violence, in this case the IRA and the INLA. The desire for cathartic relief from the intensity of these disturbing and potentially poisonous and self-destructive emotions may be satisfied symbolically by storytelling that emphasises the emotional realities of victimhood in order to 'set the record straight', in opposition to what are felt to be the misrepresentations of the perpetrators.

This has been the project of the FAIR group in telling *The True Story of South Armagh:* one of 'untold misery, bloodshed, and the pain of a[n Ulster Protestant] community who have been under siege for the past thirty years' (FAIR [1999:4]). At its centre are the stories of 'three of the worst massacres carried out in South Armagh during the period 1970s-1990s: at Tullyvallen Orange Hall (1975), Whitecross (1976) and the Mountain Lodge Pentecostal Church at Darkley (1983) (FAIR [1999:3]).[10] These events are described as 'totally indiscriminate sectarian attacks which typified the fanatical nature of Republican death squads' (FAIR [1999:3]).

Undoubtedly these attacks warrant their description as sectarian atrocities. The Darkley attack, for example, was condemned by the leaders of the four main churches in Northern Ireland as 'an act of sectarian slaughter on a worshipping community which goes beyond any previous deed of violence' (McKittrick et al. 1999:963). Nevertheless, they were exceptional events, not typical examples of the IRA's conduct of its 'armed struggle', despite their representation as such by British counter-insurgency propaganda (Nairac 1977:369). In FAIR's account, intensely emotive, even vitriolic rhetoric is deployed to express and contain the fear, anger and outrage attached to the memory of the attacks, whilst simultaneously discrediting conventional Republican heroic discourse. The victims of Tullyvallen are 'innocent men' who meet their death 'like lambs to the slaughter'; while the gunmen – far from being 'brave soldiers or courageous volunteers' – are 'cowardly', 'psychopathic killers' and 'bloodthirsty, evil gangsters who were faceless, gutless and heartless' (FAIR [1999:4]). By highlighting their most extreme atrocities, the 'evil Republican death squads' can be represented as lacking 'any moral justification' [11], in contrast with 'the protectors of life and guardians of law and order', the UDR [7], and the persecuted but enduring community as a whole: 'During the past 30 years only commitment to our existence, coupled with unequalled bravery and a belief in God has resulted in the Protestant population not becoming extinct at the hands of a carefully orchestrated campaign to "ethnic cleanse"' [3]; 'Our aim is to ensure that the great sacrifice of the Protestant community in South Armagh will never be forgotten' [11].

Re-articulated as a memory of collective victimhood in this way, the narrative of 'ethnic cleansing' expresses a psychic reality of pain, trauma and damage that demands recognition within the terms of the government's new settlement for victims, as an essential component of reparation and peace-building. At the same time, this recapitulation of war memories expresses deep antagonism and enmity and, emphasising the damage done to 'our community', tends to undercut fragile attempts at building cross-community understanding, recognition, dialogue and co-operation, necessary to the process of conflict resolution. Making peace politically with Republicans requires a shift in perception that many members of the Protestant and Unionist victims' groups have been unable to make, due to an endemic distrust underpinned by the trauma of victimhood. For others, an initial optimism was eroded by the loss of forward momentum in the unfolding of the peace process, and the build-up of suspicion and discontent about its dynamic, that affected increasing numbers of Protestants and Unionists.

The persistence of fear, anger and hurt, attached to the memories of past Republican violence and re-evoked by its continuation throughout 'the peace', helps to explain the intensity and tenacity of Unionists' emphasis on the 'decommissioning' of the IRA's arsenal. This in turn affected their responses to the peace talks and the implementation of the Good Friday Agreement itself. In the conflict that developed between the pro- and anti-Agreement wings of Unionism and loyalism, the 'No' campaign, in particular, mobilised antagonistic memories of IRA violence and made decommissioning its central theme (McInnes 2000). Protestant and Unionist victims supported both sides, but campaigned most vociferously for the 'No' camp.

FAIR, for example, joined other victims' groups in an umbrella organisation, Northern Ireland Terrorist Victims Together (NITVT), which organised the 'Long March' of June–July 1999 from Derry to Drumcree, where it linked up with the Orange Order's 'right to march' protest. The Long March focused demands for 'a declaration by the IRA that the war is over', the decommissioning and destruction of paramilitary weapons, and the disbandment of terrorist groups (Smyth 2000:131–2; see also Ryder and Kearney 2001). During the late summer of 1999 Ulster Unionist Council delegates debating the conditions for establishing an Executive that included Sinn Féin, were sent a copy of a video, 'An Appeal to You from The Victims': an overt attempt to mobilise memories of Republican violence in order to swing Unionist political opinion against support for Sinn Féin's involvement in government. The Long March, with its banner logo of an eye and an tear, featured in the video, which promoted the idea that Protestants and Unionists harmed by the IRA were the 'Real Victims' of the Troubles and 'a voice for real justice in Northern Ireland' ('An Appeal to You from The Victims' [September? 1999]).

Perceptions of injustice in the conduct of the peace process also caused the voices of Protestant and Unionist victims to be raised in opposition to another policy at the centre of the Agreement: the early release of 'terrorist prisoners', particularly Republicans (Lynch 2000:1; see also Page 2000). This was a catalyst for the formation of a tranche of Protestant and Unionist victims' groups, including FAIR and West Tyrone Voice, in the months after April 1998. As Hazlett Lynch (2000) describes it:

[T]here was the feeling that these people who plunged many people in Northern Ireland into bereavement, into loss, into trauma, suffering and pain, were now getting out, they were being in a sense rewarded by the Government ... whereas those of us who have carried the wounds and the scars of their activities have been left, still with the pain. And there didn't seem to be any justice or fair play[... T]here was a feeling ... throughout the border counties of Northern Ireland in particular, that something will have to be done in order to ensure that *we* as victims are not forgotten. (1)

Emotionally, the release of prisoners impacted on victims by re-awakening memories of the original incident, undoing the positive psychic effects that stemmed from judicial retribution, and provoking fear that the released terrorist might be re-encountered. These concerns prompted a FAIR demonstration at Stormont in September 1998 to protest that 'the insensitive release of terrorists who caused so much grief has reopened old wounds which were never properly healed' (*Irish News* 1998). From the summer of 1999, hostility to the prisoner-release scheme meshed with disillusionment at the lack of progress on arms decommissioning, disappointment at the failure to form an Executive, and anger at the proposals of the Patten Report on the reform of the RUC (another policy that provoked highly emotive memories), to crystallise growing opposition to the Agreement (de Bréadún 2001:238–301).[11]

This emotive antagonism to Republicans has also affected the responses of Protestants and Unionists to those representing nationalist and Republican victims of violence, such as Relatives for Justice or the Loughgall Truth and Justice Campaign. Their rejection of moral equivalence between those who have fought for and against the Northern Ireland state, and their appropriation of the epithet 'the *real* victims' on behalf of their own dead, effectively denies any valid use of the term, 'victim', to members of the IRA or INLA, to their relatives, or to nationalist groups which have any connection with Republican volunteers or ex-prisoners. FAIR also demonstrated at Stormont in 1998 against a government minister meeting relatives of the IRA unit killed by the SAS in the Loughgall ambush of 1987 (Smyth 2000:131). When invited to send a representative to the Touchstone Group, set up by the VLU to advise about policy formulation on victims' issues, FAIR declined, according to Eilish McCabe of Relatives for Justice, 'because we've a representative on it [... A]nd they don't recognise us as victims' (McCabe 2000:35, Smyth 2000:131).[12]

An associated assumption in Protestant and Unionist culture, that only the deserving – meaning terrorists and their accomplices – have been harmed by state security forces, leads to difficulties in accepting the evidence even of well-documented atrocities against nationalist civilians, such as Bloody Sunday.[13] Where nationalist campaigns like the Bloody Sunday Justice Campaign have had some success, as in the establishment of the Saville Inquiry or the official investigations into the assassination of the human rights lawyers, Pat Finucane and Rosemary Nelson, this is often experienced as a denial and exacerbation of the Protestant and Unionist communities' memories of trauma, suffering and loss (Wilson [1999]:5.7.1, Finlay 2000b:13–14, Frazer 2000).

This kind of response to 'the other side' telling 'their' story, has ensured that the emerging discourse and debate about victimhood has quickly become a new battleground. To the extent that the Protestant and Unionist victims share in this, they too are engaged – in the words of Colm Barton (2000) of the Bloody Sunday Trust – in 'fighting the war by other means'.

There is nevertheless a sharp paradox here. While their voicing and mobilisation of highly charged memories of the Troubles might be said to keep alive the hurts, grievances and suspicions of the war years, thus generating difficulties for peace-making and the transition to a just social and political settlement of the conflict, the memorywork of these Protestant and Unionist victims' groups is indispensable to any inclusive process of conflict resolution. They constitute a new kind of voice from below in Northern Ireland that tells stories about the 'things that we need to hear' (Damian Gorman, quoted in Dawson 1999:186).[14] The articulation of these stories has deeply contradictory effects: inevitably so, given the history of the conflict and the depth of the damage inflicted and sustained. As well as reproducing the fixed positions and understandings inherited from the past through cultural memory, the voices of the Protestant and Unionist victims also speak from new positions and express new, emergent meanings, that open up possibilities for 'reparative remembering' on a number of levels (Dawson 1999: 196–7).

The primary contribution made by these victims' groups lies at the personal level, in their importance and value for members; not only in practical terms, but in offering safe arenas in which it becomes possible to reflect on, feel, discuss and make sense of what has happened over the last 30 years, through personal storytelling. It is not necessary to endorse the political narrative of 'ethnic cleansing' in which this remembering is often cast, in order to recognise its value. The testimony of former UDR soldier, Leslie Finlay, will resonate with many others who have joined these groups, when he speaks of sleepless nights sitting on the edge of his bed, experiencing flashbacks of 'them things [you can see] every time you close your eyes', haunted by the row of UDR headstones in Castlederg graveyard where he helped to bury his mates one after the other, and realising that 'I need help' – which he found in West Tyrone Voice (Finlay 2000a).[15]

In terms of public politics and the state, the voices-from-below of the Protestant and Unionist victims are not neatly reducible to old political positions and lines of antagonism. They tell stories and ask questions that pose problems for all those who benefited from the silence of the victims. These are awkward voices for Republicans, who embrace an agenda of human rights and equality but resist attempts to probe for 'the truth' about IRA activities, by confronting them with the human consequences of the Republican 'armed struggle'.[16] They are awkward, too, for the Unionist establishment: for Protestant church leaders, for those who manage the UDR Benevolence Fund, and in particular for Unionist politicians, who are the object of deeply sceptical memories about their cynicism and ineffectiveness in dealing with victims' issues (Black 2001:30, Wilson [1999]:5.1, Frazer 2000, Lynch 2000, and Finlay 2000b:10–17). They raise uncomfortable issues for the British state and government, since they call into question the workings of 'justice' in Northern Ireland, and with it the long-standing strategy of containment which kept them safely silent, so promoting a sceptical memory about the workings of the state itself (Lynch 2000:4–5). The voices of the victims also ask difficult questions of the Republic of Ireland state, in demanding a public inquiry into the Irish government's relationship to the development of the Provisional IRA in the early 1970s.[17] Ultimately, these challenging questions raised by the Protestant and Unionist victims' groups will need to be addressed in a peace process that is formally committed to tackling the legacy of the conflict in terms of 'truth', 'justice' and 'human rights'.

Lastly, the Protestant and Unionist victims' groups of the border regions open up new possibilities for reparative remembering within their local communities, through a process that may be largely invisible to outsiders. These are traumatised communities, scarred by decades of violence, the effects of which have yet to be properly addressed. They are now struggling for their own 'collective self-esteem' (Wilson [1999]:5.9.6) in the face of alienation, disillusionment and a profound sense of threat to their British identity and heritage, posed by the new political dispensation in Northern Ireland and the transformation in the fortunes of Irish Republicanism (see also Wilson [1999]:1.2.2, and McKay 2000:303 and *passim*). While for many of the Protestant and Unionist victims it is 'too early' for reconciliation with those who remain political antagonists, victims' work can make an immediate contribution to building self-respect, confidence and reconciliation *within* their own communities (Frazer 2000). The rebuilding of 'morale and self-confidence' (Wilson [1999]: 5.9.5) in communities damaged by the Troubles necessarily involves them in the endeavour to make their peace with the past. This imperative applies no less to the young who are now growing up in the times of 'imperfect peace'[18] but find themselves grappling with the 'postmemory' of the war (Hirsch 1997), as it does to their elders who face the task of coming to terms with the aftershocks of a war they survived personally, and reconciling its memories with the world that is slowly emerging through conflict resolution.

The victims' groups provide local agencies dedicated to tackling the contradictions and difficulties inherent in this work of reparation and regeneration. Their understanding that the commemoration of those who did not survive the conflict is a fundamental part of its resolution has informed visions like that of FAIR's projected Living Memorial Centre for the victims of Republican violence in South Armagh. This is imagined as:

> [a] resource in honour of the victims ... to keep faith with the dead ... They call out to be remembered in dignity, not in a bare stone or empty mausoleum, but a place that is alive with tribute, memory and affection ... where we can recall our loved ones to memory and where strangers might come to know them. (Wilson [1999]: 5.8.1)[19]

Commemoration, however, cuts both ways. While it may allow ghosts to be laid to rest in a dignified acknowledgement of the permanence of loss, it may also keep alive the memory of the hurt inflicted on the Protestant and Unionist people of the border areas, in ways that continue to fuel current grievances and antagonisms. The challenge of the politics of victimhood, as it evolves in the future, will be how to mobilise the contradictory energies released by these victims' groups, both for the psychic work of reparation, and for the political work of building a peace that can be trusted.

ACKNOWLEDGEMENTS

This research was supported by the British Academy, the Leverhulme Trust, and the Arts and Humanities Research Board.

NOTES

1. Graham Dawson, *Making Peace with the Past? Cultural Memory, the Irish Troubles and the Peace Process*. Manchester: Manchester University Press, forthcoming.
2. Political violence has nevertheless continued to flourish in numerous forms: see Darby 2000.
3. I am indebted to Arlene Foster of FEAR, Willie Frazer and Jonathan Larner of FAIR, and Hazlett Lynch and Leslie Finlay of West Tyrone Voice, who gave generously of their time, knowledge and hospitality. I have drawn extensively on our informal conversations as well as recorded interviews, and other material provided by them. I would also like to thank members of the Families Against Crime by Terrorism (FACT) group in Lisburn for a moving and instructive meeting.
4. See, for example, Holland (2000) where it is barely mentioned, and Coogan (1996) which makes no mention of it at all.
5. Rev. Ivan Foster, speaking at a memorial service for two local UDR soldiers held in Enniskillen Free Presbyterian Church, September 1972.
6. See Graham Dawson, 'British Identity and the Popular Memory of "Genocide" and "Ethnic Cleaning" on the Northern Ireland Border', in Robert Phillips and Helen Brocklehurst (eds) *History, Nationhood and the Question of Britain*. Basingstoke: Palgrave Macmillan, forthcoming.
7. For the interrelationship of personal storytelling and trauma, see Rogers et al. 1999. For the development of such thinking in the Northern Irish context, see Dawson 1999:184–91, McKimm 2001.
8. The full interview transcript with Mr and Mrs Gillen (pseudonyms), from which this quotation derives, is included in the 'Personal Stories' section of FEAR [1997].
9. For a theorisation of the psychic dimensions of social recognition in relation to storytelling, see Dawson 1994:22–52. For discussion of recognition and emotional catharsis in the context of the Troubles, see Dawson 1999:187–8, and Kulle 2001.
10. For detailed accounts of these atrocities, see Harnden 1999:132–40, McKittrick et al. 1999:571–3 (nos 1455–8, 1461), 611–14 (nos 1566–75), 963–4 (nos 2578–80).
11. For Unionist reactions to the publication of the Patten Report, see *News Letter* 1999. For the Report itself, see Dickson 2000.
12. Relatives for Justice has argued against what it sees as a 'hierarchy of victims', in which British and Unionist deaths are held to be more important and meriting recognition than those of nationalists and Republicans: see *Justice* 2000:2, Thompson 2000:3, McCabe 2000:11.
13. See, for example, McKay 2000:325–6, 'Victims Were Gunmen, Says Peer', *Guardian* 2002b.
14. Damian Gorman was founder of *An Crann*/The Tree; see *An Crann*/The Tree (ed.) 2000.
15. For Castlederg cemetery, see also Finlay 2000b:22, 23, 39.
16. On the resistance by Republicans to 'truth-telling' about the war, see, for example, Morrison 1998.

17. See, for example, the interview with Willie Frazer of FAIR, 'Five Members of My Family Were Murdered by the IRA. Why Has the World Forgotten?', *Belfast Telegraph* 1999. The call for an inquiry was also a demand of the 'Long March' (Smyth 2000:131–2).
18. Secretary of State, Mo Mowlam, quoted in *An Imperfect Peace*, broadcast BBC Radio 4, 3/10 December 2001.
19. Also, crucially, the Living Memorial Centre would 'prevent the memory of the victims from being lost to the collective consciousness of a younger generation that may be the first to see peace' (Wilson [1999]:5.8.2).

REFERENCES

Adams, Gerry. 1986. *The Politics of Irish Freedom*. Dingle, Co. Kerry: Brandon.
Ahmed, Akbar S. 1995. ' "Ethnic Cleansing": A Metaphor For Our Time', *Ethnic and Racial Studies* 18(1):1–25.
An Appeal to You from The Victims [September? 1999], video, no date or production details, available in Linen Hall Library, Belfast.
An Crann/The Tree (ed.). 2000. *Bear in Mind: Stories of the Troubles*. Belfast: Lagan Press.
Barton, Colm. 2000. (Project Coordinator, Bloody Sunday Trust), in conversation with the author, 26 March.
The Belfast Agreement. 2000. Reproduced in Cox et al. *A Farewell to Arms? From 'Long War' to Long Peace in Northern Ireland*. Manchester: Manchester University Press: Appendix 2:301–25.
Belfast Telegraph. 1999. 'Five Members of My Family Were Murdered by the IRA. Why Has the World Forgotten?', 8 May.
Black, Mary. 2001. 'Current Work with Victims and Survivors', in J. Magowan and N. Patterson (eds) *Hear and Now ... and Then ... Developments in Victims and Survivors Work*. Belfast: Northern Ireland Voluntary Trust:27–33.
Bloomfield, Sir Kenneth. 1998. *We Will Remember Them: Report of the Northern Ireland Victims Commissioner, Sir Kenneth Bloomfield*. Belfast: Stationery Office Northern Ireland.
Bolton, David. 2001. 'Welcome and Introduction to Conference Participants', in J. Magowan and N. Patterson (eds) *Hear and Now ... and Then ... Developments in Victims and Survivors Work*. Belfast: Northern Ireland Voluntary Trust:3–10.
Coogan, Tim Pat. 1996. *The Troubles: Ireland's Ordeal 1966–1996 and the Search for Peace*. London: Arrow.
Cox, Michael, Adrian Guelke and Fiona Stephen (eds). 2000. *A Farewell to Arms? From 'Long War' to Long Peace in Northern Ireland*. Manchester: Manchester University Press.
Daily Telegraph. 30 October 1997.
Darby, John. 2000. 'The Effect of Violence on the Irish Peace Process', in M. Cox et al. (eds) *A Farewell to Arms? From 'Long War' to Long Peace in Northern Ireland*. Manchester: Manchester University Press:263–74.
Dawson, Graham. 1994. *Soldier Heroes: British Adventure, Empire, and the Imagining of Masculinities*. London and New York: Routledge.

——. 1999. 'Trauma, Memory, Politics: The Irish Troubles', in K. Rogers et al. (eds) *Trauma and Life Stories: International Perspectives*. London and New York: Routledge: 180–204.

de Bréadún, Deaglán. 2001. *The Far Side of Revenge: Making Peace in Northern Ireland*. Wilton, Cork: Collins Press.

Dewar, M. W., John Brown and S. E. Long. 1967. *Orangeism: A New Historical Appreciation*. Belfast: [Grand Orange Lodge of Ireland].

Dickson, Brice. 2000. 'Policing and Human Rights After the Conflict', in M. Cox et al. (eds) *A Farewell to Arms? From 'Long War' to Long Peace in Northern Ireland*. Manchester: Manchester University Press:104–15.

European Commission. 1998. *Peace and Reconciliation: An Imaginative Approach to the European Programme for Northern Ireland and the Border Counties of Ireland*. Luxembourg: Office for Official Publications of the European Communities.

FAIR. n.d. [1999]. *The True Story of South Armagh*. Armagh: Families Acting for Innocent Relatives. [no page numbers in the original]

FAIR website. 2000. 'Testimony of a Darkley Gospel Hall Survivor', <www.victims.org.uk/darkleytestimony.html>, visited 14 September.

Fay, Marie-Therese, Mike Morrissey and Marie Smyth. 1999. *Northern Ireland's Troubles: The Human Costs*. London and Sterling, VA: Pluto.

FEAR Fermanagh Ltd. n.d. [1997]. 'Research Document and Development Plan: "People, They Don't Realize the Hurt of Having to Leave What You Have Worked for All Your Life".'

Finlay, Leslie. 2000a. Treasurer, West Tyrone Voice, in conversation with the author, 27 March.

Finlay, Leslie. 2000b. Treasurer, West Tyrone Voice, transcript of personal interview, conducted jointly with Hazlett Lynch, Coordinator, West Tyrone Voice, 27 March.

Foster, Arlene. 1999. Secretary, FEAR, transcript of personal interview, 29 July:2.

Frazer, Willie. 2000. Vice-Chairperson, FAIR, in conversation with the author, 24–5 March.

Guardian. 2002a, 'Bloody Sunday Costs Will Not Be Capped', 16 January.

Guardian. 2002b. 'Victims Were Gunmen, Says Peer', 15 March.

Harnden, Toby. 1999. *'Bandit Country': The IRA and South Armagh*. London: Hodder and Stoughton.

Hirsch, Marianne. 1997. *Family Frames: Photography, Narrative and Postmemory*. Cambridge, Mass. and London: Harvard University Press.

Holland, Jack. 2000. *Hope Against History: The Ulster Conflict*. London: Hodder and Stoughton.

Impartial Reporter. 1997. 21 August.

Irish News. 1995. 12 April.

Irish News. 1997a. 12 August.

Irish News. 1997b. 6 November.

Irish News. 1998. 22 September.

Irish Times. 1997. 26 August.

Jackson, Andrew. 2000. Pseudonym, FACT member, in conversation with the author, 1 March.

Jarman, Neil. 1997. *Material Conflicts: Parades and Visual Displays in Northern Ireland*. Oxford and New York: Berg.

Justice: Newsletter of Relatives for Justice. 2000. Issue 2.

Kulle, Dorte. 2001. 'Victims and Survivors: A Study of the Dynamics of the Victims Debate in Northern Ireland', in J. Magowan and N. Patterson (eds) *Hear and Now ... and Then ... Developments in Victims and Survivors Work*. Belfast: Northern Ireland Voluntary Trust:79–87.

Lynch, Hazlett. 2000. Coordinator, West Tyrone Voice, transcript of personal interview, conducted jointly with Leslie Finlay, Treasurer, West Tyrone Voice, 27 March.

McCabe, Eilish. 2000. Relatives for Justice, transcript of personal interview conducted jointly with Mark Thompson Coordinator, Relatives for Justice, 4 April.

McInnes, Colin. 2000. 'A Farewell to Arms? Decommissioning and the Peace Process', in M. Cox et al. (eds) *A Farewell to Arms? From 'Long War' to Long Peace in Northern Ireland*. Manchester: Manchester University Press:78–92.

McKay, Susan. 2000. *Northern Protestants: An Unsettled People*. Belfast: Blackstaff Press.

McKimm, Cathie. 2001. 'Narrative, Imagination and a Pluralist Vision', in J. Magowan and N. Patterson (eds) *Hear and Now ... and Then ... Developments in Victims and Survivors Work*. Belfast: Northern Ireland Voluntary Trust.95–103.

McKittrick, David, Seamus Kelters, Brian Feeney and Chris Thornton (eds). 1999. *Lost Lives: The Stories of the Men, Women and Children Who Died as a Result of the Northern Ireland Troubles*. Edinburgh and London: Mainstream Publishers.

Magowan, James, and Norma Patterson (eds). 2001. *Hear and Now ... and Then ... Developments in Victims and Survivors Work*. Belfast: Northern Ireland Voluntary Trust.

Morrison, Danny. 1998. Interviewed by Fergal Keane, *Resigning Issues*, broadcast BBC Radio 4, 13 October.

Nairac, Captain Robert. 1977. 'Talking to People in South Armagh', British Army Briefing Paper, reproduced in T. Harnden. 1999.'*Bandit Country': The IRA and South Armagh*. London: Hodder and Stoughton:367–72.

News Letter. 1997. 26 August.

News Letter. 1999. 10 September.

Observer. 1997. 2 November.

Orange Standard. 1992 'Ethnic Cleansing on Our Own Doorstep – Molyneux', September.

Orange Standard. 1993. 'Ethnic Cleansing Along the Border', April.

Page, Michael von Tangen. 2000. 'A "Most Difficult and Unpalatable Part" – the Release of Politically Motivated Violent Offenders', in M. Cox et al. (eds) *A Farewell to Arms? From 'Long War' to Long Peace in Northern Ireland*. Manchester: Manchester University Press:93–103.

Peake, Sandra. 2000. Director, WAVE Trauma Centre, Belfast, transcript of personal interview, 6 April.

Rogers, Kim Lacy, Selma Leydesdorff and Graham Dawson (eds). 1999. *Trauma and Life Stories: International Perspectives*. London and New York: Routledge.

Ryder, Chris and Vincent Kearney. 2001. *Drumcree: The Orange Order's Last Stand*. London: Methuen.

Smyth, Marie. 2000. 'The Human Consequences of Armed Conflict: Constructing "Victimhood" in the Context of Northern Ireland's Troubles', in M. Cox et al. (eds) *A Farewell to Arms? From 'Long War' to Long Peace in Northern Ireland*. Manchester: Manchester University Press:118–35.

Smyth, Marie and Marie-Therese Fay. 2000. *Personal Accounts from Northern Ireland's Troubles: Public Conflict, Private Loss*. London and Sterling, VA: Pluto.

Thompson, Mark. 2000. Coordinator, Relatives for Justice, transcript of personal interview conducted jointly with Eilish McCabe, Relatives for Justice, 4 April.

VLU Newsletter. 1999. 'Further Funding Package for Victims Announced', 2 November.

West Tyrone Voice. n.d. [1998]. Information Leaflet.

Wilson, S. J. and Associates. n.d. [1999]. 'A Needs Analysis of Families Acting for Innocent Relatives'.

8 'In the Name of the Victims': the Politics of Compensation in the Work of the South African Truth and Reconciliation Commission

Lars Buur

When I interviewed people who had been part of the South African Truth and Reconciliation Commission (hereafter the Commission or TRC) process in 1996 and 1997, they often referred to themselves as 'victims of apartheid'. In 1999 they would state, 'I am a victim of the TRC.' This last sentence can mean two different things. On the one hand, it can refer to the people the Commission had defined as victims of gross human rights violations. On the other, it can refer to people who felt betrayed by the Commission because they became victims of its work. I hope to give some answers to this shift in meaning and also to how we can understand the relationship between the Commission and the people it represented.[1]

The experiences of people who handed in statements and engaged in the Commission's public hearings process – where they were given the opportunity to speak and thereby have their stories documented in an official state setting (Wilson 1996:16) – were generally positive. There are many examples of how people felt relieved after giving public testimonies (see for example Krog 1998, Tutu 1999, Villa-Vicencio and Verwoerd 2000). This scenario changed considerably when they were promised 'substantial compensation' for their efforts and the African National Congress (ANC)-led government declined to pay out reparation grants promised by the Commission. In contrast, Commissioners and high-profile staff members of the Commission have been celebrated all over the world and have taken up lucrative positions in the state apparatus. Furthermore, most of South Africa's socially marginalised population has not experienced any real change in its socio-economic situation.

However, promises were made even before the question of financial reparation began to surface. One of the more painful results of the disparity between what was promised, besides financial compensation, and what was done, was that during hearings, Commissioners often guaranteed victims proper investigations into what had happened to them or their missing relatives. These pledges were not kept and served only to raise victims' expectations unrealistically and unnecessarily.

The great hopes for a better and different life, which the Commission incarnated, have made many people from the most marginalised population groups feel disappointed. Over the last few years people formally identified as victims by the Commission have begun to organise themselves and make their voices heard. They are claiming their rights to promised compensation through petitions and demonstrations. The emergence of victims as *political actors* can be seen as dispersed, partial, and largely uncoordinated forms of resistance on the part of those subjected to formal and technocratic nation-building processes. In my opinion, however, an attempt to understand the emergence of organised defiance solely in relation to unfulfilled promises raised by the Commission is likely to be unfruitful. Instead, I will suggest that the emergence of victims as political actors exists in the social matrix of the Commission (its language and practices) and its interaction with the group of people that became 'victims of the TRC' and were caught up in the complex, ongoing relationship between the TRC and the ANC.

In other words, I will suggest that if one wants to understand the emergence of 'victim groups' as political actors, and how the elected embodiment of all poor people in South Africa – in other words, the ANC – has finished up in a situation where they had to turn down the promises made on behalf of 17,500 people found to be victims by the Commission, then we first have to understand both the issues underpinning the development of the group of people and the wider grammar of liberal-democratic representivity embedded in the work of the Commission.

THREE VECTORS

To begin to untangle this challenge we will have to account for a social field constituted by three principal vectors: *objectification*, *taxonomy* and *release*. By objectification I refer to a set of institutionalised techniques for objectification that had to be in place so that the Commission could sort out who were proper victims and who were not. By taxonomy I refer to the development of a human rights violation taxonomy which more or less matched the experiences of the abused people who came forward to the Commission. Finally, release refers to the possibility of escape for people classified as victims of human rights violation. The classification 'victim' invited an escape not only for people who had suffered from human rights violations so they could gain access to a better life, but also for the Commission, who needed 'victims of apartheid' to come forward and participate in the Commission process.

My use of the concept *vector* is influenced by the work of Ian Hacking (1998). According to Hacking, the origin of the word 'vector' is in mechanics, but I use it (as he does) as a metaphor. In mechanics, a vector is 'a force acting in a direction. When there are several forces acting in different directions, the resultant force is the product of the different forces and their directions' (81). I will suggest that the emergence of victims as contested objects in South Africa can best be understood if we account for how different kinds of phenomena act in different ways. The result, however, may be a social field in which promised compensation, 'victims of the TRC' and new controversies over the status of victimhood can interact.

OBJECTIFICATION

A substantial system of identification and selection had to be in place. People who had suffered human rights violations during apartheid had to be proven to be victims on the TRC's terms. Those who handed in a statement alleging that they were victims of gross human rights violation (GHRV) were systematically subjected to scrutiny as to whether their statements were 'within mandate' or 'out of mandate'. In order for individual apartheid experiences to be deemed a GHRV they had to fit an established taxonomy, their allegations had to be proved and these had to materialise as 'objective' evidence. In the Commission the process of objectification was organised and structured by what is known as the Information Management System (hereafter IMS).

The IMS is at its most basic level concerned with what Ian Hacking (1982) calls 'statistical analysis of regularities of population' (50). This does not mean that one necessarily generates statistics. It means that one treats 'information' in a particular manner, focusing on the generation of exclusive categorisations and generalised profiles of representative 'groups' or 'populations' – in this case victims – on which representational democracy allocates entitlements and political rights (van Beek 2001). In order to do so, it is necessary to define the kind of representative groups about which one is searching for information. In a human rights data-collection process this is intimately related to what constitute human rights data. For Patrick Ball (1996), who is a researcher at the Science and Human Rights Program of the American Association for the Advancement of Science (AAAS) and the main architect of the database of the Commission, human rights data are the 'representation of acts of violence which allows human rights researchers to make systematic, comparative analyses of patterns of violations in time, space and social structure' (4). Such data are aimed at objectifying 'trends' in the material concerned with 'who did what to whom' – the 'global truth'. For this to be done, decisions have to be made under the 'controlled vocabulary' emerging from the legal mandate. This brings me to the second vector: taxonomy.

TAXONOMY

Many of the people who had experienced human rights violations during the apartheid era fitted into the TRC taxonomy (or 'controlled vocabulary') of violations which was only one of a range of possible taxonomies. The 'controlled vocabulary' of violations determined how a given incident in the 'real world' appeared in the coded data (Ball 1996:33). The Commission operated with four main categories in its taxonomy of what constituted a GHRV: 'torture, killing, abduction and severe ill-treatment' (Act 1995:1). The issue of gross human rights violations did not replace existent systems of classification, but it did invite debates around issues such as: 'What is a gross violation of human rights?'; 'Into which part of the established taxonomy should people coming to the Commission be fitted?'; 'What should happen to victims of human rights violations who did not fit the taxonomy?'; 'What were the implications of changes in the taxonomy which created inconsistent and contradictory patterns of inclusion and exclusion over time?' Let me give an indication of the complexities related to classification.

Each of the overall categories of 'torture', 'killing', 'abduction' and 'severe ill-treatment' was divided into a range of sub-categories. Depending on the position of a staff member in the Commission hierarchy, the history of the taxonomy applied by the Commission was either chaotic or controlled. Seen from the bottom of the hierarchy, it was rather chaotic. During the Commission's lifespan the taxonomic structure that lower-level staff worked with developed from two pages to ten (Buur 2001).[2] Nearly every week new categories were added or removed, or previous interpretations of categories re-worked.[3] However, while higher levels of the Commission's bureaucratic structure made these revisions, information about the changes was not always passed on to the lower-level staff who had to implement the changes in their daily work. When a change did filter down, it generally took one to two weeks to reach the base of the IMS.

To classify actual experiences according to the taxonomic system created problems in the work of the Commission when the system met with the manner in which local conflicts and human rights violations were configured. For the statement-takers, the problems related to definition and interpretation were particularly severe when the Commission worked in rural areas. The reason was that the Commission's interpretation of the normative definition of political context did not include racial violations as GHRV if they were not:

[Advised], planned, directed, commanded, ordered or committed by ... any member or supporter of a publicly known political organisation or liberation movement on behalf of or in support of that organisation or movement, in furtherance of a political struggle waged by that organisation or movement. (TRC Report 1998, Volume 1:82)

In the rural areas human rights violations seldom involved known political organisations as such, but they were nonetheless closely related to and informed by racism:

We rejected many, many, many cases which came to us simply because they were not falling within the political act of the Commission [or part] of the political ambits. For instance most cases of violations in the rural areas were ... along racial lines. For instance a person comes to you and reports that he [one day] was walking in the street in one of the 'dorpies'[4] and he was shot by a white man. The problem with it (this case) is that there is no political connection into the violation, because it's a civilian or an individual that just shot someone. So there is no political motive. (Extract from interview with a statement taker, 1997)

The dilemma described in this quote was not unique. The tensions between the interpretation of the normative framework of the Act and the realities encountered at statement-taker level were prolonged, as Commissioners took considerable time to decide whether or not to change the operational interpretation of the political context. This made statement-takers question the definition of GHRV put forward by the Commission and the very foundation of their work:

> [What] is a human rights violation and what makes it gross? A lot of people couldn't accept the fact that because of what this 'white' person did to them it is not a gross human rights violation... Politics wasn't like the order of the day or the main things that the Commission was looking for ... the racial issue was never addressed in terms of what happens to people because [they were] discriminated against racially. (Ibid.)

The result was that statement-takers felt they bore the burden of turning away person after person who had clearly suffered from violations of rights. The ambivalent position they were placed in was difficult to manage because they were aware that another policy change by the Commissioners could easily mean that the following week they could have accepted them and classified them as 'victims'. How did statement-takers react to this situation?

Some of them followed the Commission's interpretation and turned people away, particularly in the rural areas, the area most affected by the Commission's interpretation of political context. Other statement-takers tried to bypass the interpretation. They thought it unfair to block a huge section of the population, who were already excluded from access to resources. This implies that even though a well-known global management system and a comprehensive taxonomy were implemented, one cannot just infer that the system ran smoothly without interference from local priorities and concerns. This entailed a series of negotiations between staff, Commissioners and the taxonomic system in which contradictions arose due to the fact that interpretations evolved over time.

RELEASE

To be classified as a 'victim of GHRV' by the Commission invited an escape for a fragmented and dispersed group of people. The classification could be an escape for people who often were, and still are, living in extreme poverty without access to basic needs, jobs and education. They could, if classified, get access to future entitlements, welfare programmes – a better life. The classification 'victim of GHRV' provided an opportunity to soothe the staff's bad consciences over not offering any real change in the life perspectives of victims, and for being part of a deeply unjust amnesty process – even if the amnesty process where victims' rights to pursue civil claims or justice were denied was necessary for the South African transition. In addition to this, the classification of 'victim of GHRV' also provided the Commission with a source of legitimacy; it badly needed people to come forward and hand in statements. Without statements it was difficult for the Commission to claim legitimately the right to speak on behalf of the 'victims of apartheid' and to justify the massive financial expenditure which was the real cost of the process. When the classification 'victim of GHRV' became concentrated around the issue of *monetary* compensation these diverse forces took on a life of their own, and a range of other forces came into play. Let me indicate how some of these forces played themselves out within the Commission between 1996 and 1998.

MONETARY COMPENSATION

Although the well-known public hearings of the Commission were considered to be a huge success (Wilson 1996), in fact far fewer victims than expected came forward to the Commission. At the outset around 100,000 statements were expected. During an internal workshop on the Final Report run by the Research Department of the Commission in September 1996, Research Director Charles Villa-Vicencio said that the Commission had expected about 80,000 people to come forward.[5] In the end only around 22,000 people came forward. This was still more than any other official Truth Commission has been capable of documenting, but seen in relation to the expected influx, it was considered to be an embarrassment within the Commission.

The first statement-protocol formula did not have any specific Reparation and Rehabilitation section. It plainly asked alleged victims 'How much do you want?' As formulated by a staff member from the briefing unit, 'It was a grandiose position for the Commission to ask victims, "What do you want?" and then imply that we would provide it – because the Commission did not expect victims to ask for money' (interview with a member of the briefing unit, 1997). As a matter of fact, people coming to the Commission *did* ask for money, and on a grand scale. Hereafter, the question was changed, and a special section from the Reparation and Rehabilitation (R and R) Committee was included under the headline 'Expectations'. However, even though it deliberately focused on *symbolic reparation* instead of *monetary compensation,* monetary compensation was very much part of the picture, even though it was written out of the statement protocol.[6]

Just a few days before the Commission had been in operation for one year, it announced a proposal to implement what came to be known as 'Urgent Interim Reparation Measures'.[7] Nevertheless, it would be a further two years before the first urgent interim reparations were paid out to victims of apartheid. Even though both the Danish and the Swiss governments contributed 1 million dollars each to the establishment of some kind of structure which could manage payments, the Commission and the ANC-led government were unable to reach agreement on the process.

With the amnesty process, however, which began in 1996 and involved multiple hearings, the question about monetary compensation continued to surface. The rationale behind the demand was *morally* anchored. People felt that it was necessary to counterbalance the amnesty processes because, according to the Act, amnesty included protection against civil claims from victims. In addition, many of the amnesty applicants secured state funding for legal representation in amnesty hearings. For victims, on the other hand, even though they were promised the restoration of their dignity and self-respect from the process of telling their story, truth-telling would not change the life conditions under which they lived.[8]

The rate of incoming statements was slow, and by February/March of 1997 the Commission in Cape Town was faced with severe problems in getting victim statements for three upcoming hearings. At the same time there were discussions among concerned researchers, committee members and Commissioners about the classification of apartheid as a crime against humanity. Some felt it would somehow be a hollow classification when the Commission had gathered fewer than 7,500 statements from a population of around 40 million (see TRC Report 1998, Volume 1:167).

Then, on 3 April 1997, a briefer from the Commission told me that the R and R Committee had decided to propose that victims should receive a *substantial* amount of money in reparation. When the rumour reached the statement-taker unit the following day, the first reaction was: 'Ag, they're just trying to get statements' (the quoted source was a statement-taker from the Cape Town office). But the new proposal had concrete effects. By 7 April 1997 the issue of money was raised as a possible form of compensation in the 'Expectations' section of the victim statement protocol. At a Hearings Meeting the following day, an R and R Committee member told statement-takers:

> Reparation and statements have to be connected. They (victims) may lose out on reparation if they do not make a statement; they jeopardise the possibility of receiving reparation if they do not make a statement. So statement-takers have to make this clear when they speak to victims. (Fieldwork notes, 1997)

It was, in other words, official policy, at least within the Commission, that reparation and money were intrinsically connected and that the issue of money could be used to 'persuade' victims, as it was called. In the following months the connection between victims, statements, money and reparation became everyday policy. Of course the fact that so far it was only a *proposal*, a recommendation the R and R Committee would make to the government, was spelled out to victims, for example in statement-taking sessions and briefing sessions; but the sense was that government would not and could not turn down the recommendation; they would lose credibility if they did. Still, the expected flood of statements did not come, and the end of the statement-gathering process, September 1997, was only months away.

Then on 23 October 1997 the Commission called for a press conference at the Cape Town headquarters where its monetary and symbolic reparation and rehabilitation policy proposal (R and R proposal) was presented. It was here stressed that according to its proposal the government should grant people 'judged to have suffered human rights violations under apartheid' a minimum reparation payment of 17,000 rand annually for six years with a maximum close to 33,000 rand. The recommended individual reparations were based on an average annual household consumption of 21,700 rand.[9] The plan would cost about 3 billion rand to implement, and a projected 22,000 victims would benefit (fieldwork notes, 23 October 1997). The Commissioners present stressed that the Commission had held numerous meetings with members of the Government and the Ministry of Justice in charge of overseeing the work of the Commission. Desmond Tutu made it clear that his impression was that the government was fundamentally sympathetic: 'We are pushing at a door that is open' (*Electronic Mail and Guardian* 1997). The R and R proposal was then reproduced in a 'Summary of Reparation and Rehabilitation Policy' pamphlet, which was made available by the TRC in 1998. Here there was a warning that read: 'Please remember that these are proposals to the President. The President and Parliament will make a final decision on them'(5).

In the last months of the statement-taking process, which officially (after several extensions of the mandated period) ended in December 1997, the Commission managed to get around 6,000 statements amounting to a 27 per cent increase in just two months. This, of course, cannot only be assigned to the promise of money, but the promise was an important factor. For example, quite a few of the statements came from KwaZulu-Natal, where the IFP, having boycotted the Commission process from its outset, decided at the last minute to encourage their members to address the Commission, so they would not lose out on possible financial compensation (see Buur 2000, Chapter 5).

DEMOCRATIC REPRESENTATION AND NEW DOMAINS OF STRUGGLE

The brief run through the three vectors is in no way comprehensive, but it illustrates how different forces come together in a complex constellation which structures the emergence of the 'victims of the TRC'. My point is that the knowledge generated by the style of reasoning applied by the Commission is based on the official grammar of representative samples. It is the task of institutions like the Commission to generate the exclusive categorisations and generalised profiles of representative groups on which representational democracy allocates entitlements and political rights.

It is exactly on this point of representivity that the Commission and the ANC have continually clashed since the release of the Final Report in 1998. The ANC's response has been to problematise the limited accessibility of potential 'victims' to the Commission. Thabo Mbeki's statement to Parliament on 25 February 1999, after the release of the Final Report, raised the question of representivity in an accusation that the Commission had only identified '*some* of the people who were entitled to receive reparation' (Mbeki 1999, emphasis added). The problem Mbeki and the ANC encountered with regard to the work of the Commission was exactly the objectification of the 'some'.

When the ANC/government had not yet made a clear commitment to the Commission's R and R proposal by mid-2000, the rationale was that many applicants who came to the Commission were *not eligible* for relief, which they thought they were entitled to simply because they had appeared before the Commission as witnesses. The full consequences of this argument have since come to the fore, in that the Commission by 26 May 2000 had to acknowledge that it 'had to make negative decisions, which affected approximately 4,500 people. These negative decisions relate to those incidents which fall outside the mandate period or do not constitute a gross human rights violation' (*TRC Mailing List* 2000). This means that roughly 20 per cent of the 22,000 statements the Commission received from alleged victims had to be turned down. Perhaps even more controversial was the ANC argument that many of the people who had participated in the struggle had not applied for reparations, because they felt they had *fought for a democratic society*, not for money (Mann 2000). The ANC is trapped between doing something for 'everybody' and, as Mamdani (1996) puts it, doing a lot for the 'few'. Which, as the political and economic reality is presently configured, means doing *nothing* for everybody.

Criticism has been mounting against the ANC government's reluctance to pay out the reparation grants promised by the Commission. Among the fiercest of these critics were former Chairperson of the Commission, Desmond Tutu, and Anglican Archbishop Njogunkulu Ndungane, who accused the government of 'betraying those who fought apartheid' (Njogunkulu Ndungane quoted in Mann 2000). In this way both the TRC and the government positions speak on behalf of the 'proper victims', claiming that they represent them. The tragedy is that on a symbolic level it would be sufficient for the Commission to objectify a representative sample, to symbolically 'stand in' for the suffering of the nation. In relation to the level of material compensation, representative samples are not sufficient. The point is that the Commission can create symbolic reparation for everybody, but the ANC/government cannot create material reparation for everybody if the few 'stand in' for all – this would be politically unjust.

THE GRAMMAR OF CONFLICT

The controversy between the Commission and the ANC is indicative of a wider *problématique* in that the principle that is supposed to lay the foundation for peace and justice – in the form of generating knowledge about the past and present – produces new conflicts.

At least two fairly well-organised victim/survivor groups have emerged on the scene. One is the Ex Political Prisoners and Apartheid Human Rights Violations Survivors group based in Cape Town; another is the largest, oldest (it started up before the Commission was implemented) and best organised, known as the Khulumani Support Group.[10] They have tried by various means to keep a dialogue open with the Commission and the government over the issue of reparation. When people who were classified as 'victims of apartheid' began to classify themselves as 'victims of the TRC', it was not the representation as 'victim' they reacted against so much as the way the representative sample had been made and the fact that the compensation they were promised failed to materialise. It has been stressed that: 'Not all of us were afforded the opportunity to give a statement to the TRC. This opportunity needs to be extended and the additional people deserving reparations be included' (*Newsletter* 2000:1).

It is important to stress that the objectification of victim groups has not directly created violence; on the contrary it points to one of the unintended success stories of the Commission. The emerging victim groups have so far followed democratic rules for stating their discontent, such as delivery of petitions, holding marches and demonstrations, organising meetings between key protagonists and so on – and will probably continue to do so in the future. Thus the language in which discontent has been expressed has been an active engagement in a democratic learning process where the status of the proper representational groupings both gets accepted and is itself subject to democratic processes of contestation.

One of the most intriguing aspects of giving voice to emerging groups of 'proper victims' in South Africa has been the simultaneous fragmentation and diffusion of wider claims of people living on the margins of the nation-state. One should not forget, in the world-wide celebration of the Commission, that the group of people formally entitled to reparation represents only a small section of all the 'victims of apartheid'. In South Africa the economic gap between social groups is widening.[11] Inequalities in employment, wealth and empowerment are not new, of course, but as long as the real living conditions of people's lives are leading to a widening of the gap between groups in spite of the new dispensation on citizenship, democracy and human rights, processes like the Commission can easily end up becoming enmeshed in the general sense of disillusionment. Stated slightly differently, the new South African dispensation suggests formal equity which, under capitalism and a neo-liberal market economy, cannot but lead to new kinds of contestation. The national project, founded on constitutional democracy, a variety of government policy programmes and the TRC, offers a new framework of shared language, rules and practices to contest such inequalities. However, when claims are contested by multiple segregated movements, or sucked up in internal disparities and conflicts over who the right and legitimate voices are, they become fragmented. In this context, conflict over reparations can be described as an intricate process of depoliticisation and repoliticisation of past conflicts, recast in a new language and drawing on a new set of practices (Buur 2000).

The dilemma is that there is a need to allocate resources and entitlements according to the representation of communities. Here the most coherent representational groupings which have emerged on the scene are the groupings emerging from the Commission process. It is of particular interest that even though the Commission and the ANC are in conflict over the status of the victims objectified by the Commission, they share the same *grammar* for allocation and representivity.

THE BENEVOLENT STATE

What was at stake in these twisted encounters was nothing but the legitimacy of not only the Commission, but also the new South African state. The public victim hearings and gathering of statements from victims had an important mission. As Alex Boraine, who became the Vice-Chairperson of the Commission, formulated it as early as 1995:

This will be the first experience of many survivors of a compassionate state, which goes out to people. Survivors will be received, respected and given a cup of coffee. Before, if they went to the police, magistrates or the military they would receive a hostile treatment. (Alex Boraine quoted in Wilson 1995:44)

The dilemma confronting South Africa and the Commission was that the state's institutions were deeply involved in committing human rights violations and enforcing the former apartheid government's institutionalised hierarchy and segregation. The new government inherited, so to speak, a state 'suffering from a legitimisation crisis' (Wilson 1996:9).

As stated by Boraine, the Commission was one of the vehicles, both on a symbolic level and also materially, for reconceptualising the state as *benevolent* using a range of meetings to take statements from people, listen to their testimonies and decide on future entitlement to reparation and rehabilitation grants. The benevolent impression of the new state that Alex Boraine saw as an important aspect of the work of the Commission can easily become tarnished by non-fulfilment of its (or indeed the Commission's) promises.

ACKNOWLEDGEMENTS

Generous grants from The Danish Institute of Foreign Affairs and the Danish Research Council for Development Research made it possible for me to conduct the research for this chapter (from 1997 to 1999). The contours of this chapter took shape during my stay with the South African Truth and Reconciliation Commission and my subsequent time as guest researcher at the Centre for Development Research (CDR) in Copenhagen. I am therefore grateful to the Commission, the Research Council, the Institute and the Centre. Thanks also to Alison Stent, Mark Anderson, Paul Gready and Steffen Jensen for editorial comments, insightful critique and highly useful suggestions.

NOTES

1. This chapter is based on ethnographic fieldwork material from South Africa undertaken between 1996 and 1999.
2. At higher levels of the Commission the 'controlled vocabulary' was actually reduced, not augmented, from over 200 violations to fewer than 50, of which only 25 were used in any meaningful way when the Commission presented its findings (based on internet discussions with one of the creators of the database, Patrick Ball, in 1999). One explanation could be that a range of sub-categories that were developed for each of the main categories in the 'controlled vocabulary' were regrouped towards the end of the Commission and the extensive network of GHRV sub-divisions in this sense was simplified.
3. For example, statement-takers and data processors in the beginning of the work of the Commission did not register what later became a sub-category 'detention without trial' under the main GHRV category 'severe ill treatment'. At a later stage of the process they were informed that half

a year in prison without trial would be a GHRV. At the end of the Commission process 14 days in prison without trial was sufficient to be classified as a GHRV. Whether the definition changed again later I do not know.

4. 'Dorpie' is an Afrikaans word for small village.

5. Ball, who was part of the implementation of the IMS, mentions in his book from 1996 that the Commission hoped to take 75,000 statements (25).

6. Here it is sufficient to mention that symbolic reparation was concerned with memorials, changing of street names, public holidays and so on.

7. It was immediately picked up in the media. The message was: 'The Truth and Reconciliation Commission this morning unveiled its first proposals for reparations for victims of apartheid-era human rights abuses.' What was revealed was 'The Policy Framework for Urgent Interim Reparation Measures' aimed at paying financial compensation to victims of human rights abuses whose immediate situation was such that they could not wait for the Commission to tender its final report. Truth Commission R and R Committee chair Hlengiwe Mkhize did stress that 'the policy framework is a recommendation to the office of President Nelson Mandela and Parliament, as the committee does not have the power to make decisions on the implementation of its recommendations'. Finance for a more structured proposal 'would be dealt with by government' (*Electronic Mail and Guardian* 1996).

8. This was something many people in the Commission were well aware of. A range of internal workshops about reparation took place, as well as discussions between the Commission and the NGO sector. Some of these meetings were known as the 'Think Tank' run by the R and R Committee where concerned academics, NGOs and others met with members of the Commission in order to discuss, for example, the question of monetary compensation. As early as July and August 1996 minutes and draft plans refer to reparation in the form of money, indicating that it was not a sudden decision. These circulating draft plans operated within a range of parameters for measurement which included kind of violation, size of household and income scale. However, at the cliff-face, where statement-takers met victims, these plans had no impact. The Commission had so far in statement-taking sessions focused on symbolic reparation. Alleged victims were asked, 'What do you expect from the Commission?'. They were then told that the question was concerned with 'symbolic reparation'. Statement-takers were aware of the discussions, but they had been told not to mention direct financial compensation.

9. The Commission decided that a standard amount should be paid to people judged to have suffered, because it would be impossible to measure the degree of suffering.

10. Both groups are closely affiliated to well-known NGOs. The Cape Town-based group is affiliated to the Trauma Centre for Survivors of Violence and Torture in Cape Town. The Johannesburg-based group is affiliated to the Centre for the Study of Violence and Reconciliation in Johannesburg.

The two groups had by late 2000 merged in order to put pressure on the government over the question of reparations.

11. See Howard Barrell 2000. The article is based on economic figures from the Wharton Economic Forecasting Association, which, as far as I have been able to follow the debate, have not been contested.

REFERENCES

Act. 1995. Statutes of the Republic of South Africa – Constitutional Law. Promotion of National Unity and Reconciliation. Government Gazette, Act No. 34 of 1995 as amended by Act, No. 87 of 1995. South Africa.

Ball, P. 1996. *Who Did What to Whom?* American Association for the Advancement of Science. Washington: AAAS.

Barrell, Howard. 2000. 'Black Elite Benefit Most From Democracy', *Electronic Mail & Guardian,* 31 January 2000.

Buur, Lars. 2000. *Institutionalising Truth: Victims, Perpetrators and Professionals in the Everyday Work of the South African Truth and Reconciliation Commission.* Ph.D. dissertation submitted to the Department of Ethnography and Social Anthropology, Aarhus University, Denmark. July 2000.

——. 2001. 'The South African Truth and Reconciliation Commission – a Technique of Nation-State Formation', in Thomas Blom Hansen and Finn Stepputat (eds) *States of Imagination.* Durham and London: Duke University Press.

Electronic Mail and Guardian. 1996. 'TRC Announces First Reparations Proposal', 11 November 1996.

Electronic Mail and Guardian. 1997. 'R3bn for Apartheid Reparations', 23 October 1997.

Hacking, Ian. 1982. 'Language, Truth and Reason', in Martin Hollis and Steven Lukes (eds) *Rationality and Relativism.* Oxford: Blackwell.

Hacking, Ian. 1998. *Mad Travelers. Reflections on the Reality of Transient Mental Illnesses.* Charlotteville and London: University Press of Virginia.

Krog, Antjie. 1998. *Country of my Skull.* Johannesburg: Random House.

Mamdani, Mahmood. 1996. 'Reconciliation without Justice', *Southern Review of Books,* November/December 1996.

Mann, Steven. 2000. 'Govt Hedges on TRC Reparations', *Electronic Mail and Guardian,* 11 May 2000. <www.mg.co.za>.

Mbeki, Thabo. 1999. 'Statement of the President of the African National Congress, on the Report of the TRC at the Joint Sitting of the Houses of Parliament, Cape Town'. 25 February 1999.

Newsletter. 2000. 'Ex Political Prisoners and Apartheid Human Rights Violations Survivors', No. 12:1.

TRC. 1998. 'A Summary of Reparation and Rehabilitation Policy Document. The South African Truth and Reconciliation Commission Proposal for Reparation and Rehabilitation'.

TRC Final Report. 1998. *Final Report. Volumes 1–5. Truth and Reconciliation Commission of South Africa.* Cape Town: Juta.

TRC Mailing List. 2000. 'TRC: Advisory on HRV Findings', 26 May 2000.

Tutu, Desmund. 1999. *No Future Without Forgiveness*. New York, London, Toronto, Sydney & Auckland: Doubleday.

van Beek, Martijn. 2001. 'Beyond Identity Fetishism: "Communal" Conflict in Ladakh and the Limits of Autonomy', *Cultural Anthropology* 2000 15(3).

Villa-Vicencio, Charles and Wilhelm Verwoerd. 2000. *Looking Back Reaching Forward*. Cape Town: University of Cape Town Press and London: Zed Books.

Wilson, Richard. 1995. 'Manufacturing Legitimacy. The Truth and Reconciliation and the Rule of Law', *Indicator SA* 13(1).

——. 1996. 'The Sizwe Will Not Go Away. The Truth and Reconciliation Commission, Human Rights and Nation-Building in South Africa', *African Studies* 55(2).

9 The Construction of Voice and Identity in the South African Truth and Reconciliation Commission

Fiona C. Ross

PROLOGUE

On 14 June 1996, at a meeting called between the South African Truth and Reconciliation Commission and members of Cape Town's civil society and NGOs to address women's participation in the Commission's process, Commissioner Mapule Ramashala expressed her concern about an emergent pattern in testimonies given before public hearings into human rights violations. She said:

> Now, having had the first round [of hearings], I've been very disturbed that women witness stories about other people, and are totally removing themselves. Part of this has to do with the male-dominated structure of the Truth Commission, and the lack of probing questions ... Women are articulate about describing their men's experiences but are hesitant about themselves ... The pain expressed has been the pain of others, not of themselves. Are we colluding by not providing space for women to talk? ... *If women do not talk then the story we produce will not be complete.* (emphasis added)

By October 1998, the Commission was able to publish findings on women:

> The state was responsible for the severe ill treatment of women in custody in the form of harassment and the deliberate withholding of medical attention, food and water.
>
> Women were abused by the security forces in ways which specifically exploited their vulnerabilities as women, for example rape or the threat of rape and other forms of sexual abuse, threats against family and children, removal of children from their care,

false stories about illness and/or death of family members and children, and humiliation and abuse around biological functions such as menstruation and childbirth.

Women in exile, particularly in the camps, were subjected to various forms of sexual abuse and harassment, including rape. (TRC Report 1998, Volume 5:256)

The prologue describes two moments in time, separated by 28 months of intensive investigation into gross violations of human rights (henceforth, GVHR) in Southern Africa. It points to the emergence of a categorisation of 'women' as a point of concern within the South African Truth and Reconciliation Commission's process and in its findings. The chapter considers the implications of the construction of voice and identity in the Commission's work, demonstrating the ways that women's experiences, activities and identities are condensed, erased from or obscured in public recall.

DEFINING VICTIM AND VIOLATION

An examination of GVHR committed between 1960 and 1994, the South African Truth and Reconciliation Commission (henceforth, the Commission) was a specific, *public* form of bearing witness to violence and its consequences, a process of remembrance and a forum in which identities were articulated, negotiated and reformulated in the aftermath of institutionalised apartheid. The Commission offered a particular discourse within which to place, describe and understand the violence of the recent past. Three committees dealt with the Commission's tasks of documenting the nature, cause, patterns and extent of GVHR, making recommendations on reparation and rehabilitation, and granting amnesty. The Commission's work bifurcated violence: 'perpetrators' committed acts of violence and 'victims' suffered the consequences. The chapter focuses on the latter.

In terms of the Commission's definition of GVHR, victims represented the locus of inflicted power. An imputation of passivity, exemplified in the second epigraph with which I opened the chapter, was built into its definitions and work.[1] The Act's definitions of violence and violation were narrow: GVHR were defined as killing, abduction, torture and severe ill-treatment. Notwithstanding provisions in the Act for recognition of pecuniary harm and other forms of damage, the Commission resolved that its mandate was to focus attention on what the Report retrospectively describes as 'bodily integrity rights':

> rights that are enshrined in the new South African Constitution and under international law. These include the right to life ... the right to be free from torture ... the right to be free from cruel, inhuman, or degrading treatment or punishment ... and the right to freedom and security of the person, including freedom from abduction and arbitrary and prolonged detention. (TRC Report 1998, Volume 1:64)

A focus on the body raises a variety of problems. It suggests a natural relationship between the subject and the experience of violence and prioritises the authenticity of physical harm over damage caused to social relationships. The triangulation of 'experience', 'subject position' and 'authenticity' in the context of bearing witness to harm raised complex problems in the Commission's work that were not entirely resolved. Two such were to focus attention on the spectacular dimensions of apartheid, particularly on the suffering of men, and to differentiate between 'victims' (of GVHR) and those who suffered apartheid's onslaught. I explore these claims in more detail below.

SPEAKING PAIN

The Act tasked the Commission with

> establishing and making known the fate or whereabouts of victims and restoring the human and civil dignity of such victims by granting them an opportunity to relate their own accounts of the violations of which they are the victims, and recommending reparation measures in respect of them.

People whose experiences fit the definitions of GVHR were invited to make statements (see Buur 1999 and this volume). By December 1997, the Commission's Committee on Human Rights Violations had received 21,298 statements concerning 37,672 violations from victims of violence, their kin, friends and witnesses (TRC Report 1998, Volume 1:166). Approximately 10 per cent of those who made statements were invited to testify in 76 public hearings that began in April 1996 and continued until mid-1997. Seated on a stage facing a panel of Commissioners and committee members, accompanied by 'briefers', testifiers described the violations they and others had suffered. Behind them, flags proclaimed the Commission's mission — 'Truth, the road to reconciliation'. Hearings were widely broadcast in diverse local and international media.

The Commission's work explicitly linked voice ('relating their own accounts', 'testifying' or 'telling one's story') with the restoration of dignity and thence with the constitution of the subject in the post-apartheid era. This formulation of the 'healed' subject as the speaking self is not unusual (Achille Mbembe (2000) argues it is distinctive of post-slavery, post-colonial and post-apartheid discourse) but it raises complex problems in relation to constituting the subject, particularly in the light of assumptions that speaking pain enables 'reintegration' for the individual and has a juridical role in society.[2] These assumptions lie at the basis of the projects generically described as 'truth commissions'.

In South Africa, testimonial practices of relating experiences of GVHR for the public were often portrayed as healing. Described as 'story-telling', a motif that ran through the Commission's process, such practices were constituted as an authentically 'African' mode of communication. Archbishop Tutu, the Chair of the Commission, stated,

> Storytelling is central, not only to many religious practices in this country but also to the African tradition of which we are a part. Ellen Kuzwayo is quoted ... as saying: 'Africa is a place of story-telling. We need more stories, never mind how painful the exercise may be ... Stories help us to understand, to forgive and to see things through someone else's eyes.' (Tutu 1997:7)

The Commission explicitly used 'story-telling' as part of its methodological approach to both healing and to ascertaining 'truth':

> By telling their stories, both victims and perpetrators gave meaning to the multi-layered experiences of the South African story ... In the (South) African context, where value continues to be attached to oral tradition, the process of story telling was particularly important. Indeed, this aspect is a distinctive ... feature of the legislation governing the Commission ... The Act explicitly recognised the healing potential of telling stories. (TRC Report 1998, Volume 1:112)

Commission posters that decked the walls of hearings outlined the harms that might result from an inadequate knowledge of the past. For example, one read, 'The truth hurts: silence kills'; and another stated, 'Revealing is healing.' The implication is that it was a civic and moral duty to narrate one's experiences of violation and pain, and, by so doing, to bring about personal healing and the healing of a nation often described in terms of wounds, scars and suppuration. The biomedical metaphor was frequently linked with two others – Christian notions of forgiveness and redemption, and the healing of a national psyche[3] through revelation. Narratives of harm were the threads that connected individual and society:

> People came to the Commission to tell their stories in an attempt to facilitate not only their own individual healing processes, but also a healing process for the entire nation. Many of those who chose not to come to the Commission heard versions of their stories in the experiences of others. In this way, the Commission was able to reach a broader community. (TRC Report 1998, Volume 5:169)

The Act established a direct relationship between experience ('gross violation of human rights') and the resultant subject position ('victim'), constituted through voice (statement or testimony). Most striking about the relationship between 'experience' and 'testimony' was that the narration of experience was assumed to be a simple act, a release of 'stories' of pain that already existed intact within those who had experienced violations. All that was apparently required was a forum through which the 'stories' could be released and channelled. But, as I demonstrate below, the recounting of stories of harm is not simple.

NAMING HARM

Testifiers' accounts were constructed by the rules of admission (such as the definitions of GVHR and of victims), the interpretation of these rules in process (see Buur 1999), cultural patterns of witnessing and the narrative forms of testimonies (Ross forthcoming). The convergence of the Commission's methodology and conventional practices of bearing witness produced marked patterns in testimonial practices, most distinctive of which was that women testified mainly about the violations suffered by men and initially seldom testified about their own experiences of GVHR. When women did testify about their own experiences of GVHR, their experiences usually fell into the category of 'severe ill-treatment' (TRC Report 1998, Volume 4:286), a category that came under considerable debate and scrutiny within the Commission (see TRC Report 1998, Volume 1:64–5, Volume 5:12–13 and Ross 2001b).

Prior to August 1996 women gave scant testimony about their own brutal experience. In the hearings that I attended,[4] only 28 of 210 women testifiers spoke about violations they had suffered.[5] Some Commissioners and feminist activists expressed concern that women did not report violations, particularly those of a sexual nature. A position paper on gender (Goldblatt and Meintjes 1996) had been submitted to the Commission in March 1996, prior to the first hearings. The authors pointed out that it was unlikely that women would easily come forward to share their experiences of pain and argued that the Commission should

> reject a gender-neutral approach towards its analysis of evidence and in all other aspects of its brief. This means that gender must be incorporated into the TRC's policy framework for without this framework, gender issues, and women's voices in particular, will not be heard and accurately recorded.

Researchers and activists argued that women's apparent silence about violation should not be read to mean that women did not suffer human rights abuses, but rather to indicate that a different kind of social intervention was necessary to extract stories of harm told by women about women. The gender submission seemed to have little effect in shaping the Commission's response to deponents (Owens 1996) until marked patterns in testimonial practices were evident.

Some Commissioners were sensitive to the interpretation that in the absence of women's 'stories' of their own violation the Commission was not capturing what it called 'the complete story', more frequently glossed as 'the Truth'.[6] They recognised that the operational definitions of the Commission's work seemed to preclude full analysis of apartheid and its differential and gendered effects. Yet, despite suggestions that some of the definitions (such as that of severe ill-treatment) remained sufficiently open-ended as to accommodate a more complex reading of apartheid (see Goldblatt and Meintjes 1996, Coalition of NGOs 1997, Asmal, Asmal and Roberts 1996), the Commission retained a narrow focus on infringements of the right to bodily integrity.

By April 1997, the Commission had included a warning to women deponents:

IMPORTANT:
Some women testify about violations of human rights that happened to family members or friends, but they have also suffered abuses. Don't forget to tell us what happened to you yourself if you were the victim of a gross human rights abuse. (Statement Concerning GVHR, Version 5, 1997:3)

Presuming that the absence of women had to do with the nature of the 'space' provided by the Commission, rather than with the requirement that people give voice to violent experience, the Commission devised alternative hearings – 'Special Hearings on Women'. The hearings, held in Cape Town (8 August 1996), Durban (24 October 1996) and Johannesburg (29 July 1997),[7] were aimed at eliciting descriptions of women's experiences of violation, particularly rape. A total of 40 people testified or offered submissions to the Commission at the three hearings. Four of them presented three submissions to the Commission. Two men testified about women's experiences. Three women testified about the deaths of sons. Twenty-six women described violations committed against them. Most of the women were affiliated with liberation organisations or mass democratic movements. They described horrific torture: rape, threats of rape or sexual violation, torture with electric shocks, separation from families and children. They stated that the lives of children and close kin were threatened. Some women who testified before the women's hearings described being shot during 'unrest' or protests. Others placed their experiences within the framework of their political activities and commitments. In Durban, young women who had been raped spoke from behind screens. The media were asked to protect their identities and not to reveal their names. A number of women who testified stated that other women they knew had been sexually violated, particularly during periods of detention and in the conflict between the ANC and Inkatha Freedom Party in KwaZulu-Natal. Most of the women identified the state and its agents as perpetrators of violations. Four women who testified about their own experiences were members of armed movements (two were members of *uMkhonto weSizwe*, MK, 'Spear of the Nation', the ANC's armed wing; one was a member of the Bonteheuwel military wing, an organisation with links to the ANC; and one was a member of the Armed Revolutionary Movement). One woman, an ANC member, implied that she had been a cadre in MK.

The Women's Hearings were an effort to capture the 'whole Truth': a supplementary action specifically devised to counter the phenomenon of women testifying as 'secondary witnesses'. Of course, the knowledge that women had been subjected to violence was not new. Documents published by the Detainees' Parents Support Committee in the mid-1980s described violence inflicted on women (see DPSC 1988) as did 'alternative' newsletters such as *Crisis News*. The South African Institute of Race Relations' Annual Review of Race Relations has a limited record of women's experiences in detention (SAIRR, 1960–1990, Ross 2000). What I have described here however, is the emergence of 'women' as a salient category within the Commission's workings. It was not a neutral category, but one that carried with it assumptions about the nature and severity of particular harms, particularly sexual violence.[8] Rape and sexual violation were represented in the hearings and in public discourse as defining features of *women's* experiences of GVHR. Sexual violation was located as an experience about which women *could* and *should* testify, and about which they *would* testify under certain conditions. The Commission and members of civil society considered it incumbent upon *women* to describe in public the kinds of sexual harms to which they were subjected.

The importance accorded to accounts of sexual violence is clearly demonstrated in the reformulation of testimonies in the final TRC Report. For example, Zanele Zingxondo testified on 12 August 1996 at a public hearing in Beaufort West. She described political events in 1985 in the small towns along the Cape's East Coast. In particular, she described her treatment in detention where she was brutally interrogated about the death of a Development Board worker, Africa Nqumse, who was burned to death in George in March 1986 during community conflict over forced removals (see TRC Report 1998, Volume 3, Chapter 4: Paragraph 212). Part of the interrogation she endured included sexual torture and attempted rape by a policeman. She spent a year in prison and was re-detained as she left the prison, held overnight in a police cell and charged with public violence. She was released on 100 rand bail and was eventually acquitted. She told the Commission, 'My late mamma died, not knowing if I was innocent or guilty, she died having a question mark whether her daughter was a murderer or not. I was not.'

Extracts from her testimony were used in four places in the Commission's Report, and all concern the event of sexual violation. In two instances, she is named and in the other two instances the act of torture is described in her words but her name is not given. The newspaper reports that described the hearing highlighted that incident of torture (SAPA 1996), rather than, for example, her age at the time of the violation (16 years), her claims of innocence, the duration of her detention or the failings of the medical and legal systems. This patterning is not unique (see Ross 1999 and forthcoming).

WORDS AND EFFECTS

It was clear both during the Commission's work and from its subsequent report that the experience of violence is not easily put into words. The effects of narrating experience are more complex than scholars yet recognise. When women did testify before the Commission, their words were not necessarily straightforwardly received. The 'release' offered by narrating harm might be short-lived. We do not yet know how therapeutic the testimonial interventions offered by the Commission have been, nor are there easy ways to measure efficacy in the contexts of deprivation that are apartheid's enduring legacy. Studies that report positively on testimonial interventions (for example, Agger and Jensen 1990) have usually been conducted with women in exile – people who encounter difficulties quite different from those of the intimacies of the spaces in which the women I worked with reside. Many women have reported to me that the aftermath of telling has been difficult, even traumatic. Their experiences are not always validated by their families and in their communities and their decisions to testify are not always accorded respect. Some feel that their voices have been appropriated. The presumption of authenticity that accompanies voice may not work in a testifier's best interests when the experiences they voice are imbued with negative social or cultural value.

Even with the institution of Women's Hearings, some women did not make statements to the Commission. Notions of social propriety,[9] a fear of public humiliation, and pride in their roles in resisting the apartheid state informed their decisions.[10] Other women found it difficult to describe violation. For example, introducing the Women's Hearing in Johannesburg on 29 July 1997, Thenjiwe Mthintso, a former Commander in MK and now a member of the Gender Commission, told the panelists:

> When today [testifiers] make their sobs, they must know that there's a flood of tears from those who did not even dare to come here today ... because we are not yet ready to make those outward sighs of pain. As they try to free themselves today of the burden, they must know that they are freeing some of us who are not yet ready, Chairperson. I speak as one of those ... I could not sleep last night, because I sat with myself, I sat with my conscience. I sat with the refusal to open those wounds.

Her description of refusal draws on the key metaphor in the Commission's work: opening and cleansing wounds in order to heal them. The biomedical metaphor, as already mentioned, was frequently linked with two others – the healing through revelation of both the individual and a national psyche, and Christian notions of forgiveness and redemption. The problem with metaphors is that they anticipate concrete responses (for example, willingness or even a responsibility to talk about violence in order for society to be 'healed') and have a naturalising effect. When their promise is not fulfilled, the appropriateness of the metaphors is seldom reassessed.

A CATEGORY WITH A HISTORY

Over the duration of the Commission's process, then, 'women' emerged as a category of deponent and testifier that sanctioned particular attention in the search for 'the Truth'. Gradually, as a pattern of testimonial practices in which women testified about sons and husbands emerged and solidified, their position was glossed as 'mothers'[11] and 'wives' and then as 'secondary witnesses'. It was only later in the Commission's process that women were categorised and identified as potential 'victims' who had suffered a particular form of GVHR.

The Commission's approach to 'gender'[12] was a supplementary intervention designed to rectify the absence of women testifying about their own experiences of GVHR. Debates about the efficacy of supplementary practices have long troubled feminists, who have found themselves caught between the need to address the absence of women in arenas of power and the need to address the power of dominant and exclusionary discourses (for example, Scott 1991). The author of the chapter on women in the Commission's Report (1998, Volume 4, Chapter 10: Paragraphs 15–19) attempted to circumvent the critique of supplementation by acknowledging that

> The Commission went some way towards meeting the criticisms of gender bias. Nonetheless, there were those who argued that it did not go far enough ... The inclusion of a separate chapter on gender will be understood by some readers as sidelining, rather than mainstreaming, the issue. Women will again be seen as having been portrayed as a 'special interest group', rather than as 'normal' members of the society ... To integrate gender fully, however, would have required the Commission to amend its understanding of its mandate and how it defined gross human rights violations.

Criticism has, however, been (justly) levelled at the Commission's approach to gender matters. For example, Beth Goldblatt and Sheila Meintjes (1999), authors of the gender submission to the commission, state that in the Report, 'gender is considered in the narrowest possible terms' (1) and argue that,

> The failure to adopt a gendered analytical framework means that a seemingly neutral approach ... has resulted in the exclusion of women's experiences ... [and that] the historical role of patriarchy in shaping the society we have today is almost entirely left out. (4)

They add that the inclusion of women's experiences as a single chapter (Volume 4, Chapter 10) in the Commission's Report 'serves to create a ghettoised female subjectivity' (6). The emergence of 'women' as a result of marked patterns in testimonial practices and the intervention of concerned Commissioners, NGO workers and academics, is a demonstration that giving accounts of harm is neither simple nor neutral. The Women's Hearings succeeded in drawing attention to particular forms of violence that were characterised as specifically gendered. Simultaneously, however, diverse identities, activities and experiences were obscured through the emphasis on sexual difference and harm. The result is an overemphasis on the similarity of bodily experience at the expense of an understanding of the subjectivities produced through apartheid and resistance to it. There are two linked effects of this movement: the subject of political violence is construed as 'naturally' gendered; and the socio-logical problem to be explained becomes women's experiences rather than violence itself.

CONSTITUTING THE SUBJECT

My critique, discussed in preceding sections in relation to the category 'women', applies more broadly. The Commission's work generated and fixed a range of identities, differentiating between victim and perpetrator, female and male victims, and also between victims and those who suffered apartheid's onslaught. During the Commission's process, Pamela Reynolds and I (1997) predicted that: 'The Commission's work and final report run the risk of too simple a translation of the memory of pain from the intimate to the public, the risk of generating fixed positions' (7). The emphasis on the violated body rather than apartheid's subjugated subject may have the effect of sanitising apartheid and limiting recognition of the duration of its harmful *social* consequences. It may also have an unanticipated effect: that of reinscribing gender differences through simultaneously foregrounding, homogenising and essentialising women and displacing practices of resistance and questions of class, race, age and ethnic differentials. Recording stories of harm through bureaucratic processes may fix identities in particular ways, con-straining the range of expression and acknowledgement and imposing narrower limits on an understanding of agency than might be possible, necessary or desirable. The notions of person and of harm that underlie the Commission's work do not recognise the complexity of the constitution of the subject during and after apartheid.

Let me end speculatively. If, indeed, its work has reinscribed gender differences, the Commission may be a powerful socialising agent in the production of new forms of belonging based on nationalist premises. Anne McClintock (1995), for example, suggests that nationalism is inevitably gendered, invented and dangerous (352) and argues that the nation represents the sanctioned institution of gender difference (353). Amina Mama (1996:26) points out that throughout Africa, women's roles as political agents are concealed. She implies that the post-colonial state relies, at least partially, on women's invisibility in political struggle. The South African example offers a different but no less worrying perspective.

NOTES

1. Ironically, in order to regain their dignity those who could be defined as victims were encouraged to speak of the harm inflicted on them – in other words, to act – but in doing so were imputed to have been passive.
2. Ingrid Agger and Soren Jensen (1990) consider testimony to be a universal 'ritual of healing' with personal, private and public, and judicial components (see also Felman and Laub 1992, Herman 1992, Agger 1994, Fitzpatrick and Gellately 1997, Minow 1998).
3. Michael Ignatieff (1996) questions these links, arguing that the most that a truth commission can hope to do is to limit the range of possible lies.
4. East London (15–18 April 1996); Cape Town (22–25 April 1996); Johannesburg (29 April–3 May 1996); Durban (7–10 May 1996); Kimberley (10–11 June 1996); Worcester (24–26 July 1996); Cape Town (5–7 August 1996); Beaufort West (12–14 August 1996); Upington (2–4 October 1996); Paarl (October 14–16 1996); Cape Town (26–28 November 1996 and 20–22 May 1997), at which 390 testifiers spoke of 416 incidents of violation. These hearings account for 16 per cent of the total number of Victim Hearings and 75 per cent of those held in the Western and Northern Cape Region.
5. Thirteen women reported injury: ten by police and three in bomb attacks instigated by the ANC or PAC. Fifteen women reported having been detained: ten were assaulted or tortured. Two reported having been sexually violated while in detention and several others hinted at sexual violence.
6. Many Commissioners had been involved in human rights organisations in the 1980s and drew from knowledge informed by those experiences to hypothesise about what was missing from 'the whole truth'.
7. The Eastern Cape office did not hold a woman's hearing, a factor that 'could, in itself, distort the picture as the Eastern Cape is known as an area in which treatment in prison was particularly brutal' (TRC Report 1998, Volume 4:283).
8. The focus owes something also to the climate of violence against women and children in South Africa throughout the duration of the Commission's work (see Shifman, Madlala-Routledge and Smith 1997:2 for statistical data on violence against women).
9. Generally, in African societies it is considered inappropriate for women to speak publicly about their bodies. In some African societies, talk about past violence is considered suspicious: violence is believed to cause symbolic pollution that may contaminate the community unless purification rites are performed.
10. Other factors included an antipathy to the individual-centred nature of the Commission's work, an unwillingness to be identified as victims, a desire to 'leave the past behind', and a dissatisfaction with the political settlement that had produced the Commission.
11. Motherhood is a significant factor in the shaping of adult women's public identities in South Africa.
12. In the Commission Report, 'gender' and 'women' are frequently used interchangeably.

REFERENCES

Agger, Inger. 1994. *The Blue Room: Trauma and Testimony Among Refugee Women. A Psycho-Social Exploration* (trans. Mary Bille). London: Zed.

Agger, Ingrid and Soren Jensen. 1990. 'Testimony as Ritual and Evidence in Psychotherapy for Political Refugees', *Journal of Traumatic Stress* 3:115–30.

Asmal, Kader, Louise Asmal and Ronald Suresh Roberts. 1996. *Reconcilation Through Truth: A Reckoning of Apartheid's Criminal Governance.* Cape Town: David Philip.

Buur, Lars. 1999. 'Monumental History: Visibility and Invisibility in the Work of the South African Truth and Reconciliation Commission', paper presented at the conference, *The TRC: Commissioning the Past.* University of the Witwatersrand, 11–14 June 1999.

Coalition of NGOs. 1997. *Submission to the Truth and Reconciliation Commission Concerning the Relevance of Economic, Social and Cultural Rights to the Commission's Mandate.* Submission by NGOS including: Community Law Centre, University of Western Cape; Development Action Group; Legal Resources Centre; Black Sash; Centre for Human Rights (University of Pretoria); NGO National Coalition; National Land Committee; National Literacy Cooperative; Peoples' Dialogue; Urban Sector Network. <http://www.truth.org.za/submit/esc6.htm>.

Coleman, Max (ed.) 1998. *A Crime Against Humanity: Analysing the Repression of the Apartheid State.* Cape Town: Human Rights Committee, Mayibuye Books and David Philip.

DPSC (Detainees' Parents Support Committee). n.d. *'Unzima Lomthwalo': A Handbook on Detention.* Johannesburg: DPSC.

DPSC. 1988. *Cries of Freedom: Women in Detention in South Africa.* London: Catholic Institute for International Relations. Previously published as *A Woman's Place is in the Struggle, Not Behind Bars.* Johannesburg: DPSC/DESCOM.

Felman, Shoshana and Dori Laub. 1992. *Testimony: Crisis of Witnessing in Literature, Psychoanalysis and History.* New York: Routledge.

Fitzpatrick, Sheila and Robert Gellately (eds). 1997. *Accusatory Practices: Denunciation in Modern European History, 1789–1989.* Chicago: University of Chicago Press.

Goldblatt, Beth. 1997. 'Violence, Gender and Human Rights: An Examination of South Africa's Truth and Reconciliation Commission', paper presented to the annual meeting of *The Law and Society Association*, St Louis, Missouri.

Goldblatt, Beth and Sheila Meintjes. 1996. *Submission on Gender to the Truth and Reconciliation Commission.* Johannesburg: University of the Witwatersrand.

Goldblatt, Beth and Sheila Meintjes. 1999. 'Women: One Chapter in the History of South Africa? A Critique of the Truth and Reconciliation Report', draft paper presented to the conference, *The TRC: Commissioning the Past.* University of the Witwatersrand, 11–14 June 1999.

Herman, Judith. 1992. *Trauma and Recovery.* London: Basic.

Ignatieff, Michael. 1996. 'Articles of Faith', *Index on Censorship* 5:110–22.

Lawyers Committee for Human Rights. 1986. *The War Against Children: Apartheid's Youngest Victims*. New York: Lawyer's Committee for Human Rights.

Mama, Amina. 1996. *Women's Studies and Studies of Women in Africa During the 1990s*. Dakar, Senegal: CODESRIA.

Mbembe, Achille. 2000. 'Memory and African Modes of Self-Writing', paper presented at the international conference, *Memory and History: Remembering, Forgetting and Forgiving in the Life of the Nation and the Community*. University of Cape Town, August 2000. Published online at <http://www.fl.ulaval.ca/celat/cadre130.htm>.

McClintock, Anne. 1995. *Imperial Leather: Race, Gender and Sexuality in the Colonial Conquest*. New York: Routledge.

Minow, Martha. 1998. *Between Vengeance and Forgiveness: Facing History after Genocide and Mass Violence*. Boston: Beacon Press.

Olkers, Ilze. 1996. 'Gender-Neutral Truth: A Reality Shamefully Distorted', *AGENDA* 4:61–7.

Owens, Ingrid. 1996. 'Stories of Silence: Women, Truth and Reconciliation', *AGENDA* 5:66–72.

Promotion of National Unity and Reconciliation Act. No. 35 of 1995. Cape Town: Government Printers.

Ross, F. C. 1997. 'Blood-Feuds and Childbirth: Reflections on the Truth and Reconciliation Commission', *Track Two* 6(3–4):7–10.

——. 1999. 'Women and the Politics of Identity: Voices in the South African Truth and Reconciliation Commission', paper presented to the Nordic African Institute conference, *Conflict's Fruits*. Copenhagen.

——. 2000. *Bearing Witness. Women and the South African Truth and Reconciliation Commission*. Unpublished doctoral dissertation, University of Cape Town.

——. 2001a. 'Speech and Silence: Women's Testimony in the First Five Weeks of Public Hearings of the South African Truth and Reconciliation Commission', in Arthur Kleinman, Veena Das and Margaret Lock (eds), *Remaking the Everyday*. Berkeley: University of California Press.

——. 2001b.'Using Rights to Measure Wrongs': A Case Study of Method and Morals in the Work of the South African Truth and Reconciliation Commission', paper presented to the *Association of Social Anthropology* conference. University of Sussex, Falmer, April 2001.

——. 2003. *Bearing Witness*. London: Pluto.

Ross, Fiona and Pamela Reynolds. 1999. 'Wrapped in Pain: Moral Economies and the South African Truth and Reconciliation Commission', *Context* 3(1):1–9.

SAIRR (South African Institute of Race Relations). 1960–1990. *Annual Review of Race Relations*. Johannesburg: SAIRR.

SAPA. 12 August 1996: <SAPA960812M.htm>.

Scott, Joan W. 1991. 'The Evidence of Experience', *Critical Inquiry* 17:773–97.

Shifman P., N. Madlala-Routledge and V. Smith. 1997. 'Women in Parliament Caucus for Action to End Violence', *AGENDA* 36:23–6.

South African Truth and Reconcilation Commission. 1998. *Report of the South African Truth and Reconciliation Commission* (five vols). Cape Town: Juta.

Taylor, Diana. 1997. *Disappearing Acts: Spectacles of Gender and Nationalism in Argentina's 'Dirty War'*. Durham: Duke University Press.

Tutu, Desmond. 1997. 'Forward', in H. Russel Botman and Robin M. Petersen (eds) *To Remember and To Heal: Theological and Psychological Perspectives on Truth and Reconciliation*. Cape Town: Human and Rousseau.

Walker, Cheryl. 1993 (1982). *Women and Resistance in South Africa*. Cape Town: David Philip.

Part III
Re-making Space

10 Remembering Ordinary Agency Under East German State Socialism: Revelations of the Rostock District Record, 1978–89

Joan Hackeling

INTRODUCTION

Social scientists writing about the arrangements of ordinary life in the former East Germany (GDR) have tended to focus either on their overall uniformity or their deeply fragmented and largely private character. This has contributed to an image of extremes: of ritualised public conformity or private manoeuvre and retreat among family and friends. As a problem of generalisation, such simplifications are an old and familiar concern. The matter takes on renewed significance as these more extreme accounts show up to explain and justify events and circumstances in the east after 1990. Thankfully, critics have begun to challenge such accounts as too static – that they tend to lose sight of the movement and ongoing contention in which residents were also engaged.

This chapter takes a closer look at some of the more ordinary conflicts between residents and local authorities, here in the case of the northern city and district of Rostock during the last decade of the GDR. It focuses, in particular, on certain geographical forms of negotiation and the flexibility that residents generated for themselves as a result, aside from the more well-known 'free spaces' (*Freiräume*) and 'niches' cultivated among smaller circles of intimates or under the protection of the church.[1] The exchanges that I present here do not fit well within the frameworks of public or private concerns or 'front-stage' and 'back-stage' events.[2] They are more likely to have breached such distinctions. Yet they remained geographical in decisive ways. I suggest we pay attention to these geographic aspects of practical agency for two reasons: (1) recognising *how* ordinary East Germans negotiated their differences with the local state has the effect of re-animating the real places in-between;[3] (2) it is also a useful reminder, in times of transition and transformation, of what was generative, of what Martin Jay has described as the 'capacity to begin something new that was not the case in the past' (Jay cited in Minkley and Legassick 2000:5).

There is a growing body of work on the GDR that takes seriously the issue of ordinary or practical agency.[4] Kocka has argued, for example, that although life in the GDR was shaped by dictatorial control, it was not determined by it, and he suggests that the limits to its 'penetration' deserve more careful study (see Kocka 1994a, 1994b). In a similar vein, Jessen (1997) observes that images of state socialism in both east and west tend to dramatise its bureaucratic forms. This makes it all the more striking, according to Jessen, just how far state socialism had departed, even in the GDR, from Max Weber's ideal type of bureaucratic rule. Lindenberger (1999) also urges scholars to pay attention to the question of agency so that the history of the GDR not be reduced to 'the effects of a single political force, namely, the will of the party' (4).[5]

The standard works of Pierre Bourdieu and Michel de Certeau provide us with some useful ways to think about the notion of practice as negotiation and inventive application of rules of order (Bourdieu 1990; de Certeau 1984). For Bourdieu, context – circumstances as experienced in time and place – must constrain what people say and do in significant ways. Still, the people he has in mind must also *grasp* their situation and resolve to act in one way rather than another, although they may not be able to give reasons for having done so. Their actions just made sense (Bourdieu 1990:36–7). Bourdieu believes that this position separates his work from earlier structuralist or existentialist theories that would 'sweep away the urgency, the appeals, the threats, the steps to be taken, which make up the real, really lived-in world' (82). De Certeau provides a more explicit account of this generative capacity of practice in terms of *tactics* and *bricolage* within limited fields of action. I use the idea of ordinary or practical agency more or less in this way, as generative or productive practice that has people moving about, altering, manipulating or otherwise engaging and affecting their surroundings and existing arrangements near-to-hand.[6] In broad terms, this ongoing process fits well within the purview of geography, if we define that field of inquiry as the study of how people, even under conditions of repression, go about humanising their environment, making the world their 'home' (Tuan 1991).

SETTING THE CONTEXT

In many respects, the scope and effects of ordinary agency in East Germany were quite limited. Repression is also understood to have been more severe there than in other Eastern Bloc countries. Yet circumstances throughout the east during the 1980s were exceptional. Indeed, the regime was in crisis. With the emergence of fledgling peace and environmental activism in the GDR, the Solidarity Movement in neighbouring Poland, renewed antagonism between east and west and a worsening economic situation, tensions within East German society were on the rise. These troubles of the state all predated the reformist era of *Glasnost* and *Perestroika* heralded in by Gorbachev in 1985.

The northern district of Rostock, the area to be considered here, encompassed the entire East German coastline along the Baltic, sharing borders with the Federal Republic to the west and Poland to the east (Figure 1). It included the city of Rostock, East Germany's main port and one of the fastest growing cities in the GDR (Voigt 1998:184). Its population essentially doubled between 1949 and 1989, reaching 250,000 in 1987. The surrounding provinces, however, known historically as Mecklenburg and Vorpommern, were, and remain, overwhelmingly rural, familiar to most Germans for their position 'on the margins'.[7] The region has also been one of the traditional poorhouses of Germany, at least since the Thirty Years War, and is often remembered for having been one of the last bastions of feudalism in Europe (Albrecht 1992; Braun 1998). In fact, large agricultural estates were so predominant in the region through World War II that fully 40 per cent of the territory designated for land reform within the Soviet-Occupied Zone in Germany was located there (Jahnke 1987:78).

Since (re)unification in 1990, the coastal district has become part of the state of Mecklenburg-Vorpommern, one of five new German states in the east, and one of the poorest regions within the European Union as a whole. It surpassed only four European provinces, two in Greece and two in Portugal, in terms of average per person gross domestic product (Braun 1998:137). Uecker-Randow, the poorest county in Mecklenburg-Vorpommern, has been ranked as the single poorest county in the entire European Union. The state as a whole,

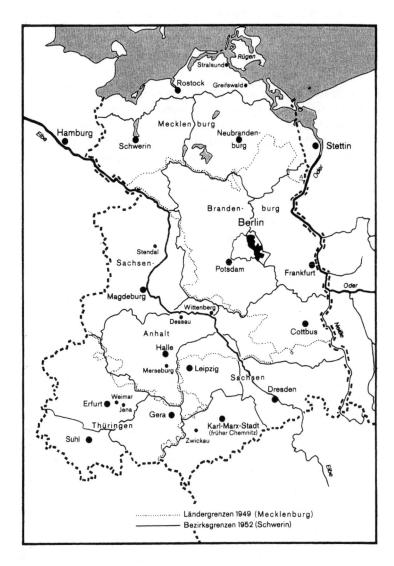

Figure 1   The German Democratic Republic: Political-Administrative Boundaries in 1949 and 1952

....   State (*Land*) borders in 1949
———   District (*Bezirk*) borders as of 1952

Reprinted with permission of the Böhlau Verlag

along with Brandenburg, has also gained a reputation for xenophobia and right-wing extremism.[8] With this as background, I now turn to discuss some of the geographic forms of practical agency in greater detail.

NEGOTIATING DIFFERENCES GEOGRAPHICALLY

Residents of this northern East German city and district operated in ways that suggest a particularly useful role for *place* as an organising framework and as a basis for negotiating differences with authorities. In the most straightforward sense, residents couched their criticisms and complaints using the state's own rhetoric of equality and sameness across places and persons. The capital city of Berlin provided a favourable standard of comparison, and residents of Rostock readily took the position that they deserved to be treated just as well as the residents of Berlin. In the words of one resident from a small coastal city in the district, 'I experience socialism in Stralsund and not in Berlin. With what right are Berliners given preferential treatment? Are we second-class citizens?' (BStU-AR 255.000312, 16 December 1986).[9] Today, residents refer to the special status of Berlin, capital once again, with a renewed sense of irony, if not outright indignation.

More often, however, residents negotiated ordinary conflicts with authorities by moving potentially questionable activities to alternate locations or by not showing up in the appropriate places at the appropriate times. It appears they found some advantage in the inability of officials to monitor and control activities equally and effectively across places, despite all claims that their coverage was spatially uninterrupted (*flächendeckend*), complete, and 'without holes' (*lückenlos*). It is these less discursive geographic forms of negotiation that I want to develop here.

MOVING CONTROVERSIAL ACTIVITIES

Consider the following scenario. An East German woman wanted her child baptised. Though not particularly religious, it seems the baptism mattered 'for the sake of tradition' (Interview, Rostock, 21 May 1998). The state, as we know, discouraged affiliation with the church. The fact that this woman's husband served as an officer in the military only increased the risk of censure. What did she do?

It turns out that this woman, a resident of Rostock, travelled to her home town for the baptism, far away in another part of the GDR. It must have seemed reasonable that what could not be done in Rostock without unpleasant repercussions could, in fact, be done elsewhere without too much risk. In other words, the differences between these two places, or rather the change in context, seemed to provide some measure of flexibility. No overriding sense led this woman to believe that her activities would be subject to the same scrutiny no matter where they took place.

Residents did not always move their activities so surreptitiously. In 1988 as many as 70 students from Rostock's university left their dormitories to occupy several vacant buildings in the oldest part of that city. In the words of the local police and Stasi, 'They are removing themselves from state control', as if such a thing were possible just by moving across town (BStU-AR 282.000034, 15 June 1988). This particular situation appears to have been resolved in the short term when local police called upon these students to register the buildings they occupied as their second addresses. For this, no formal housing assignments would be required.

MOVING THE CONVERSATION

Residents also moved or changed address under more ordinary, though no less acute, circumstances. In the following example, one family met and corresponded with officials for several years about their housing situation before picking up and moving themselves into a vacant apartment. This case is of particular interest for the way these residents engaged both local and extra-local state institutions to resolve their concerns.

The exchange seems to have been initiated with a letter of petition to the Mayor of Rostock in May of 1978. It began: 'I write to you with an urgent request, with the hope that you will be able to help us. Our living circumstances are desperate' (Stadtarchiv Rostock – hereafter Stadtarchiv – 2.1.1.6804, 2 May 1978). After paying the family a visit in early July of that year, city officials agreed and urged the couple to approach housing authorities at their places of work for further assistance. This was the usual channel for housing allocations. In the meantime, the city proceeded to condemn their building as uninhabitable, and residents were asked to vacate the premises.

After appealing to workplace housing authorities without success, the family wrote to state officials in Berlin. Officials in Berlin then contacted Rostock's mayor directly, requesting that he review the situation and report back. By January 1980, the petitioners wrote to the mayor's office once again, this time with the accusation that the mayor's account to officials in Berlin had 'not conformed to the facts'. They demanded another appointment to discuss the situation. Furthermore, they explained, 'We view this letter here as a petition as well, which means that the matter must be addressed within four weeks', as specified by law. Finally, 'in the event that a decision is reached that does not lie in our interests, we reserve the right to take further steps'. Two months later all local parties – petitioners, workplace officials and city officials – met again. In June 1980, with no official resolution in sight, the petitioners decided to move themselves across town. If they believed the matter resolved, they were wrong. In August, the family called upon the mayor's office once again, construing their situation in the following way:

> We were living in a condemned building, and since no one was able to help us, we moved ourselves, without permission, into an apartment in June, one that had been standing vacant for more than a year. We've paid rent, have registered with the police, and signed our names in the building's log ... Then on 3 August, a woman from the city council visited us and threatened to have us removed forcibly. (Stadtarchiv 2.1.1.6804, 13 August 1980)

What these petitioners managed to do was shift the burden of action and resolution to local officials. The family would have to be forced to leave. Eventually, the case seems to have been resolved, but only after the couple contacted the media (albeit the state-run East German media). In fact, the last letter on file to the couple from local housing authorities appears to have been the city's response to an appeal for help made by the couple to one of the East German television programmes, PRISMA.[10] So, while city housing officials were careful to point out in this letter that they had full authority over the distribution of housing within their jurisdiction, they also saw fit to offer the family one of the coveted newly constructed apartments in the city.

In the end these residents seem to have negotiated with officials to some effect in at least two important ways: by moving themselves, and by shifting the scope of the conversation to engage progressively more senior officials and extra-local state institutions. In these respects, they were not unique. East Germans petitioned local authorities and party officials in Berlin with great regularity, and have continued to do so at twice the rate of their West German counterparts (Golz 1997; Staadt 1996). It also turns out that, by the late 1970s, residents were directing more of their petitions and complaints to more prominent officials removed from the immediate circumstances at issue: to the mayor, the city council, or party officials in Berlin, bypassing local authorities altogether. 'People are saying that petitions sent directly to the mayor or to central authorities are being processed more carefully and often more positively' (Stadtarchiv 2.1.1.8310, 15 February 1978). It seems they had come to believe that petitions submitted to officials positioned differently in relation to the matter in question received more sympathetic treatment. The number of petitions directed or redirected by residents to higher party or state officials continued to climb through 1989.[11]

Officials came to agree that it mattered to whom a petition was sent, but for rather different reasons. They also took steps to exercise greater control over these exchanges by structuring their interactions with residents in particular ways. Just as residents sought some advantage in the intervention and mediation of extra-local authorities, officials saw their own advantage increasingly in the context of a personal conversation. This was not just local practice. It became state policy – an important component of this 'socialist democracy at work', as the petitioning process was called (Stadtarchiv 2.1.1.5066, 30 November 1961; 2.1.1.8449, 'Beratung ...' 1989).[12] 'Experience shows', according to one 1980 report, 'that having a personal conversation with the petitioner ... often leads to a quicker resolution of the problem, and the citizen gets the feeling that his or her problem is being dealt with conscientiously' (Stadtarchiv 2.1.1.8310, 'Analyse der Eingaben 1980'). So, while Rostock officials met with only 54 per cent of local petitioners in 1979, by 1984 that figure had risen to 90 per cent. By 1985, it had become proper procedure to process petitions by way of personal conversations with residents (Stadtarchiv 2.1.1.8130, 23 December 1985). In 1989, the proportion had reached 95 per cent. Also noteworthy is the fact that some petitioners, 77 out of several thousand in 1989, refused to meet with local authorities, insisting that officials respond to their complaints in writing (Stadtarchiv 2.1.1.8130, 8 May 1989).

NEGOTIATING 'PUBLIC' PARTICIPATION

If residents relocated some of their activities in response to conflict with official norms, on other occasions they simply did not show up, did not stay, or threatened not to appear in the appropriate places at the appropriate times: at school, at work, for various meetings, or even for the vote. In 1979, for instance, it made sense to at least 190 petitioners to threaten not to go to the polls unless their complaints were addressed. This amounted to more than 15 per cent of the 1,207 petitions submitted that year by Rostock city residents prior to the local elections. In 1984, 164 residents made their act of voting dependent on the outcome of their petitions, although 97 of them withdrew their threat in the course of a personal conversation with local officials (Stadtarchiv 2.1.1.8310, 'Vorbereitung auf der Wahl zur Stadtverordnetenversammlung, 6 May 1984'). According to the city's own analysis, 'The majority of these petitioners saw, in their threat not to vote, an opportunity to dramatise their usually justified concerns to the state' (Stadtarchiv 2.1.1.8310, 'Vorbereitung auf der Wahl zur Stadtverordnetenversammlung, 6 May 1984'). Prior to the elections of May 1989, 283 residents (of the 2,347 who lodged petitions in preparation for the elections) tried to exact leverage by the same means (Stadtarchiv 2.1.1.8130, 8 May 1989). Bear in mind that residents were under considerable pressure to turn out for the vote.

These tactics were not confined to the vote. In 1980 the East German Ministry of Education saw the need to revise its list of categories used to classify what were termed 'Unusual Circumstances' (*Besondere Vorkommnisse*) in the schools. Added was a new category: 'organised absences of any larger group of students from school' (Stadtarchiv 2.1.1.7526, 1 February 1980). In fact, it had become less 'unusual' for youths not to show up at school, although these and other infractions tended to occur in certain neighbourhoods more than others (Stadtarchiv 2.1.1.7526, 2 April 1980; 2.1.1.7526, 22 August 1983; 2.1.1.7526, 'Analyse ... v.1.1.1983 bis 15.2.1984'; 2.1.1.7527, 'Analyse ... für das Jahr 1984').

Regarding the workplace, workers may have shown up for work, but they didn't always stay. This practice was in itself a form of negotiation with state policy in the face of shortages of certain goods. For example, women employees at a district bicycle factory often abandoned their shifts to shop for goods in short supply. This had the effect of slowing production. The same women, however, refused to sacrifice their personal time to work additional shifts. 'We need that time for shopping as well', they countered, 'and anyway, there would be little to buy with the additional income' (BStU-AR 42.000057–8, 20 October 1982). Security reports also indicated that working women tended to favour food rationing cards for such goods as meat, butter and infant food, so that at least these items would be distributed more equitably.

By 1985 special shopping trips during work hours had become the norm (BStU-AR 194.000304, 22 March 1985). One impromptu visit to the construction site of a nuclear power plant in the district found more than 1,000 employees had left work several hours early to shop (BStU-AR 273.000151, 6 November 1987). Similar forms of negotiation or 'hidden bargaining', in which larger work brigades threatened to leave their work sites altogether, have been documented by others for earlier decades.[13]

Officials also took note of an overall decline in certain kinds of volunteerism, and here we find further and explicit connections made between place and participation. In the workplace, for example, supervisors were generally responsible for organising the education, support and surveillance of 'criminally endangered' or criminally prone individuals within their area of jurisdiction (BStU AR 279.000041, 23 August 1989; Stadtarchiv 2.1.1.6449, 'Bericht über die Entwicklung der Kriminalität im Jahre 1988'). However by 1988, fewer workplace collectives were prepared to take on and 'resocialise' such problem employees (Stadtarchiv 2.1.1.6449, 31 January 1983 and 9 March 1987). Residents were also less willing to exercise the expected socialising influence on, and otherwise integrate, 'asocial' or 'criminally endangered' individuals in their neighbourhoods. Such people, they came to argue, should be housed instead on the outskirts of the city. The same report suggests that this development came on the heels of an intensified effort to cultivate an atmosphere of intolerance toward breaking the law (Stadtarchiv 2.1.1.6449, 'Bericht über die Entwicklung der Kriminalität im Jahre 1985 in der Stadt Rostock'). Shortly before the elections in May of 1989, a number of residents registered their dissatisfaction once again. City documents indicate that two city neighbourhoods were of particular concern. 'Living together with difficult citizens presents a special problem. It is demanded, especially in the Kröperliner-Tor-Vorstadt and in Evershagen, that a concentration of these people no longer be allowed' (Stadtarchiv 2.1.1.8130, 8 May 1989).

CONCLUSIONS

At this point, we might draw conclusions about the state's waning legitimacy and a failure of socialisation. Such conclusions were drawn by Rostock officials themselves as early as 1981: 'We convey knowledge, but we are not shaping personalities' (Stadtarchiv 2.3.3.7, Kulturbund der DDR, Kreisleitung Rostock, 'Protokoll, Arbeits-ausschußsitzung am 28.1.1981'). Still, this was a state with totalitarian ambitions. So while it is important to know that the system may have failed in its goal to 'create socialist personalities', it is also worth noting the forms that such failures took. Put another way, how did ordinary residents 'fail' to conform to the rules and 'fail' to live up to the expectations of authorities?

Residents did negotiate their more ordinary differences with local authorities, and they did so in a variety of ways. Some of these ways took geographical form, as residents sought to broaden (or narrow) the scope of their projects and concerns. People also moved contentious activities to alternate locations, failed to present themselves at the appropriate places and times, or no longer performed the roles expected of them in those places. In all likelihood, Rostock is typical of the East German experience in this regard.

Given the grand project of state socialism and the restrictions on political life *in general*, it is not surprising that residents so often cast their own projects and found opportunity for negotiation in relation to the partial limits represented by context, place and the personal.[14] More striking is the fact that these tactics so often confounded officials and seemed to take them by surprise. This chapter begins to tell us why. As total and as spatially continuous as the state's control was to have been, residents' movements and other geographic forms of negotiation are an indication that the exercise of this control remained place-based in crucial ways.

While these sorts of practical agency may not satisfy those who prefer to find activism and 'civil courage' (*Zivilcourage*) in the form of heroic gestures or some apparently more rational and purely discursive oppositional stance, they remain one of the decisive legacies of life in East Germany. They are part of the crucial, though often mundane, 'prehistory' to events in 1989 and thereafter (Höffer 1997:6). They also provide East Germans with some familiar precedent for active engagement in shaping the arrangements of life in post-unification Germany (Golz 1997; Staadt 1996). Here, however, there are real grounds for caution. We need to recognise, but then also be critical of this legacy, as these geographic practices and forms of negotiation may be used to promote social exclusion.

NOTES

1. The idea of private niches in the GDR has been explored by others, most famously by Günter Gaus 1983. For related, though critical, considerations of the idea, see Diewald 1995, Neubert 1997, Pollack 1997 and Zastrow 1990.

2. The idea that GDR citizens withdrew into such private arenas is too simple, as others have argued as well. See Neubert 1997:41, Maier 1998:43, and Wolle 1998:338. One might also refer to the work of J. C. Scott (2000) for his discussion of 'non-state spaces'.

3. For an extended discussion of the status of places as *in-between*, see Entrikin 1991.

4. On this point, see, for example, Beck 1997, Jarausch 1999, Jessen 1997, Lindenberger 1999, Markovits 1995, Mayer 1995, Merkel 1997, Pollack 1997 and Wolle 1998.

5. All translations are my own, unless otherwise noted.

6. See Markovits (1995) for her discussion of the discretion exercised by judges in East Germany's civilian courts. She concludes that 'Whatever judicial independence existed in this scheme of things was thus restricted to the decision of the case at hand' (71).

7. For a valuable collection of essays about changes in the region since 1990, see Werz and Schmidt (eds) 1998.

8. For articles in the popular press, see, for instance, 'Riots in Rostock', *Washington Post,* 27 August 1992; 'Germany for Germans? (Anti-Foreigner Riots in Rostock, Germany)', *Time* 140(10) 7 September 1992; 'Gallier am Ostseestrand', *Der Spiegel* 34(32) 1997.

9. These comments were included in the regular reports prepared by local and district officials working for state security or Stasi. BStU-AR refers to *Der Bundesbeauftragte für die Unterlagen des Staatssicherheitsdienstes der ehemaligen Deutschen Demokratischen Republik – Aussenstelle Rostock* (see bibliography).

10. For more on letters of petition sent to PRISMA, see Merkel 1997.

11. No doubt this also reflected the fact that power was highly centralised and associated with particular people, as Jessen (1997:69) suggests.

12. I include abbreviated titles only for those documents without specific dates.

13. See Soldt (1998) for his discussion of the leverage that workers exercised at some of the large construction sites and production facilities during the late 1950s and early 1960s in the GDR. See also Sabel and Stark 1982.

14. This does not exclude those instances in which residents presented their concrete demands as consistent with state policy and the interests of socialist society as a whole.

REFERENCES

Archives

Bundesbeauftragte für die Unterlagen des Staatssicherheits-dienstes der ehemaligen Deutschen Demokratischen Republik – Archiv der Aussenstelle Rostock, abbreviated as BStU-AR (Federal Authority for the Documents of the State Security Service of the former German Democratic Republic – Archives of the Rostock Branch Office)
Stadtarchiv Rostock (Rostock City Archives)

Secondary sources

Albrecht, W. 1992. 'Mecklenburg-Vorpommern: Mezzogiorno der BRD? Oder rettet der Tourismus den ländlichen Raum?', in *Mecklenburg-Vorpommern: Tourismus im Wandel.* Greifswald: Geographisches Institut der Ernst-Moritz-Arndt-Universität.

Beck, U. 1997. 'Eigenes Leben im Sozialismus – oder die Kunst des Informellen', in U. Beck, U. Erdmann Ziegler and T. Rautert *Eigenes Leben: Ausflüge in die unbekannte Gesellschaft, in der wir leben.* Munich: C.H. Beck Publishers.

Bessel, R. and R. Jessen (eds). 1996. *Die Grenzen der Diktatur, Staat und Gesellschaft in der DDR.* Göttingen: Vandenhoeck and Ruprecht.

Bourdieu, P. 1990. *The Logic of Practice* (trans. R. Nice). Stanford: Stanford University Press.

Braun, G. 1998. 'Wirtschaftsstandort Mecklenburg-Vorpommern', in N. Werz and J. Schmidt (eds) *Mecklenburg im Wandel: Bilanz und Ausblick.* Munich: Olzog Verlag.

de Certeau, M. 1984. *The Practice of Everyday Life* (trans. S. Rendall). Berkeley and Los Angeles: University of California Press.

Diewald, M. 1995. '"Kollektiv", "Vitamin B", oder "Nische"? Persönliche Netzwerke in der DDR', in J. Huinink, K. U. Mayer, M. Diewald, H. Solga, H. A. Sorensen and H. Trappe (eds) *Kollektiv und Eigensinn.* Berlin: Akademie Verlag.

Entrikin, J. N. 1991. *The Betweenness of Place: Towards a Geography of Modernity.* Baltimore: Johns Hopkins University Press.

Eppelmann, R., H. Möller, G. Nooke and D. Wilms (eds). 1997. *Lexikon des DDR-Sozialismus* Vols 1–2. Paderborn: Verlag Ferdinand Schöningh.

'Gallier am Ostseestrand'. 1997. *Der Spiegel* 34(32).

Gaus, G. 1983. *Wo Deutschland liegt: eine Ortsbestimmung.* Hamburg: Hoffmann and Campe.

'Germany for Germans? (Anti-foreigner Riots in Rostock, Germany)'. 1992. *Time* 140(10).

Golz, H.G. 1997. 'Eingabenfreudige Ostdeutsche: Jahresbericht des Petitionsausschusses', *Deutschland Archiv* 30(5):700–1.

Grossman, A. 1997. '"Sich auf die Kindchen freuen." Frauen und Behörden: Auseinandersetzungen um Abtreibung, 1967/68', in A. Lüdtke and P. Becker (eds) *Akten. Eingaben. Schaufenster. Die DDR und ihre Texte: Erkundungen zu Herrschaft und Alltag.* Berlin: Akademie-Verlag.

Höffer, V. 1997. '"Der Gegner hat Kraft." MfS und SED im Bezirk Rostock', *BF informiert* No. 20. Berlin: Der Bundesbeauftragte für die Unterlagen des Staatssicherheitsdienstes der ehemaligen Deutschen Demokratischen Republik.

Huinink, J. 1995. 'Individuum und Gesellschaft in der DDR – Theoretische Ausgangspunkte einer Rekonstruktion der DDR-Gesellschaft in den Lebensverläufen ihrer Bürger', in J. Huinink, K. U. Mayer, M. Diewald, H. Solga, A. Sorensen and H. Trappe (eds) *Kollektiv und Eigensinn*. Berlin: Akademie-Verlag.

Jahnke, K. H. 1987. 'Rezension: Geschichte der Landespartei-organisation der SED Mecklenburg 1945 bis 1952', *Beiträge zur Geschichte der Stadt Rostock, Neue Folge*, No. 8.

Jarausch, K. 1999. 'Die gescheiterte Gegengesellschaft. Überlegungen zu einer Sozialgeschichte der DDR', in *Archiv für Sozialgeschichte* No. 39. Bonn: Verlag J.H.W. Dietz Nachf.

Jay, M. 1999. 'Mendacious Flowers', *London Review of Books* 21 (29 July).

Jessen, R. 1995. 'Die Gesellschaft im Staatssozialismus: Probleme einer Sozialgeschichte der DDR', *Geschichte und Gesellschaft* 21(1): 96–110.

——. 1997. 'Diktatorische Herrschaft als kommunikative Praxis. Überlegungen zum Zusammenhang von "Bürokratie" und Sprachnormierung in der DDR-Geschichte', in A. Lüdtke and P. Becker (eds) *Akten. Eingaben. Schaufenster. Die DDR und ihre Texte: Erkundungen zu Herrschaft und Alltag*. Berlin: Akademie-Verlag.

Kocka, J. 1994a. 'Crisis in Germany – How Germany Changes', *Daedalus* 123(1):173–92.

——. 1994b. 'Eine durchherrschte Gesellschaft', in H. Kaelble, J. Kocka and H. Zwahr (eds) *Sozialgeschichte der DDR*. Stuttgart: Klett Cotta.

Lindenberger, T. 1999. 'Die Diktatur der Grenzen: Zur Einleitung', in T. Lindenberger (ed.) *Herrschaft und Eigen-Sinn in der Diktatur. Studien zur Sozialgeschichte der DDR*. Zeithistorische Studien No. 12. Cologne: Böhlau Verlag.

Lüdtke, A. and P. Becker (eds). 1997. *Akten. Eingaben. Schaufenster. Die DDR und ihre Texte: Erkundungen zu Herrschaft und Alltag*. Berlin: Akademie-Verlag.

Maier, C. 1998. *Dissolution: the Crisis of Communism and the End of the GDR*. Princeton: Princeton University Press.

Markovits, I. 1995. *Imperfect Justice: An East-West German Diary*. Oxford: Clarendon Press.

Mayer, K. U. 1995. 'Kollektiv *oder* Eigensinn? Der Beitrag der Lebensverlaufsforschung zur theoretischen Deutung der DDR-Gesellschaft', in J. Huinink, K. U. Mayer, M. Diewald, H. Solga, A. Sorensen and H. Trappe (eds) *Kollektiv und Eigensinn*. Berlin: Akademie-Verlag.

Merkel, I. 1997 'Beschwerdebriefe an das Fernsehen der DDR in den 1980er Jahren', in A. Lüdtke and P. Becker (eds) *Akten, Eingaben, Schaufenster. Die DDR und ihre Texte: Erkundungen zu Herrschaft und Alltag*. Berlin: Akademie-Verlag.

Minkley, G. and M. Legassick. 2000. '"Not Telling": Secrecy, Lies, and History', *History and Theory* 39(4):1–10.

Neubert, E. 1997. 'Erfahrene DDR-Wirklichkeit', in R. Eppelman, H. Möller, G. Nooke and D. Wilms (eds) *Lexikon des DDR-Sozialismus* Vol. 1. Paderborn: Ferdinand Schoeningh.

'Riots in Rostock' (1992) *Washington Post* 27 August.

Pollack, D. 1997. 'Die konstitutive Widersprüchlichkeit der DDR. Oder: War die DDR-Gesellschaft homogen? Eine Fortsetzung der Diskussion zwischen Sigrid Meuschel and Ralph Jessen', *Geschichte und Gesellschaft* 24(1).

Sabel, F. and D. Stark. 1982. 'Planning, Politics, and Shop-Floor Power: Hidden Forms of Bargaining in Soviet-Imposed State-Socialist Societies', *Politics and Society* 11(4):439–75.

Schroeder, K. with S. Alisch. 1998. *Der SED-Staat: Geschichte und Strukturen der DDR*. Munich: Bayerische Landeszentrale für Politische Bildungsarbeit.

Scott, J. C. 2000. 'Hill and Valley in Southeast Asia ... or Why the State is the Enemy of People who Move Around ... or ... Why Civilizations Can't Climb Hills', prepared for the conference on *Development of the Nation-State 2000: Asia Initiative*, Washington University in St Louis.

Soldt, R. 1998. 'Zum Beispiel Schwarze Pumpe: Arbeiterbrigaden in der DDR', *Geschichte und Gesellschaft* 24:88–109.

Staadt, J. 1996. 'Eingaben. Die institutionalisierte Meckerkultur in der DDR', *Arbeitspapiere des Forschungsverbundes SED-Staat* 24. Berlin: Freie Universität Berlin.

Tuan, Yi-Fu. 1991. 'A View of Geography', *Geographical Review* 81: 99–107.

Voigt, P. 1998. 'Die Veränderungen der Sozialstruktur', in N. Werz and J. Schmidt (eds) *Mecklenburg-Vorpommern im Wandel*. Munich: Olzog.

Werz, N. and J. Schmidt (eds). 1998. *Mecklenburg im Wandel: Bilanz und Ausblick*. Munich: Olzog Verlag.

Wolle, S. 1998. *Die heile Welt der Diktatur: Alltag und Herrschaft in der DDR 1971–1989*. Bonn: Bundeszentrale für Politische Bildung.

Zastrow, V. 1990. 'Die Legende von der "Nischengesellschaft in Sozialismus"', *Frankfurter Allgemeine Zeitung* 12 July:29.

11 Insinuating Spaces: Memories of a Madrid Neighbourhood During the Spanish Transition[1]

Steven Marsh

TRANSITION

The Spanish 'Transition' has long been characterised as a model of untraumatic progression from dictatorship to democracy. Studies of the period have tended to follow one of two paths: either that of viewing Spain as an example to be compared with other transitions corresponding roughly to the same chronological period and region (for example, Greece and Portugal) or, alternatively, as a sociological and political 'phenomenon'; that is to say, as an exemplary and peaceful transition, marked by a historical reconciliation between ideological forces negotiated against the odds by all the country's political representatives under the tutelage of the King, and Francisco Franco's chosen successor, Juan Carlos de Borbón.

Although the strictly formal concept of the 'Transition' is generally considered to be that period from the death of the dictator in November 1975 to the ratification of the democratic constitution in 1978, in this chapter I want to discuss a period roughly covering the whole decade of the 1970s, which in the case of the city of Madrid had significant consequences beyond its municipal parameters. Primarily I want to look at how the discourse of democracy has been employed, among other things, to construct a notion of national space, distinct (although not discontinuous[2]) from that national space of the Francoist period, and how the device of the 'Transition' has been subsequently employed to bind the population to this specific project. The 'Transition', in the case of Spain, is of course, a temporal construction with locational specificity, a shaping of chronological time and a space carved in and from history as a social representation. The key element of the discourse of the 'Transition', 25 years after the death of Franco, has been that of welding the population within a consensus concerning the existence, not only of a new 'time' called democracy, but of a new national 'space' called democratic Spain: the production, that is to say, of a social space.

The media, the regular and repeated commemorations and anniversaries as well as the abundance of politicians' testimonies and historical chronicles of the period both serve to stimulate and shore up this process of renewal and contribute to a *desmemoralization* (collective amnesia) among the population, particularly of those born after the death of Franco. Perhaps, though, of equal importance has been the concomitant silencing of those who lived through the period. Michel de Certeau (1984) writes: 'Official historiography – history books, television news reports, etc ... tries to make everyone believe in the existence of a national space' (125).

The abundance of televised coverage of the 'Transition' has, thus, been at the forefront of contributing to and bolstering a notion that everything that occured on the plane of Spanish politics in the mid-1970s was the product of an ongoing and tense negotiation between the monarchy, the reformist elements within Francoist institutions, the political parties of the opposition and the leadership of the clandestine trades unions, with the threat of an extreme right-wing counter-opposition backed by the military looming in the background.

Victoria Prego's celebrated 13-part documentary series about the 'Transition' (and entitled *La Transición*) made for the state broadcasting company Televisión Española and shown in 1995 in commemoration of the twentieth anniversary of Franco's death, exists, in the popular imagination, as the definitive rendering of events. While, in general terms, this version is not a falsification (and the series, in my view, is very good indeed) it inevitably ignores the complex experiences of those who, while resisting, did not appear on television, whose role in events is thereby marginalised. It is perhaps relevent that Prego wrote and presented the one-off special follow-up to the series, broadcast in November 2000, to commemorate 25 years of the monarchy. Television coverage, like statistical inquiry (as we shall see below), homogenises history.

Conversely, oral history both helps give voice to those people considered unremarkable by journalists and historians, and provides ample evidence of how history and historiography itself are complicated matters. This kind of testimony pits real memory against popular constructions such as anniversaries and television documentaries and poses an alternative set of arguments to those provided by the statistics of political scientists.

It is a much remarked feature of the post-dictatorship period, for example, that participation in the democratic process has dropped, not simply in terms of votes but also with regards to active membership in community organisations and political parties. The mobilisation of 'the people', on the other hand, has proved a fundamental and much employed instrument in the Spanish state's offensive against Basque nationalism to the point to which it was precisely in Vallecas (the suburb of Madrid which is the subject of this chapter and where the armed Basque separatist organisation, ETA, placed a bomb, killing six people in 1995), where the residents' associations, together with the local government, organised one of the first of many huge demonstrations in protest.[3] Two things can be observed immediately of these circumstances. First, the state has responded by the employment of leftist discourse in defence of the unity of Spanish national territory, the like of which only entered dominant discourse in Spain, in any legal sense, during the transitional period (erstwhile member of the Falange and current Prime Minister, José María Aznar, is fond of quoting Brecht following ETA attacks). Second, the relationship between the state and the 'people' is a two-way process, one of appropriation and even ideological cannibalism: many of the initiatives and slogans that have arisen from genuine popular outrage concerning the activities of ETA have subsequently been seized upon and 'made use of' by the representatives of the state themselves.

INSINUATING SPACES

My argument, thus, resides in how the local inflects upon the national and the complexities of the relationship between the population and its political representatives. Of equal importance is the fact that it is from out of this complex relationship of political institutions and dominant discourse that subaltern operations emerge. Subaltern groups, I will argue, never consume passively, they function from within, insinuated inside both the ideological and physical space of dominant groups. It is precisely the suggestion of insinuation that has gone unnoticed by statistical evidence, indeed, '[S]tatistical investigation', in the words of de Certeau (1984), grasps the material of [popular] practices, but not their *form*; it determines the elements used, but not the 'phrasing' produced by the *bricolage* (the artisan-like inventiveness) and the discursiveness that combine these elements ... Statistical inquiry ... 'finds' only the homogenous. (xviii)

Space, in the thinking of de Certeau, comes to resemble a source of contestation; something simultaneously emergent, residual and subject to the vectors of time and place.[4]

If the concept of the 'Transition' suggests a relation between time and space, of inflections of time upon a spatial scenario, then it also suggests that this scenario can be traversed and transgressed by mobile beings, by the weak and the dispossessed 'making use' of time, by practices, ruses and operations. It is within this context that de Certeau traces a distinction between 'strategy' and 'tactic'. 'A strategy', he says:

assumes a place that can be circumscribed as *proper* (*propre*) and thus serve as the basis for generating relations with an exterior distinct from it. (1984:xix)

A tactic, on the other hand 'insinuates itself into the other's place, fragmentarily, without taking it over in its entirety, without being able to keep it at a distance'. And, he adds: 'Many everyday practices (talking, reading, moving about, shopping, cooking etc.) are tactical in character' (xix).

VALLECAS

The district of Vallecas sprawls along the south-eastern fringes of Madrid. A large working-class area, Vallecas today provides a home to around 200,000 people, many of whom originally emigrated to the city throughout the 1950s and 1960s – from the regions of Andalusia and Extremadura – in search of work and settled in shacks constructed illegally in outlying fields.[5] Vallecas is, in turn, divided into several subdistricts of which Entrevías, Palomeras and El Pozo del Tío Raimundo form a nucleus; partly because they are physically adjacent to one another but also because these three neighbourhoods were the most deprived and were at the forefront of the resistance to the Francoist state throughout the late 1960s and 1970s. It was shortly following the arrival of the first batch of new migrants in

Madrid that the 1964 Law of Associations, which permitted the founding of neighbourhood groups for strictly non-political purposes, came into force.

Jenara Alonso (67) and Hilaria Alonso (64) are two sisters who I have known for many years. Together with their family they were rehoused in the neighbourhood of Entrevías in the late 1960s having lived in the shanty town of Tetuan in the north of Madrid since the end of the Civil War. Their father had been a member of the Socialist trade union, Unión General de Trabajadores (UGT), and had fought in defence of the second republic during the war. Hilaria, like many working-class people of her generation, spent five years as a factory worker in Germany as a *Gastarbeiter*, returning in 1965. She was and remains an active member of the trade union Comisiones obreras. Jenara was instrumental in the creation of La paz y la viña residents' association which covered her street and those surrounding where the family lived in Entrevías. Their younger brother – who now lives in Barcelona – was jailed for 18 months in the early 1970s following his arrest on an illegal demonstration.

Jenara and Hilaria on occasions collaborated with one of the most significant figures in the residents' association of El Pozo del Tío Raimundo, the members of which worked with those of Entrevías, José María de Llanos. Llanos was a Jesuit priest who had been a fervent supporter of the Regime[6] and briefly, in 1951, acted as Franco's personal confessor. In September 1955 Llanos moved to El Pozo del Tío Raimundo where he set up a shack as a chapel and in time would become one of the founder members of *Comisiones obreras* and a member of the Communist Party (PCE). Llanos was among the first of several generations of worker-priests who would work and reside in the neighbourhood. Llanos, himself, wryly but aptly described the contested view of the area that occured within his very person when, in an interview shortly before his death in 1992, he said of the people of El Pozo del Tío Raimundo: 'I have not known how to teach them to be Christians but they have taught me to be a Communist' (González-Balado 1992:150).[7]

TACTICS

The residents' associations tactically 'made use', in de Certeaun ways, of the expertise provided by both the church and the political organisations of the Left (particularly the PCE). On one level the church provided valuable alibis and was a useful ally in times of repression.

Hilaria Alonso told me of one occasion when she took part in the occupation of the emblematic Jesuit church in Madrid's city centre[8] in protest at new restrictions placed on visits to the political prisoners held in Carabanchel Prison. The church was surrounded by the police and the protesters were saved from the customary heavy-handed treatment by the intervention of the Jesuits from El Pozo del Tío Raimundo:

> Hilaria: *On that occasion we were not arrested. The police were waiting outside to beat us but the priests from El Pozo came and escorted us back to the neighbourhood and from there we made our own way back home.*

By the same token the residents' associations provided a training ground for a generation of future democratic political leaders who were, first, unable to work openly in their illegal organisations and, second, lent professional expertise to the associations. The political parties[9] and the church provided most of the technical and professional assistance required for the plans to rebuild the different neighbourhoods. Thus it was that the future head of state security and number 2 in the Interior Ministry during the first Socialist government (elected to power in 1982), Rafael Vera, worked as a volunteer surveyor in Vallecas; the defence attorney for those members of the Civil Guard in the Basque Country convicted of torture and murder in the year 2000, Jorge Argote, began work as a labour lawyer in Palomeras; and the then communist and future deputy mayor of the city Ramón Tamames drew up the economic feasibility study for the Entrevías railway station at the behest of the Entrevías and El Pozo residents' associations. One of the leading figures of the El Pozo residents' association was José Luis Palacín, himself an erstwhile Jesuit, who would later work under the Socialist government minister José Barrionuevo, first in the Ministry of Interior and then in the Ministry of Transport, Tourism and Communications.[10]

The El Pozo del Tío Raimundo residents' association, which had sought first and foremost to pressurise the local council to install sewage and running water facilities in the neighbourhood and to achieve guarantees that the authorities would not evict them from the area, was central to the construction process of the new district following Franco's death. It was here, from 1977 onwards, that the tactical operations described by de Certeau came to take on a quite literal form. The very first publically funded family planning clinic in Madrid was established in Entrevías thanks to the demands of the

La paz y la viña residents' association, many of whom worked voluntarily in it. The residents' associations organised the drawing-up of the neighbourhood census both as a means of guaranteeing that residents would be officially registered as members of the community and also to clarify the nature of the housing to be built. In a remarkably enlightened (albeit shortlived) urban policy and one put into practice by the authorities only under extreme pressure, the residents, who for decades had provided a workforce for the city's building sites, quite literally designed their own homes.

> Jenara: *Until then when a neighbourhood was rehabilitated, the residents were not consulted. The area was done up, you were assigned your house, the administration set the rents and that was the end of it. However we had the architects and surveyors who drew up the projects. Once the projects were drawn up they were taken to the IVIMA,* [the Madrid Public Housing Institute] *approved and then, once construction began, the architects from the associations followed up the work and made sure everything was being carried out according to their plans.*

> Hilaria: *El Pozo was constructed in that way because as the census was being drawn up, the members of the association asked the people how they wanted to live, whether in tower blocks or in duplexes or in two-storey houses.*[11]

NAMING

In the same vein as de Certeau describes the workings of television newsreels and documentaries, street names have a populist function, insofar as they help to fix occasions in the popular imagination. Throughout Spain there are streets and public buildings (schools, hospitals) that commemorate events and personalities in recent history. Madrid, itself, is peppered with streets named after generals, former prime ministers and monarchs. De Certeau has remarked upon the nominative function of discourse which, in urban planning, once more takes on a literal form. Interestingly, the case of Vallecas under the influence of the residents associations and the subsequent counterattack by the authorities helps clarify the political content of nominative practices.

> Jenara: *Here in Palomeras, what is now called Madrid-Sur, almost all the streets have been named after films. That is because of the local*

councillor in the City Hall. The associations wanted the names to more or less follow the list of Miguel Hernández, Pablo Neruda, Rafael Alberti etc.,[12] *but she said, 'No way!' And so as not to cause more problems than were absolutely necessary – she wasn't going to impose names that the people did not want – they gave them the names of films and that was that.*

Although phrased in terms of urban space, De Certeau's concept of 'strategy' is about making discursive what was previously non-discursive. Interestingly the earlier quote on 'strategy' is de Certeau plagiarising himself. In a previous book, *The Writing of History* (1975) he uses the same terms to make quite explicit the discursive nature of strategy and its function as that of re-channelling transgression:

The task of doctors or exorcists is one of nomination, which aims at categorizing the interlocutors, confining them in a place circumscribed by these doctors' or exorcists' knowledge. (1975:247)

De Certeau's spatialising of discourse is suggestive in the context of the historiographical operation that has been named the 'Transition'. The case of Vallecas is exceptional insofar as the nominative function has been partially wrested from the authorities and certainly lays bare the vertebrae of hegemonic relations. The untroubled aura with which dominant discourse usually enshrouds itself is unfurled and is clearly subject to contestation, albeit non-discursively, in certain pockets of the district. The street names of El Pozo del Tío Raimundo and Palomeras constitute a veritable litany of the memory of resistance: Calle del Lele del Pozo, Calle del Padre Llanos, Calle de la Cooperativa Eléctrica and the Federica Montseny Health Centre.[13] In the case of 'Lele', an affectionate nickname for Juan Antonio Jiménez who is mentally handicapped, the local regulations have been sidestepped. According to a Madrid bye-law, street names can only be granted in honour of those who either no longer live in a particular neighbourhood or have died. After almost 40 years Lele continues to reside in El Pozo del Tío Raimundo where he sells lottery tickets. Jenara and Hilaria know Lele and recalled him in the following terms:

Jenara: *Lele was a backward lad, he is still alive, he is mentally disabled ... At the beginning in El Pozo there was no water in the houses and he used to deliver water from the well in large pitchers and jugs. When the*

Association began he was involved. I am sure he is the mentally disabled person who knows most about politics and clandestinity.

Hilaria: *I remember Lele from the labour movement. We used to have union meetings at Llanos' place and Lele used to be outside wandering about and ready to warn us if the police appeared. Because of his disability the police used to think he was completely harmless and never paid any attention to him.*

The very square where Jenara and Hilaria now live in Palomeras is popularly known as *La Plaza Roja* (Red Square). Indeed eight years after they were rehoused in the new neighbourhood it remained officially unnamed until, in 1997, the city council, against the wishes of the residents' association, erected street signs bearing the words *La Plaza de la Constitución Española* ('Spanish Constitution Square'), in a move clearly timed to coincide with the impending twentieth anniversary of the 1978 Constitution: the set-piece of the 'Transition'. To date the city mayor, José María Alvarez de Manzano, has still not visited the area to inaugurate the square and all local references (posters and advertisements in the press, political parties announcing public meetings, *fiestas*) still refer to it as *La Plaza Roja*.

INSIDE OUT

It is this sense of contested space that defines the Vallecas of the post-dictatorship period. If the struggles that ensued prior to the death of Franco revolved around basic needs and human rights, those that have persisted since then have been more a question of political control over the 'space' of the district. De Certeau (1984) neatly defines *space* as *practiced place* and says:

> [I]n relation to place, space is like the word when it is spoken, that is when it is caught in the ambiguity of an actualization, transformed into a term dependent upon many different conventions, situated as the act of a present (or of a time), and modified by the transformations caused by successive contexts. (117)

Clearly for de Certeau 'space' has none of the static, unitary sense of the 'proper'; that which pertains to his concept of 'strategy'. In the case of Vallecas the post-dictatorship period has been marked, in part, by the efforts of the dominant group to reassert itself spatially, to establish its 'place' within the district. Just as the former Vallecas councillor, according to the version of Jenara Alonso, sought to neutralise politicisation of the nominative function in naming streets, or the 'Transition' as concept is appropriated so as to justify state terrorism in the Basque Country (or to reassert a different ideology in the square where Jenara and Hilaria live), the installation of the glittering new Madrid regional parliament building in Palomeras Bajas (which opened in September 1998) on the very site which once played host to the city's largest shanty town, owes as much to ideological renewal as it does to its urban counterpart. There is in this a sense of re-conquest of the district. As Jenara Alonso pointed out, the name Palomeras Bajas no longer exists. The area has been re-baptised *Madrid Sur*. Also, it should be noted, the residents' association of Palomeras Bajas is distinguished not only by having been *the* pioneering neighbourhood association, the very first to be established in the city, but also because in 1976, a matter of months after the death of Franco it became[14] the very last to be closed down by the Regime for subversion.[15]

When de Certeau (1984) wrote of people being 'put in motion by the remaining relics of meaning, and sometimes by their waste products, the inverted remainders of great ambitions' (105), he probably did not have in mind the latest remnant of the discredited Borbón dynasty, distaste for which united both large swathes of the opposition and many acolytes of the Regime throughout the almost 40 years that the dictatorship endured. The monarchy has proved, nonetheless, to be a linchpin in the populist discourse of the 'Transition' which has, in turn, proved vulnerable to insinuating subaltern operations.

In December 1995, at the request of the residents' associations and particularly of Communist Party councillor (and aptly named[16]) Felix López Rey, 20 years after the death of the dictator, Juan Carlos de Borbón was finally cajoled (against the wishes of the local government) into making a two-day visit to the outlying regions to the south of the capital and particularly to the districts of Vallecas, Villaverde and Orcasitas. In this case the residents' associations of El Pozo del Tío Raimundo, Entrevías, Orcasitas and others, dominated and led by republicans, made use of the institution of the monarchy to expose the cuts in public spending in the region implemented by the local authorities (the local authorities in this instance being the Socialist Party (PSOE) which, at the time, governed the Madrid

Autonomous Region, and the Partido Popular (PP), which governed the City – and continues to do so).

In 1970 the then 22-year-old López Rey, president and one of the founders of the Orcasitas residents' association, caused a minor scandal when he was interviewed live on Radio España and was quoted live as saying: 'How is it possible that while man reaches the moon, those of us who live in Orcasitas still have to shit in a tin can?' Now he found himself, a republican and left-wing councillor, accompanying the King through the same neighbourhood. The visit of Juan Carlos to Vallecas is itself an example of the community *making use* of an institution that is by its very nature both undemocratic and populist, in order to draw attention to the social problems of the neighbourhood. The King's presence in Vallecas was taken advantage of tactically by the dispossessed within space, almost as an invisible riposte to the planned establishment of the regional parliament in the heart of Palomeras Bajas.

There is, moreover, a certain symbolic irony in the fact that, while the administrative centre of the nation's capital should shift into the space of Palomeras, it has also been displaced (other than for ceremonial occasions) from one of its previous locations in the geographically central Puerta del Sol – that had also formally housed the *Dirección General de Seguridad*, the notorious police centre where, among others, Hilaria Alonso and her brother had once been held – quite literally to an area once condemned to neglect at the margins of city life. Even though the surnames of those who run the city are the same as those who have run it since 1939[17] there is also a sense that, amid the indelible memories and the disputed street signs, the metropolis has been turned inside out.

NOTES

1. I am greatly indebted to Esther Alonso without whose intimate knowledge of Vallecas this chapter would never have been written.
2. It should be noted that in Spain there was no purge of the police or of the armed forces. Neither has there ever been an assessment of the crimes of the dictatorship. At no point has there been anything resembling a 'Truth Commision' and those police officers notorious for abuses and the use of torture remained in the force during the democratic period. Former Prime Minister Felipe González has often insisted, in the face of evidence of state terrorism in the Basque Country during his period of office, that such activities were the work of renegade officers operating independently of the government and that they had commenced during the dictatorship.

3. Following the killing by ETA of *El Mundo* newspaper columnist José Luis de Lacalle, in June 2000, Victoria Prego was the person charged with publically reading the condemnation issued by the Madrid press association.

4. De Certeau (1984) writes: 'Totalitarianism attacks what it quite correctly calls *superstitions:* supererogatory semantic overlays that insert themselves "over and above" and "in excess" and annex to a past or poetic realm a part of the land the promoters of technical rationalities and financial profitabilities had reserved for themselves' (106).

5. Much of the land on the fringes of Vallecas was restricted by law to agricultural purposes and building was not legally permitted.

6. Llanos' two brothers were arrested and executed by leftists during the Civil War and his father, an army officer, was held prisoner in Madrid for the duration of the conflict. Franco later promoted him to the rank of General.

7. All the translations in this text are mine.

8. The same church which, on 20 December 1973, the then Prime Minister Luis Carrero Blanco left moments before a bomb planted by ETA in Claudio Coello Street blew up the car in which he was travelling. The killing of Carrero Blanco is often considered to mark the beginning of the end of the Francoist Regime. Victoria Prego's television series, for example, commences with this event.

9. The most active political parties at work in the residents' associations of Vallecas were the Communist Party (PCE) and the Revolutionary Workers Organisation (ORT). The PCE won 61 per cent of the vote in El Pozo del Tío Raimundo in the first democratic municipal elections to be held in Madrid.

10. In 1998 Barrionuevo and Vera were convicted of having ordered the kidnapping of Segundo Marey 15 years previously. Marey was a French businessman with no connections to Basque nationalism who was mistaken for an ETA leader. In his book, *2001 días en Interior*, Barrionuevo claims that on the night Marey was seized by hired mercenaries of the *Grupos Antiterroristas por la Liberación* (GAL) he was Palacín's guest for dinner in the shack he inhabited in Entrevías (94–6) and only learned of Marey's capture the following day. Argote who at the time of the 'Transition' was a member of the ORT entered the Minister of the Interior's legal department following the Socialist Party (PSOE)'s general election victory in 1982. He served as legal adviser to most of the Ministry's members and particularly those Civil Guards accused and convicted of the torture and murder of ETA members, José Antonio Lasa and José Ignacio Zabala. Argote himself stood trial and was acquitted of having participated in the subsequent cover-up. Ramón Tamames is generally held to be one of the most important Spanish economists. He spent several years in prison during the dictatorship because of his membership of the PCE. However since the restoration of democracy he has moved to the right. He served as a local councillor in Madrid representing the Communist Party before joining the PSOE and in recent years has declared his support for the ruling conservative Partido Popular. Palacín, who lived in El Pozo del Tío Raimundo for many years, is today

a successful businessman and no longer a resident of the neighbourhood. In spite of Barrionuevo's claim he has never lived in Entrevías.

11. In spite of the influence of the Jesuits in the area, El Pozo del Tío Raimundo is unique among the districts of Madrid in not having a patron saint. The neighbourhood *fiestas* are programmed to coincide with 1 May, Workers' Day.

12. Pablo Neruda and Rafael Alberti provide names for the two main thoroughfares in Palomeras, Miguel Hernández is the name of an underground railway station. All three are named after poets who participated in the Spanish Civil War in defence of the second republic and all three were members of the Communist Party. Hernández died in prison, Alberti went into exile and Neruda returned to his native Chile.

13. To this day electricity is supplied to El Pozo del Tío Raimundo by a workers' cooperative, created in 1958, to supply the neighbourhood with energy at a rate 20 per cent cheaper than that provided by the city's private companies. Federica Montseny was a leading member of the anarcho-syndicalist trade union, CNT, during the 1930s and was appointed Minister of Health in the Republican government of 1936.

14. In October 1976 the Civil Governor of Madrid Juan José Rosón suspended the Palomeras Sureste and San Blas residents' associations. Rosón would later serve as Minister of Interior in the last Unión del Centro Democrático (UCD – Union of the Democratic Centre) government under Prime Minister Adolfo Suárez (who, together with the King, is often considered the architect of the Spanish 'Transition') and was Barrionuevo's immediate predecessor. The UCD was the name of the ruling coalition that formed a series of Spanish governments between 1977 and 1982.

15. It subsequently renewed its activities and continues to function today.

16. The Spanish word *rey* means king.

17. Alberto Ruiz Gallardón, the President of the Madrid Autonomous Region at the time of writing, is a representative of the third generation of a family that has dominated right-wing politics in the city since the end of the Civil War.

REFERENCES

Barrionuevo, José. 1997. *2001 días en Interior*. Barcelona: Ediciones B.

Cabrerizo, Maite. 1998. *Treinta y tantos: La lucha del movimiento vecinal en Madrid, desde sus comienzos hasta hoy*. Madrid: Editora Vecinos de Madrid.

Castells, Manuel. 1977. *Ciudad, democracia y socialismo: la experiencia de las asociaciones de vecinos en Madrid*. Madrid: Siglo XXI.

de Certeau, Michel. 1975. *The Writing of History*. New York: Columbia University Press.

——. 1984. *The Practice of Everyday Life*. Berkeley, Los Angeles and London: University of California Press.

González-Balado, José Luis. 1992. *El cura que bajó al Pozo: aventura y recuerdo de José María de Llanos*. Estella, Navarra: Verbo Divino.

Instituto de la Vivienda de Madrid. 1987. *Vallecas, un nuevo distrito: la remodelación de Palomeras*. Madrid: Instituto de la Vivienda.

McDonough, Peter, Samuel H. Barnes and Antonio López Pina. 1998. *The Cultural Dynamics of Democratization in Spain*. Ithaca and London: Cornell University Press.

Redero San Román, Manuel (ed.). 1994. *La transición a la democracia en España*. Madrid: Asociación de Historia Contemporánea.

Vallecas Todo Cultura (ed.). 1999. *Ponencias de las jornadas de recuperación oral de la historia de Vallecas*. Madrid: Vallecas Todo Cultura.

Vázquez Montalbán, Manuel. 1996. *Un polaco en la corte del Rey Juan Carlos*. Madrid: Extra Alfaguara.

12   Public Bad, Public Good(s) and Private Realities

Carolyn Nordstrom

There are experiences where time, place and history are erased, where they are actively un-constructed.

This is an intentional process; it is an act of power, and an abuse of power. This process seeks to ensure that certain realities do not – in the public realm – exist. Private realities are publicly erased and politically denied.

People populate these erased realities: they work and fear, survive and suffer, act and forge lives in ways that are 'made' invisible. Those who populate these invisible worlds do not do the acts of erasing, they seldom self-silence; they do not challenge their own realities.

Those who prosper from acts of silencing and erasure are the architects of invisibility. These are political acts, they are acts of profit, and they are avenues to struggles over power. This is, then, the politics of invisibility.

The impact of constructing invisibility is extensive. At the most basic level, to be created outside of time, place and history is to be cast as being without remembrance, identity and volition. It is to be cast out of political representation by the architects of invisibility in the hopes that those rendered invisible will be unable to challenge the bases of power and profit.

If these words dance on the edges of abstraction, examples from contemporary Angola will bring the people who suffer the politics of invisibility to light – and explore why these acts of erasure are so important in global economics and politics today.

This chapter will follow a trek across a no-man's-land one hot summer day in the mid-1990s – a small journey that sums up the tremendous impact spaces created outside time, place and history have on survival, anamnesis and the reconstruction of lives in times of uncharted political transitions. The consequences are extensive and complex: some people are silenced, quite literally, to death. Others reap billions on these erasures. I have intentionally followed the traditional usage of the term 'no-man's-lands' rather than changing this to gender-neutral terms, for, as the following explorations will show, the clash of these powerful forces is profoundly gendered. Each leg of this one-day journey represents a different, yet interlinked, level of invisibility. These levels move from the most immediate ground-level experiences at the fronts of political upheaval out through national consequences to international profiteering.

*   *   *

To understand no-man's-lands, it is necessary to understand the political intersections defining Angola today and the repercussions these have had on the lives of the Angolan people. The country gained independence from Portugal in 1975, and was immediately embroiled in political contestations, the most severe and enduring between the MPLA government (thought by many Central and Southern Angolans to represent more of the interests of the urban and north-west communities of Angola), and UNITA, lead by Jonas Savimbi (who represented the interests of the peoples of central Angola, many of whom felt they had been politically and economically disenfranchised from colonial times). As the MPLA government first followed a 1970s Marxist philosophy, it found itself in the global Cold War as well: under attack by apartheid South African Defence Forces, undermined by American support for UNITA, and aided by the Communist Bloc and by Cuban soldiers. Savimbi and his UNITA forces were the recipients of extensive western aid, and found an ally in President Mobutu of neighbouring Zaire (now Democratic Republic of Congo). These international forces extended onto the battlefields themselves: accounts of battles frequently reported Cuban soldiers fighting apartheid South African troops with advisers and financial supporters from the major Cold War superpower sites (Brittain 1998, Maier 1996, Hare 1998, Human Rights Watch 1999, Minter 1994).

Cold War ideologies cloaked another set of forces that shaped Angola's war: resource wealth. Angolans often lament that they are both blessed and cursed by a land enriched by extensive valuable resources. Angola is rich in oil, diamonds, minerals, timber, seafood, energy sources and agricultural land. War and international resource extraction are linked in two major ways. First, armies need armaments and supplies, and they need hard currency to purchase these goods. The Angolan kwanza does not trade on the international market, but oil and diamonds do. Many billions of dollars have flowed out of Angola and into major cosmopolitan financial and commercial centres in procuring the means to wage decades of war (Hodges 2001, Cilliers and Dietrich (eds) 2000, Human Rights Watch 1994, Global Witness 1998, 1999).

In 1992 a Peace Accord was brokered, and both Savimbi's UNITA and the government's MPLA parties agreed to stand for elections. Before the elections were completed, Savimbi came in second in the polls, and returned to arms. A devastating war followed: in 1993 INGOs (international non-governmental organizations) estimated a thousand people were dying a day. Entire towns were reduced to ruins and starvation. Battles raged so savagely in some city centres that families could not bury their dead who had fallen in the streets and yards outside their doors. By the mid-1990s the United Nations brokered, ostensibly, a return to the Lusaka Peace Accords, and demobilisation began. People called these years a time of 'not war not peace', for periodic battles, military control of the population and militarised violence were a part of daily life. A balance of power remained.

Formal trade was decimated by the divisions of war that left one side (the MPLA government) with control over urban infrastructure and consumer goods and the other side (Savimbi's UNITA) with control over rural areas and agricultural products. Thus, those in the government-held areas had access to goods, but suffered a lack of food; those in UNITA-held areas had basic foods, but lacked 'hard goods' and supplies. What I call 'trading tomatoes for medicines' (food for goods) at the local level was crucial for survival countrywide (Nordstrom 2001). During this time of 'peace', battles raged over control of the diamond producing regions; and in Cabinda, the oil producing region, a war for independence continued. By the beginning of 1999, violence had escalated so dramatically that no one could continue to invoke the chimera of peace.

Savimbi was killed in February 2002. After decades of avoiding all attempts on his life, his ignoble end was captured on front pages of newspapers internationally: his body lying in a pool of blood with his undershorts showing above loose combat khakis. When Savimbi met his death, some 1 million people had lost their lives to this war, and a quarter of the population was dislocated. Over half the population faces malnutrition, and a handful of de-miners battle an enduring nationwide menace that given current technologies and budgets will take hundreds of years to remove.

A Peace Accord was signed immediately upon Savimbi's death. Demobilisation is now under way. Few impartial observers are as yet allowed into the core demobilisation areas, to the forced relocation centres generated in the recent battles, to the military-operated mining locales or to the population-controlled areas – perhaps peace has come to these areas, perhaps not. The optimistic think Angola is too war-weary, and the powerful now too content with their war-gains, to return to war. The pragmatists think that international interests, from oil through gems and minerals to energy and agricultural breadbaskets, will work to ensure greater political stability in the pursuit of profit. The pessimistic worry that this will be like the mid-1990s, when, on paper, it was a time of 'peace' and demobilisation – while in fact, the MPLA government controlled the urban areas and infrastructure of the country while UNITA had virtual authority over the majority of the rural areas in Angola, and demobilisation was a sham: young boys and old guns were turned in, but healthy adult soldiers and their state of the art weaponry were not to be seen in the demobilisation camps.

Critical to questions of peace, and to the analysis presented in this chapter, is the fact that war, the potential for peace and daily survival in Angola are set in global networks of exchange that variously cross the lines of legality, informality and illegality that bring in cosmopolitan-produced goods (weapons, pharmaceuticals, industrial equipment, electronics, vehicles, books, ad infinitum) and remove valuable natural resources. These vast networks run through no-man's-lands to global markets, from the anguish of front-line survival to the abuses of international profiteering. They rest on the foundations of the creation of invisibility and its links to the pursuit of power. The next four sections explore the interrelationships of these levels from the most immediate – people seeking to survive the no-man's-lands at the front of political violence, to the international – people seeking to maximise cosmopolitan gain and command.

* * *

Level 1
   no-man's-lands ...
In Angola, no-man's-lands are stretches of terrain from several to several score kilometres wide between regions held by opposing forces. To move between government and UNITA zones, people face heavily guarded military checkpoints and need passes and papers similar to any state-border

frontier. Africare graciously allowed me to travel with their agricultural team, and thus to cross the no-man's-lands.

The no-man's-lands themselves are the province of fearful traders, roving soldiers variously guarding their flanks or preying on traders, and armed bandits working their own trade routes or mini-control areas. No-man's-lands are dangerous and often lethal, and they are the lifeline for survival. Anyone wishing to cross these voids in political logic is politically suspect: they are transgressing the boundaries. For profiteers, the unarmed in no-man's-lands are prey.

No-man's-lands are about not being seen: soldiers can not be seen freely crossing lines of demarcation; traders are seen as rogue actors; and those who prey on traders do so surreptitiously. This is, as Chingono (1996) writes in his study of war-economies, 'the politics of the invisible' (127). Millions of dollars are made in these junctures of war, profit and desperation. Thousands of lives are lost.

In Angola this equation is set in life-threatening contradictions. People on each side of the no-man's-lands are dying from lack of essentials, essentials that the other side has. The more closed off the borders, the more people need to trade scarce goods to survive; but the more closed the borders, the more trading is seen as a political act. Power and privilege, and possibly the control of violence, are linked with the dangers of trade itself.

As dangerous as these conditions are, there are people who thrive in these circumstances: armed troops, roving gangs of profiteers and cross-border traders – be they mercenaries, government officials, or international mafias. Angolans frequently invoke the term *capitalismo selvagem:* capitalism of the wilds / jungle (Hodges 2001). These are the conditions of a frontier: the perilous transport of daily necessities to the millions who need them; the wild-catting of vast fortunes; and the systems of protection, usury and domination that see these various ventures to fruition (Cilliers and Dietrich (eds) 2000; Berdal and Malone (eds) 2000; Nordstrom 2001).

With such power comes exploitation, and there is another silent story in the no-man's-lands. Who is it that walks the perilous journey in the zones that defy sovereignty? Worried that anyone crossing politico-military lines for trade might not come back, authorities focused on allowing travel to those who could be 'convinced' to return. For example, in UNITA areas, I frequently heard how women who wanted to travel had to leave their children under the watchful eye of the authorities and travel alone. At best, if they did not return, they would not see their children; at worst, the children might be harmed. Numerous stories circulated of men who left their families behind to travel across political boundaries, and, when they failed to return, their families had been murdered. The prevailing opinion was that more women than men would come back for their children. So women were common traders of goods across no-man's-lands. Given the renegade troops, roving bands of armed bandits, human predators and trigger-happy armed forces, many did not survive the trip.

These unarmed women live, fight for survival and die largely unrecognised by the world. No-man's-lands are purposely constructed to erase place and history. History roots identity, it marks change over time, and in such change stories are told and understood. Without history and place, there is no public, social, or political accountability, and human rights violations are made invisible. What is the result when social practices and cultural patterns are politically rendered 'not-known'? This issue is ontological, and it is also very practical: service organisations, whether governmental organisations or INGOs, are not set up to help illicit traders suffering the ravages of no-man's-lands. This might be labelled a total eclipse of these people's lives.

* * *

Level 2
... and profit
Returning back across the no-man's-land, I saw the other side of the trade equation – the large-scale traders and profiteers. Several trucks and four-wheel drive vehicles, for example, pulled into a wide turnabout on the road. In the many hours we had been on the road, we had passed almost no vehicles, much less several at one time. 'Trade', the Angolans explained to me, 'big business and government workers often do trade: they trade, they benefit from privilege, they can grow rich, and sometimes they can die too'. One man added: 'So we people are banned from trading, and we are starving without the trade. But who do you think is running the trade in banned goods? The powerful, of course.'

This is not a phenomenon restricted to Angola. From Eastern Europe to Colombia, Sri Lanka to inner city USA and Russia, there are those who profit from political instability and the reduced legal restraints that accompany the social dislocations that war produces.

government officials, military personnel, multinational industries and consortiums with wildcatting enterprises, gem and gold runners, smugglers, mafias and international cartels are most likely to survive, and indeed thrive in, no-man's-lands and cross-border, extra-legal transactions. In many ways, these non-formal market(eer)s parallel, and even make use of, colonial-style market systems: simple extractions of labour and resources channelled along routes to the cosmopolitan centres of the world.

Black markets can function on a massive scale. At the time of the collapse of Mobutu's reign in Zaire in mid-1997, highly organised traffickers were smuggling out 80 per cent of Zaire's diamond wealth. Figures were not mentioned for Zaire's cobalt and copper trafficking, except to mention that it has amounted to a 'king's ransom'. Fully half of Mozambique's GNP is smuggled out of the country illegally, primarily gems and mineral wealth, and seafood from the coastlines. In the final years of war in Angola, upwards of 90 per cent of the country's economy was taking place outside formal state channels (Human Rights Watch 1994, 1999; Global Witness 1998, 1999; Nordstrom 2000).

One of the ironies of war economies is that politico-military institutions are networks of access. The formal sectors of politics and economy are interlaced with informal exchange. Chingono (1996), writing on Mozambique, underscores the same dynamics of war economies and non-formal economies that apply in Angola:

> The grass-roots war economy was more predictable and rational in many respects than the official one. Illegal and unrecorded trade was not haphazard but institutionalized, operating according to a system of rules known to all participants. (114)

Large-scale, non-formal trade does not take place only at the internal level between contending militaries and desperate civilian populations. This trade is linked in with the larger international trade that moves diamonds, minerals and people for the hard currency to purchase weapons, supplies and basic commodities. And along these same lines move TVs, sophisticated computer equipment, Mercedes Benz's, industrial equipment, fine champagne and a veritable supermarket of cosmopolitan goods.

*   *   *

Level 3

television sets – brokering informal goods into formal power
The drivers dropped me off in the government-held city that day. As I
walked through the city centre, I noticed a storefront with new state-of-the-
art television sets. In a town with no functioning water systems or running
water (bombed out) and sporadic electricity restricted to the urban centre
(war-depleted), in a town where people sneered at currency and asked for
payment in food or goods, in a town where hardly a building had more
than a couple of walls standing – a shop full of state-of-the-art television
sets gleamed amidst the rubble. No formal economy brought those sets
into town. Yet in the years to come, as the economy rebuilds and a regularly
functioning civil society emerges, these shops and their owners will stand
at the centre of what we perceive as the heart and soul of formal state
economies.

No political violence can take place unless the means to enact
violence exists: armies need weapons, training and supplies. Given
international accords, sanctions, exchange laws and sheer expense,
a significant percentage of military necessities flow along extra-state
channels; that is to say, outside formally and legally recognised, state-
based transactions. Gold, diamonds, oil, timber, precious metals,
technology, drugs, domestic and sex workers, and a host of other
people and commodities flow out of a country while weapons,
supplies, allies, foodstuffs and the like flow in. This is not a simple
matter of buying and selling: the networks capable of hosting such
volatile and profitable trade must be institutionalised.

The people who bring televisions sets into a war zone often have
access to contested sites of wealth: from precious resources to illegal
substances. They have access to the international markets to sell and
buy their goods. They have the power to withstand scrutiny of their
deeds in their home land. If they bring in television sets, they can as
easily bring in industrial components, vehicles, drugs, technology. In
developing war-destroyed infrastructure, such people gain personal
wealth, a wealth that can be brokered into political power. These
traders may consolidate power and the protection of wealth by
standing for political office. A cycle of power and privilege is set into
motion through the war that reconfigures political landscapes (see
Hodges 2001; Reno 1995, 1998; Bayart 1993; Bayart et al. (eds) 1999;
Berdal and Malone 2000 (eds)).

* * *

Level 4
cosmopolitan linkages

I can visit the most war-afflicted markets in Angola and purchase goods from Europe and Asia. I can walk the streets of Antwerp, Belgium and buy 'conflict diamonds' – more colloquially known as 'blood stones'. These stories link tragedy with profit on a global scale. As Chingono (1996) notes for Mozambique: 'It was the "big fish", the professional racketeers in their fancy suits and posh cars, not only from Mozambique but from other countries as far north as Zaire, Nigeria, and Sierra Leone and Germany' who really benefited from this business (106).

Many politicians and economists in cosmopolitan centres say that Angola's economy plays a small role in global affairs. This is one of the greatest illusions of current classical economic analysis. When people say 'economy', they are actually referring to 'formally state-recognised economies'. That means legally charted economies. That means about 10 per cent of Angola's complete economy.

Why is 90 per cent of Angola's economy edited out of formal UN and INGO economic factsheets on country finances and development? If this seems a small point, add up the unregulated economies globally – about one-half of Italy's, Mozambique's, Kenya's, Russia's and Peru's full economies, for example, are non-formal (Greif 1996, Ayers 1996); and then consider the impact trillions of dollars a year in unregulated monies world-wide that are exchanged, laundered and used through legal markets (for unlaundered money has no purpose beyond the paper it is printed on) has on global economic health and stability, from stock and interest rates to inflation and currency exchange rates.

Who, then, ultimately authors these censorships? Wars stimulate extra-state trade (Alves and Cipollone 1998, United Nations Research Institute 1995), trade that represents a significant proportion of the world's economy. The diamonds, oil, timber, seafood and human labour that comes from Angola (and other war-afflicted zones), and the weapons, supplies and services these valuable resources buy from cosmopolitan industries add up to considerable profits for those running the governments and industries of the cosmopolitan centres of the world. From the legal arms sales through the negotiated oil futures to the illegal diamond trade, Angola's war is, tragically, good for business in the USA and the cosmopolitan production centres of the world.

*   *   *

populating no-one's-lands ...

How much can we say we know of the cultures and conventions that sustain these networks of survival, exchange and profiteering: do we easily ponder how the person – generically labelled 'smuggler' in the international press – who moves illicit substances, pays for his children's education, arranges health care for her family, survives threats and seeks justice? Where do we turn for information on the ways acts and remembrances are formed across the boundaries of real behaviours and silenced politics; across the divides of the politically acceptable, the socially recognised and the 'made-invisible'? What battles, what contestations, shape the rendering of identity for those that walk the margins of legality and survival?

These non-state (and non-legal) networks are not undifferentiated mass phenomena. Like the licit, the non-formal is characterised by differences of power. Non-formal networks are shaped by concepts and ideals of identity, group and place. They are sites of association, loyalties, contestations and human rights abuses. These associations evolve social principles and cultural norms, from the positive to the downright abusive. Yet, while thousands of studies of formal institutions have been carried out, we know comparatively little about the systems of power and principle that influence people in non-legal endeavours.

Such a dearth of information constitutes acts of silencing, yet this does more than take away voice and representation. Say a person wanted to chart the impact of illicit exchange and laundering on economic stability and development in a war-torn economy – sufficient data simply does not exist to do this accurately. The records are not there, and so history is erased. History is change over time, and without history there is no institutional memory. Without institutional memory, there is no way to chart the impact of the illicit on development projectories, inflation, interest rates, unemployment and the like – either at a given point or over time.

Say, in addition to charting the impact of the non-legal on economic viability, a person wanted to study the power inequalities in these transactional networks and the trauma associated with basic violations of human rights that exist because of these inequalities. How many studies identify no-man's-lands as sites of culture, with social institutions to be studied and psychologies to be gleaned? Zones rendered non-transparent are not easily recognised as cultural spaces.

What political representation, what social support, what systems of economic justice can be said to exist for the women in the no-man's-lands? What power is wielded by those who reap billions behind the curtain of visibility? For places left outside time, place, and history, the answers do not yet exist. The only certainty is that people's complicity in allowing silence and invisibility is a very political act.

*   *   *

Classical analyses of power have crafted fictional dichotomies: state/informal; legal/illegal; civilised/violent. In practice, all these forms of power and action are variously layered throughout the realities of people's lives. Invisible networks of exchange and no-man's-lands extend beyond the rift between UNITA and the MPLA government into a series of global relationships whereby military and survival goods flow across uncharted boundaries into Angola while gems, labourers, gold, timber, oil, seafood and other critical and precious resources flow out along these same lines into the global economy on equally uncharted pathways of profit and profiteering.

The most invisible actors in this set of economic and power relationships – the real base of the 'politics of invisibility' – are the women and men who risk their lives daily crossing dangerous no-man's-lands to trade a gemstone, an AK-47 or their own human labour for the foods, medicines, technology and clothing to keep their families and community members alive in the midst of political turmoil. Without this labour, the exchange relationships moving military goods into war zones and precious resources out into the global economy and the cosmopolitan centres of the world would not be possible in current circumstances.

When dealing at the level of trillions of unregulated goods and dollars circulating the globe – when considering that illegal weapons alone reap $500 billion dollars a year, and that the world's largest exporters of diamonds include rebels trading gems outside national and international laws – it may be difficult to keep in mind the woman crossing the no-man's-lands trading food for antibiotics, weapons for chickens to eat, diamonds for clothing. Yet, these trillions would not circulate the globe if at ground zero someone did not carry goods across borders – borders of war, of countries, of possibility and of invisibility. The people working at this level are not profiteers; they are hungry and often desperate people seeking the basics to keep life and limb intact for themselves and their loved ones. War, poverty and desperation fill the ranks of those willing to risk their lives negotiating no-man's-lands, and thus expand the dangerous opportunities open to those who are profiteering at a large, international and much safer level. As Hodges (2001) writes, resource-rich countries are four times more likely to be embroiled in severe political violence. The rebels, the governments and the trillion-dollar illicit networks depend on these people risking their lives in no-man's-lands. And they depend on keeping these linkages invisible.

REFERENCES

Alves, G. and B. Cipollone. 1998. *Curbing Illicit Trafficking in Small Arms and Sensitive Technologies.* Geneva: UNIDIR.

Ayers, Edward. 1996. 'The Expanding Shadow Economy', *World Watch* 4:11–23.

Bayart, Jean-François. 1993. *The State in Africa: The Politics of the Belly.* London: Longman.

Bayart, Jean-François, Stephen Ellis and Béatrice Hibou (eds). 1999. *The Criminalization of the State in Africa.* Oxford: James Currey Press.

Berdal, M. and D. Malone (eds). 2000. *Greed and Grievance: Economic Agendas in Civil Wars.* Boulder: Lynne Rienner.

Brittain, Victoria. 1998. *Death of Dignity: Angola's Civil War.* London: Pluto Press.

Chingono, Mark F. 1996. *The State, Violence and Development.* Brookfield: Avebury.

Cilliers, Jakkie and Christian Dietrich (eds). 2000. *Angola's War Economy.* Pretoria: Institute for Security Studies.

Global Witness. 1998. *A Rough Trade: The Role of Companies and Governments in the Angolan Conflict.* London: Global Witness.

——. 1999. *A Crude Awakening: The Role of the Oil and Banking Industries in Angola's Civil War and the Plunder of State Assets.* London: Global Witness.

Greif, Avner. 1996. 'Contracting, Enforcement, and Efficiency: Economics Beyond the Law', in M. Bruno and B. Pleskovic (eds) *Annual World Bank Conference on Development Economics.* Washington DC: The World Bank:239–65.

Hare, Paul. 1998. *Angola's Last Best Chance for Peace: An Insider's Account of the Peace Process.* Washington DC: United States Institute for Peace.

Hodges, Tony. 2001. *Angola from Afro-Stalinism to Petro-Diamond Capitalism.* Oxford: James Currey.

Human Rights Watch. 1999. *Angola Unravels: The Rise and Fall of the Lusaka Peace Process.* London: Human Rights Watch.

Human Rights Watch Arms Project and Human Rights Watch/Africa. 1994. *Angola: Arms Trade and Violations of the Laws of War Since the 1992 Elections.* New York: Human Rights Watch.

Maier, Karl. 1996. *Angola: Promises and Lies.* Rivonia, UK: William Waterman.

Minter, William. 1994. *Apartheid's Contras: An Inquiry into the Roots of War in Angola and Mozambique.* London: Zed Books.

Nordstrom, Carolyn. 1997. *A Different Kind of War Story*. Philadelphia: University of Pennsylvania Press.

———. 2000. 'Shadows and Sovereigns', *Theory, Culture and Society* 17(4):35–54.

———. 2001. 'Out of the Shadows', in Thomas C. Callaghy, Robert L. Kassimir and Ronald K. Latham (eds) *Intervention and Transnationalism in Africa: Global–Local Networks of Power*. Cambridge: Cambridge University Press.

Reno, William. 1995. *Corruption and State Politics in Sierra Leone*. Cambridge: Cambridge University Press.

———. 1998. *Warlord Politics and African States*. Boulder: Lynne Rienner.

United Nations Research Institute. 1995. *States of Disarray: The Social Effects of Globalization*. London: UNRISD.

Part IV
Testimony and Voices

13 The Politics of Memory and International Trials for Wartime Rape

Julie Mertus[1]

The young woman sat stone-faced, staring straight ahead at the lawyer for the prosecution. She avoided eye contact with the three men accused of rape and other crimes in wartime Bosnia. She politely answered question after question in a deep monotone. She described how night after night the soldiers took her out of the room in which she was imprisoned and into the place where the beatings and rapes took place. What exactly did they do to you? How did they rape you? How many times that night? What other women were there? What did the rapists say to you? The lawyer pressed her to remember and recount every detail. She told of being forced to dance naked before cheering soldiers and paramilitary; she remembered being sold into a kind of sex slavery and being kept in a brothel for the use of soldiers; she spoke of the man who said he would help her and then betrayed her by raping her too. She gave the names of the other girls who had been sexually abused and raped, and she stated that she never directly told her family anything. After hours of witnessing, the attorney for the prosecution asked:

> Q. Can you describe why you finally decided to speak to the Tribunal?
> A. Because of my future.
> Q. Can you be more specific about what you mean?
> A. To say what happened.
> Q. And in what way is that related to your future?
> A. It will make me feel better. (Testimony:2031)[2]

TRIAL WITNESSES AS AGENTS?

Many survivors of wartime rape who testified or who sought to testify before the International Criminal Tribunal for the Former Yugoslavia (ICTY) believed giving testimony would help them heal. They did not view themselves as passive recipients of assistance, but as active agents of change who knowingly chose to use international advocacy as a personal and political tool (Sen 1999:189).[3] They did not act as supplicants to elites who would define their rights for them and bestow these from above (see Chandler 2002:109), but rather as politically mobilised survivors who, through their actions, would influence international opinion and help shape the content of international norms (see Booth 1999:61). In short, by acting as bearers, protagonists or beneficiaries of the values in question, they were exercising agency (Beetham 1996:29).

Public remembering creates an opportunity for public recognition of what happened (Minow 1998); thus, many survivors hoped that witnessing could help bring closure. 'If I can hear a judge say that what happened to me happened, I think I can stop remembering so much and learn to forget.'[4] Survivors hoped witnessing would create a public record that would not only help them, but their entire nation. Many survivors sought to create a historical record that would include their experiences and honour all women who survived similar atrocities in Bosnia and elsewhere. 'This [the prosecution of rape before the ICTY] is not just for us', explained one Croat woman from Sarajevo, 'it is for [the Comfort Women] from Japan too'.[5] Some survivors wanted to look the men who raped them in the eye and accuse them publicly. Others were less interested in facing their perpetrators, but equally invested in seeing their perpetrators held accountable. 'There will only be justice', one woman told me, 'when [the perpetrators] are in jail somewhere'.[6]

Despite their initial faith that they could use international war crimes tribunals to their own purposes, survivors have quickly become disillusioned with the adversarial process (see Mertus 2000). Witnesses almost universally experience trials as dehumanising and re-traumatising experiences. Patricia Wald, an ICTY judge, observes that participation in adversarial criminal proceedings rarely helps survivors to 'feel better'.

> Many of the witnesses are physically and emotionally fragile in the aftermath of their fractured lives. They frequently break down on the stand. The accused are there in the courtroom only a few feet away. One witness openly pled with the court to stop the accused from threatening her with his eyes ... Some of the witnesses say they are relieved to testify before us. Some express a humbling confidence that we will bring justice to their suffering.

Others seem to find the courtroom experience with its stress on legal niceties anti-climatic and frustrating. (Wald 2001:109)

Witnesses who seek supportive counselling before and during trial face the risk of defence attorneys discrediting them as being too traumatised to be credible. As the years go by, prosecutors for the tribunal face greater and greater difficulty in finding witnesses to testify (Wald 2001:109).

While survivors and their advocates have learned about the limits of the adversarial process for survivors, the (mainly western) champions of 'universal justice' have not (see Ignatieff 2000:201). A recent survey in the Harvard Law Review notes, 'Prosecution seems the sole presumptive response to violations of international humanitarian law' (Developments in the Law 2001: 1981). The vast majority of the literature on international criminal tribunals assumes that, as long as investigators focus specifically on sexual violence and procedural rules are correct and adequate protections provided, the trials will serve the interests of survivors (see, for example, Chesterman 1997, Askin 1997, Levy 1994, Pratt and Fletcher 1994).

In the domestic context, however, scholars and activists have long recognised that survivors of sexual violence cannot expect that testifying in a rape case will be a cathartic, healing experience (see, for example, Bryden and Lengnick 1997, Ward 1995, Matoesian 1993). This literature recognises that the narrative of a witness is contorted to suit the needs of the audience(s). Far from providing an opportunity for women's realities to be validated, it is through adversarial proceedings that '[w]omen are disempowered, their voices silenced, patriarchal tales validated, rapes legalized' (Taslitz 1999:11).

Just as domestic women's rights advocates recognise the futility of relying on court testimony alone for the production of a narrative that reflects women's experiences and promotes their agency (see Matoesian 1997), international women's rights advocates should explore the limitations of international tribunals and examine complementary and alternative mechanisms. Although women still may exercise agency in the context of the adversarial process, their ability to do so is stunted. In the words of one Kosovar survivor of wartime rape: 'It is like shouting from the bottom of a well.'[7] War crime trials do serve useful goals, but they do not adequately meet the needs of survivors.

This chapter explores the limitations of international tribunals for wartime rape through a case study of the celebrated case of Kunarac,

Kovac and Vukovic (known as the 'Foca case'). The International Criminal Court for Yugoslavia (ICTY) in that case sentenced three ethnic Serbs to prison for their abuse of women at a 'rape camp' near Foca, a small Bosnian town southeast of Sarajevo.[8] Heralded as a major victory by international women's human rights advocates seeking justice for wartime sexual violence, the judgment has generally proved disappointing to the women survivors themselves and to their kin back home.

STRUGGLING AGAINST THE LEGAL COUNTER-NARRATIVE

The overarching limitation of the adversarial process for survivors and their advocates is the same structural design that makes it so appealing for perpetrators and lawyers. By design, the legal process does not permit witnesses to tell their own coherent narrative; it chops their stories into digestible parts, selects a handful of parts, and sorts and refines them to create a new narrative – the legal anti-narrative. Women who have survived rape and sexual assault describe the harm committed in words that are very different from the sterile language and performance of law (see Ray 1997, Lusby 1995).

The justification commonly advanced for limiting witnessing is a patronising one: witnesses need to be protected to ensure that their suffering is not put on trial (see Ni Aolain 1997). Yet witnesses long for the opportunity to finish their story – to speak of their suffering publicly and in their own terms so it may be publicly acknowledged. At trial, witnesses do continually resist the legal counter-narrative by offering facts that are seemingly irrelevant to the crime and in sequencing their testimony in a manner that appears nonsensical. A close examination of the Foca case demonstrates that witnesses struggle to exercise their agency at all points in the trial – as they respond to both prosecutors' and defence attorney's questioning – but ultimately the adversarial process cannot alone fulfil their needs.

THE PROSECUTION: RESPONDING TO 'FRIENDLY' QUESTIONING

In the Foca trial, the prosecution forced witnesses to speak about their experiences in a truncated question-and-answer format.

> Q. [prosecution attorney] But the Court will need to know. Can you describe what he did?

A. Yes. He pushed me onto one of the beds. He asked me to put his penis into my mouth.

Q. And did he do that?

A. He did it himself.

Q. How long did that last?

A. I don't know.

Q. Did he say anything while this was happening?

A. He was saying things like: What am I afraid of? Don't I know what sex is? Haven't I done it before? That kind of thing. Let's enjoy it. That kind of thing.

Q. Were you scared?

A. Yes.

Q. Did you feel like you could do anything to defend yourself?

A. It was impossible. He had a pistol. He threatened. And even had I risked my own life there, I was afraid for my family's lives. So I didn't dare do anything.

Q. When did this stop?

A. I don't know. I can't say exactly.

Q. Did something happen?

A. I did not understand your question. Can you rephrase it?

Q. I'm sorry. I meant, did something happen to stop what he was doing to you?

A. I think so, yes. Yes. For sure something happened. But I don't know whether these two soldiers walked into the room or whether they knocked on the door before that, or whether they were clamoring in the hallway. At any rate, somebody came in and it stopped.

Q. And whoever came in, did they indicate that a bus was ready to leave?

A. Yes.   (Testimony:1243–4)

Throughout this line of questioning, the prosecutor risked reducing the witness to the role of victim. In this narrative, the woman was not relevant as her own agent, but only as her actions demonstrated something about the perpetrator. The witnesses in the Foca case who tried to deviate from the structure of legal witnessing were cut off and then steered into the preferred direction. Witness after witness was compelled to narrowly define what happened to them in line with the legal definition of rape.

Q. [prosecution attorney] When you say, 'rape' what exactly do you mean?

A. I don't understand your question.

Q. You said that this – this elderly man raped you. What exactly did he do?

A. He forced me onto the bed to take my clothes off, and then he raped me, he attacked me and raped me.

Q. Does it mean he put his penis into your vagina?

A. Yes.

Q. And these other men, did they do the same thing?

A. The same thing, yes.

Q. Were you conscious all the time when that happened?

A. I was conscious up to 10, up to the time I counted 10. Then I lost consciousness, and I know that some of them brought some water to splash over me and that I was all wet from that water when I came to, when I regained consciousness. But that didn't mean anything to them. They continued doing what they were doing. One of them came in and made me take all my clothes off, just to see what I looked like. And he said, 'That's a pity for you. You look so beautiful.'   (Testimony:1391)

The emphasis of the trial was on who did what to the witness, when and how. Because the prosecutor appropriated what the witness said to an existing schema, he was no longer listening to *her*, but rather to his own construction of victim (see Anderson and Jack 1991:19).

Q. [prosecution attorney] In which way were you raped? What did they do?

A. Durko Dubvic shut me up in a room with him. He wouldn't let anybody else enter except for him. And he wouldn't let me go the whole night. Every ten minutes he was on me and raped me.

Q. Did he rape you vaginally?

A. Yes.

Q. Anally?

A. Yes.

Q. Orally?

A. Yes.

Q. The other two persons you mentioned, when did they rape you?

A. In the morning, at dawn, early morning.

Q. Did they rape you together at the same time or one after the other?

A. One after the other. And Gaga as well.

Q. When did Gaga rape you?

A. In the morning.   (Testimony:1427–8)

In the Foca case, the main euphemism for rape was being 'taken out'; the women were taken out of their rooms for rape and other abuse. This detached language might have helped some women speak about the unspeakable, but at the same time it diminished the true nature of the horrors that repeatedly occurred. The use of euphemisms, combined with the examining attorney's failure to ask about the survivors' experiences of *themselves* numbs the reader/listener to the nature of the violence.

Q: [prosecution attorney] Were you taken out by soldiers while you were at Partizan?

A. Yes.

Q. Are you able to say how often you were taken out or how many times?

A. I don't know exactly how many, but it was often.

Q. Was it every night, every day?

A. Not every night and every day. Sometimes not for two days. But then I would be taken out every day for three days, that kind of thing.

Q. When you were taken out, how long were you kept away?

A. That depended too, depended on the situation. Sometimes for a short period, just to let them do what they wanted to with me, and at other times in flats of unknown individuals, it would last for three days. I would be shut up for three days.

Q. Whenever you were taken out, were you also raped?

A. Yes, every time.

Q. And when you say 'rape', do you mean what happened to you at the high school, the same thing?

A. Yes. Every other time it was the same thing, every time after that it was always the same thing.

Q. Do you remember the first time that you were taken out from Partizan?

A. Yes.

Q. Do you remember when it was?

A. Perhaps a day or two later, after our arrival in the Partizan.

Q. Do you remember who took you out?

A. Yes.

Q. Who was it?

A. It was what I talked about a moment ago, when I was in the WC. Two soldiers whom I did not know came, and among them was Zoran Vukovic again.

Q. When you say again, do you mean the same person who raped you at Buk Bijela?

A. Yes.

Q. Do you remember if he was armed at that time?

A. Yes, he was.

Q. Where did he take you?

A. He took me to an apartment. I assume that it had been abandoned, because I didn't see anybody there. When he brought me to that apartment, he took me into one of the rooms, which was to the left-hand side of the hallway. There was a big bed there for sleeping in. I don't remember exactly whether there was a cupboard or what there was there, but it was a bedroom. And then it happened once again; I was raped again.   (Testimony:1263)

In this line of testimony, the judge realised that the true nature of the crimes was being lost in their almost rote recitation. The judge pressed for more specifics:

A. The next time was when I was taken to a house. The house was opposite the bus stop in Foca, the bus station in Foca. There was only one bus station and everybody knew it. A group of soldiers took me off, along with three other girls from the Partizan Sports Hall. They took us into a house, which was – how shall I describe it? It was all ransacked, things all over the place. You could see that nobody lived there. And the first thing they ordered us to do was to tidy the house and they said they'd go off to see to some business and that they'd come back. And they raped us there. Each one of them raped the girl he wanted to rape, and as many times as he wanted to rape her. Everybody would pick and choose. They would say, 'Come on, you', or 'Let's go upstairs', because the house had rooms on the ground floor and on the first floor. So we would be down there until they took us off to rape us, to another room. And whenever they wanted to, they picked the girl they wanted to and raped her. I think that I was raped there three times, perhaps more. I can't remember exactly how many times, but it was dreadful. They would take their turns, one after the other. They would have breaks of 15 minutes or maybe one hour, as long as they wanted, but there were terrible things going on there. There were old people there. They were dirty people and drunken people, and they would take my friend off. He would rape her and then rape me. But they did their best to rape all of us, that each one of them raped each one of us in turn.

Q. How many different soldiers raped you that day?

A. Well, I said a moment ago that I counted up to three. All three of them were different. I was raped three times by three different men, not by one person. But they didn't pay any attention of how much my body could take. They did what they wanted until absolute exhaustion. It was absolutely terrible.

Q. How many soldiers would you say were there?

A. Well, today I can't remember the number exactly, but I do know that there were a lot of them. Perhaps a little less than ten, but there were more of them than there were us. And they took turns. So two of them would go off for a period of time and then some others would come back or they would come back. There was nothing definite. That was how it went.   (Testimony:1264)

The follow-up question to this gruesome testimony concerned the identity and reactions of the soldiers who committed the crimes, not the reactions of the women who survived them. The goal of obtaining a perpetrator-driven narrative is central to criminal proceedings (Oseil 1995: 520). Thus, even when told with greater specificity, the narrative constructed at the Foca trial focuses myopically on the actions of perpetrators. Yet, whenever witnesses saw an opportunity to step outside the legal definition of rape, quite a different story emerges. One woman who was questioned in the standard format of 'who did what' to her body defiantly disobeyed her handler. She responded instead about injury to her soul.

A. He did say something for sure, but today, eight years later, and after so many rapes, I cannot remember. I only know that he was very forceful, that he wanted to hurt me as much as possible. But he could never hurt me as much as my soul already hurt me.

(Testimony:1274)

The most devastating psychological trauma of rape is that it takes away a person's sense that life has meaning. Rape calls into question all basic human relationships and 'shatter[s] the construction of the self that is formed and sustained in relation to others'. It 'undermine[s] the belief systems that give meaning to human experience' (Herman 1993:69). Patricia David observes that '[b]eing the victim of rape affects a woman not only at the time of her attack, but also throughout the rest of her life, isolating her from her family and community, and putting her at risk of future attacks' (David 2000:1246). For rape victims who are also refugees, the experience is particularly jarring as the victims' familiar way-of-being in the world is challenged by 'a new reality of the sociopolitical circumstances that not only threatens that way-of-being but also forces one to see the world differently' (Daniel and Knudsen 1995: 1). How wartime victims of rape overcome the radical discontinuities and recreate the kind of social landscape necessary for survival is a narrative rarely heard at trial.

THE DEFENCE: RESPONDING TO UNFRIENDLY QUESTIONING

Defence lawyers are particularly uninterested in survivors' perception of what happened. Their sole purpose is to cast blame and discredit survivors. The rules for the Tribunal in the Foca case specifically prohibited testimony of prior sexual acts and thus limited the ways in which the defence attorneys could blame women for their own rapes. This 'rape shield' rule, however, did not eliminate the blaming tactic altogether. At one point the defence counsel implied that a woman who had testified that she was forced to stimulate a man so he could rape her shared responsibility for her own crime (see Testimony:1452). In another part of the Foca trial, defence counsel suggested that a woman who had spoken of a rapist deciding who to rape on a particular night and who to 'reject' must have been a jealous lover.

> Q. [defence attorney] In the course of your stay in the apartment, was there a change with respect to the sleeping arrangements amongst the individuals who were in the apartment?
> A. Yes, there were changes.
> Q. Could you tell me how this came about and what changed?

A. When he rejected me, he took AB, but he didn't keep her for long either; he rejected her. Then he took number 87, and then he spent most of his time with her.

Q. I don't understand this term 'rejected' that you use. As far as I understand it, when a man rejects a woman, it's in a romantic relationship.

A. When he had had enough of me and taking it out on me, then he didn't keep me there. He chased me away into the other room and he kept AB with him, also for a brief period. After he had had enough of her too, then he took number 87. That is what I meant.

Q. I'm afraid your answers do not correspond to my questions.

A. Then I don't understand your questions.

Q. Will you agree with me that jealousy is a psychological state, when a person imbued by it is ready to do certain things which people which are not imbued by jealousy would not consider doing?

A. I'm afraid I don't understand that question at all. What are you talking about? What do you mean by jealousy?

Q. I'm referring to the fact that you said that after four or five days, Klanfa rejected you. I said yesterday that in my understanding, when a man rejects a woman, it is usually a person he loves and not a person who has been raped.

A. How could I possibly be Klanfa's beloved? Only dead, not even dead, could I be Klanfa's beloved, or any one of theirs. That's all I could say.   (Testimony:1608)

Defence lawyers try to suggest that witnesses are untrustworthy by provoking them and pointing out inconsistencies in their testimony. Survivors of any kind of trauma, but especially those uprooted by conflict, are unable to provide a consistent and linear narrative. Courts of law, which demand that truth be told in a complete and linear fashion, mistrust the natural voice of survivors. This can be particularly devastating for rape survivors whose purpose for testifying is to make the truth public and who have made great personal sacrifice to publicly confront their abusers.

A natural result of the post-traumatic stress of rape is an inability to remember and/or to recount fully what happened. Some survivors are unable initially to speak about certain painful incidents; other survivors skip facts that appear irrelevant; and others remember differently over time. This witness was driven to testify more fully as time passed.

Q. In 1995, do you remember speaking with investigators from the Tribunal, at the end of August and the beginning of September?

A. Yes, I remember.

Q. And you gave a statement at that time about what happened to you during the war; is that right?

A. Yes.

Q. Did you tell the investigators at that time the details of what happened to you at Buk Bijela, and Zoran Vukovic?

A. I did not.

Q. Why not?

A. I don't know. Those words could not leave my mouth.

Q. Over this past weekend, on Sunday, March 26th, did you come to the Tribunal and meet with an investigator, and I was there as well?

A. Yes.

Q. Were you shown your previous statements?

A. Yes.

Q. Did you read your previous statements?

A. I read them.

Q. Were you asked at that time if you wanted to correct or add anything to your statements?

A. Yes.

Q. Did you describe what Zoran Vukovic did to you at Buk Bijela at that time?

A. I did.

Q. Why did you describe it then?

A. First of all, because of the oath I took today, that I would speak the truth and nothing but the truth. I knew I'd come to this courtroom. That's why. And secondly, let it be known that it really happened. It's not easier for me to speak about it today, but nevertheless, I wanted everyone to hear about it.   (Testimony:1247)

Another witness was able to remember some events in detail, but had no memory of other events at all. She explained that the pain at one point became so great that she stopped experiencing her own body.

Q. What happened when you were returned to that group?

A. I don't think anything happened; that is to say, it was as if I wasn't present, conscious of it all, what was happening to me.

(Testimony:1672)

Instead of recognising the cognitive processes of witnesses as understandable under the circumstances, defence attorneys attempt to pathologise their behaviour. In one exchange the defence attorney suggested that an elderly woman was ill because she could not consistently remember facts, before finding out that she was in fact ill.

> Q. [defence attorney] So you don't know whether you said that or not?
> A. I don't know. I really don't know.
> Q. Well, if you're not feeling very well, perhaps we can make a break.
> A. No, we don't have to make a break.
> Q. Well, I'm suggesting that for your well-being.
> A. No, you don't have to make a break because of me. What I know, I shall gladly state. What I don't know, I cannot say, and you can't make me say anything I don't know. If I've forgotten something, if I've made some mistakes, I don't know. I've had enough of all this.   (Testimony:1023)

Building on his depiction of the elderly woman as infirm and incapable, the defence attorney attempted to strip the witness of her agency by suggesting that she could not have possibly come to the tribunal on her own volition.

> Q. Madam, I'm very interested in finding out who brought you here at all.
> A. What I know, I know; what I don't know, I don't know. I'm ready to say what I know. What I don't know, I cannot say.
>   (Testimony:1023)

Instead of acknowledging the woman's intelligent frankness, the defence attorney scolded:

> Q. Yes, but I have to continue with my questions, because at one point you seemed to be saying one thing; at another point you say something else. You see these three men here? They have been charged for terrible crimes, and you are a witness for the Prosecution. As their Defence counsel ...
> A. My husband is not here anymore. He's no longer with us, and I'm going on living. I think that's very difficult. I've been living for the past eight years.

Q. Yes, I can understand that it is difficult for you.

A. Terrible things happened to my husband. I've never seen him again. I think that it is very hard.

The judge interrupted:

> JUDGE MUMBA: Counsel, you have to understand the state in which the witness is and simply ask her questions to elicit whatever evidence you want to elicit; otherwise we'll be here forever.
>
> MR JOVANOVIC: [defence counsel] Your Honours, with your permission, I have just two more sentences. Perhaps I've let myself go a little, but I should like to ask your indulgence. We come from those regions, from those parts. I know everything that this woman has gone through. (Testimony:1024)

Outraged at the suggestion that the defence attorney *knows* what she has been through, the old woman exclaimed, 'Nobody can know. Only I know what I have lived through. Nobody else can know' (Transcript:1025).

This exchange demonstrates that even within the confines of an adversarial system, and even when questioned by a hostile defence attorney, rape survivors are able to assert their own agency. Yet, by forcing them to fit themselves into the structure of the legal anti-narrative, the adversarial process mutes and distorts their narrative.

CONCLUSION

One of the most powerful moments of defiance in the Foca trial came when the court heard from a young woman who was only 15 at the time she was raped.

> Q: [prosecution counsel] What happened to you while you were in Karaman's House?
>
> A. Rape happened, humiliation, mistreatment.
>
> Q. When you say 'rape', what exactly do you mean?
>
> A. In the Yugoslav language in those days, which is now Bosnian, there is a word, 'silo', which means power, strength. To me, that very word, 'silovanje', because I was a child of 15. So they used force, power, strength to bring me there, and that means everything.

Everything I went through, as well as the other girls, occurred not through my will or my acquiescence but by the use of force, power and strength.

Q. But for what did they use the power and strength and force, for what?

A. To bring us there and to do everything they did.

Q. Does that mean to put their penises into your mouth, or vagina, or anus?

A. Yes.

Q. How often did that happen? Was it a daily occurrence?

A. For me, no. Of course, all of us who were there didn't – were not given the same treatment. The intensity of the forcible behaviour towards us varied.

Q. How often were you raped?

A. These are things that I have always wanted to forget. So not so frequently, but I can't tell you with precision.

Q. Who raped you; do you remember anyone specifically?

A. Yes. The first to do it was Pero Elez, Nedjo Samardzic, also a man who came and said he was Captain Dragan, that he was a Montenegrin, Zoran Samardzic. Now I simply – I could not name any others.

Q. How did this make you feel while you were in Karaman's House?

A. Awful, dreadful, helpless. But at the same time I felt dignified and proud.

Q. Of what?

A. I didn't understand the question.

Q. You said at the same time you felt dignified and proud, and what do you mean? What made you feel this way?

A. Yes. We girls, children, were hopeless. They were men under arms and they used force. But simply I did not want to be subdued. They would often describe us as slaves, but I wouldn't accept that.

(Testimony:2423–4)

Like all witnesses, this young woman had been asked to define what happened to her in narrow legal terms and to focus on the perpetrators' acts against her body. She instead offered her own definition of rape, which focused on power and not on body parts, and her own reaction to the experience, which highlighted women's defiance instead of their victimisation.

Women can exercise agency in the context of witnessing before international tribunals, but tribunals alone do not serve their need for creating a record, achieving justice, remembering or forgetting. The trial transcript is marked by what Kathryn Anderson and Dana Jack (1991) have called the 'presence of the absence' (19). Survivors need space and opportunity to 'reflect upon their experiences and choose for themselves which experiences and feelings are central to their sense of the past' (ibid.:17). Adversarial tribunals alone cannot provide this.

Alternative and complementary processes to international war crimes tribunals could include civil suits for compensation, controlled by survivors and their chosen attorneys and not prosecutors responsive to other agendas (Alvarez 1998:2103); truth commissions inspired by grassroots movements for reconciliation and justice (Rotberg and Thompson 2000, Shankar 2000, Hayner 2001); memory projects that collect and publish without judging the accounts of survivors; popular education campaigns that encourage survivors to test their voices; and psychotherapeutic testimony therapy (Friedrich 1999). As long as these alternative processes are truly driven by local needs and indigenous ideas and do not rely on international pressure, they are far more useful than trials in fostering the reconstruction of civil society. The benefits for survivors of such non-adversarial processes thus may indeed extend far beyond the outcome.

One particularly intriguing complementary mechanism would be the staging of a 'people's tribunal', such as the one held in December 2000 for consideration of Japanese military sexual slavery (Chinkin 2000). People's tribunals are the embodiment of Richard Falk's (1988) vision of law as 'an instrument of civil society' that belongs to peoples, not governments (29). 'Accordingly,' Christine Chinkin (2000) explains, 'when states fail to exercise their obligations to ensure justice, civil society can and should step in' (339). While a people's tribunal could not impose sentences, order reparations, or provide the same due process guarantees as a court of law, it could address the need of survivors for public acknowledgement of what happened. Survivors of atrocities could have more say in fashioning the rules of these tribunals and thus ensuring that they have an opportunity to present their full story. By remaining witness-focused instead of perpetrator-focused, the narrative that would be constructed by a people's tribunal would be more true to the experiences of survivors.

No single response will serve all the needs of all survivors in all circumstances. Several tools could help create a narrative that fully includes survivors' experiences and empowers them in the process.

As the editors of the Harvard Law Review have aptly noted, '[e]xaggerating just what one tool – international prosecution – can reasonably accomplish may distract attention and resources from other more suitable mechanisms and will inevitably lead to disappointment in the prosecutions' performance' (Developments in the Law 2001:1981–2). Above all, survivors themselves should take a lead in determining the nature and operation of any set of tools. Only the survivors can determine whether and how to put the past at rest, and whether and how to keep remembering.

The words of one witness in the Foca case are haunting:

> I think that I have decided to try and leave many of those things behind me somewhere, although within me, I still have and there will always be traces of everything that happened to me. I think that for the whole of my life, all my life I will have thoughts of that and feel the pain that I felt then and still feel. That will never go away.   (Testimony:1728)

No public memory project will cure the pain of this survivor and the others. However, the adversarial process alone does not honour their assertion of agency, their resistance to power and their will to survive.

NOTES

1. American University, School of International Service. The author would like to thank Lynda Boose, Orly Luben and Janet Lord for their comments and suggestion.
2. The transcript can be found at www.un.org/icty/judgement.htm.
3. That many of the survivors were also patients does not negate their ability to exercise agency. Amartya Sen observes that '[t]he fact that the agent may have to see herself as a patient as well does not alter the additional modalities and responsibilities that are inescapably associated with the agency of a person' (Sen 1999:190).
4. Interview with Albanian Kosovar woman, Kosovo, August 2001.
5. Interview with Croat woman from Bosnia, Vienna, April 1995.
6. Interview with Bosnian woman, Croatia, March 1994.
7. Author's interview, August 2001.
8. The Hague, 22 February 2001 (JL/P.I.S./566-e). The decision read in open court can be found at <www.un.org/icty/pressreal/p566-e.html>. The full transcript and text of the decision can be found at <www.un.org/icty/judgement.htm>

REFERENCES

Alvarez, Jose. 1998. 'Rush to Closure: Lessons of the Tadic Judgment', *Michigan Law Review* 96(7):2031.

Anderson, Kathryn and Dana C. Jack. 1991. 'Learning to Listen: Interview Techniques and Analysis', in Sherna Berger Gluck and Daphne Patai (eds) *Women's Words: The Feminist Practice of Oral History*. New York: Routledge.

Askin, Kelly Dawn. 1997. *War Crimes Against Women: Prosecution in International Tribunals*. The Hague: Martinus Nijhoff Publishers.

Beetham, David. 1996. *The Legitimation of Power*. Atlantic Highlands, NG: The Humanities Press.

Booth, Ken. 1999. 'Three Tyrannies', in T. Dunne and N. J. Wheeler (eds) *Human Rights in Global Politics*. Cambridge: Cambridge University Press:103–26.

Bryden, David P. and Sonja Lengnick. 1997. 'Rape in the Criminal Justice System', *Journal of Criminal Law and Criminology*, (87):1194.

Chandler, David. 2002. *From Kosovo to Kabul: Human Rights and International Intervention*. London: Pluto Press.

Chesterman, Simon. 1997. 'Never Again … and Again: Law, Order, and the Gender of War Crimes in Bosnia and Beyond', *Yale Journal of International Law* 22:229.

Chinkin, Christine. 2000. 'Women's International Tribunal on Japanese Military Sexual Slavery', *American Journal of International Law* 95:335.

Daniel, E. Valentine and John Chr. Knudsen (eds). 1995. *Mistrusting Refugees*. Berkeley: University of California Press.

David, Patricia H. 2000. 'The Politics of Prosecuting Rape as a Warcrime', *International Lawyer* 34:1223.

Developments in the Law. 2001. 'The Promises of International Prosecution', *Harvard Law Review* 114:1957.

Drakulic, Slavenka. 2001. 'Bosnian Women Witness', *The Nation* 19 March.

Falk, Richard. 1988. 'The Rights of Peoples (In Particular Indigenous Peoples)', in James Crawford (ed.) *The Rights of Peoples*. Oxford: Clarendon Press:17–37.

Friedrich, M. J. 1999. 'Addressing the Mental Health Needs of Balkan Refugees', *Journal of the American Medical Health Association* 282(5):422–523.

Hayner, Priscilla B. 2001. *Unspeakable Truths: Confronting State Terror and Atrocity*. New York: Routledge.

Herman, Judith Lewis. 1993. *Trauma and Recovery: The Aftermath of Violence from Domestic Abuse to Political Terror*. New York: Basic Books.

Ignatieff, Michael. 2000. *Virtual War: Kosovo and Beyond*. New York: Metropolitan Books.

Levy, Arden B. 1994. 'International Prosecution of Rape in Warfare: Nondiscriminatory Recognition and Enforcement', *UCLA Women's Law Journal* 4:255.

Lusby, Katherine. 1995. 'Hearing the Invisible Women of Political Rape: Using Oppositional Narrative to Tell a New War Story', *University of Toledo Law Review* 25:911.

Matoesian, Gregory. 1993. *Reproducing Rape: Domination Through Talk in the Courtroom*. Chicago: University of Chicago Press.

——. 1997. '"You Were Interested in Him as a Person?": Rhythms of Domination in the Kennedy Smith Rape Trial', *Law and Social Inquiry* 55:60–1.

Mertus, Julie. 2000. 'Truth in a Box: The Limits of Justice through Judicial Mechanisms', in Ifi Amadiume and Abdullahi An-Na'im (eds) *The Politics of Memory: Truth, Healing and Social Justice*. New York: Zed Books:142–61.

Minow, Martha. 1998. *Between Vengeance and Forgiveness: Facing History after Genocide and Mass Violence*. Boston: Beacon Press.

Ni Aolain, Finnuala. 1997. 'Radical Rules: The Effects of Evidentiary and Procedural Rules on the Regulation of Sexual Violence in War', *Albany Law Review* 60:883.

Oseil, Mark. 1995. 'Ever Again: Legal Remembrance of Administrative Massacre', *University of Pennsylvania Law Review* 144:486–8.

Pratt, Kathleen M. and Laurel E. Fletcher. 1994. 'Time for Justice: The Case for International Prosecutions of Wartime Rape and Gender-Based Violence in the Former Yugoslavia', *Berkeley Women's Law Journal* 9:77.

Ray, Amy E. 1997. 'The Shame of It: Gender-Based Terrorism in the Former Yugoslavia and the Failure of International Human Rights Law to Comprehend the Injuries', *American University Law Review* 46:793.

Rotberg, Robert I. and Dennis Thompson (eds). 2000. *Truth v. Justice: The Morality of Truth Commissions*. Princeton: Princeton University Press.

Sen, Amaryta. 1999. *Development as Freedom*. New York: Anchor Books.

Shankar, Finola. 2000. 'Gendered Spaces of Terror and Assault: The Testimonio of REMHI and the Commission for Historical Clarification in Guatemala', *Gender, Place and Culture* 7(3): 265–86.

Taslitz, Andrew E. 1999. *Rape and the Culture of the Courtroom*. New York: New York University Press.

Tetreault, Mary Ann. 1997. 'Justice for All: Wartime Rapes and Women's Human Rights', *Global Governance* 3:197.

Wald, Patricia M. 2001. 'The International Criminal Tribunal for the Former Yugoslavia Comes of Age: Some Observations on Day-to-Day Dilemmas of an International Court', *Journal of Law and Policy* 5:87–118.

Ward, Colleen A. 1995. Attitudes Toward Rape: Feminist and Psychological Perspectives. London: Sage.

14   Networks of Memory: Chileans Debate Democracy and the Pinochet Legacy Over an Internet Forum

Eliza Tanner Hawkins

On 16 October 1998 the unthinkable happened: the aging, retired Chilean general, ex-president, and senator-for-life Augusto Pinochet was arrested at the London Clinic. This action sparked a massive debate both within and outside Chile over the legacy of the Pinochet dictatorship. Besides using older forms of communication – radio, television, newspapers, magazines, speeches – these debates were carried on over national and international computer networks. As soon as the news broke the publication *La Tercera* (<www.tercera.cl>) established an online forum devoted to the Pinochet case. For the years following Pinochet's arrest and eventual return to Chile in the year 2000, Chileans from around the world used *La Tercera Internet*'s forum to argue over the meanings of justice, reconciliation, forgiveness, truth, democracy, liberty, sovereignty and human rights. More than a thousand Chileans participated in this debate in just the first three months of the forum's existence. 'What a poor memory we have', wrote one Chilean woman,

> that we have forgotten the bitter disputes between people who thought differently from that proposed by the 'Super president' Allende, have we forgotten that we were persecuted for thinking and speaking differently than them, have we forgotten the long lines for a bit of bread and many times the fights for a bit of meat while they, logically, did not know what the people were suffering, they didn't know hunger, shortages, nor lines; they were given preferential treatment, they had power ... We should be grateful since Mr Pinochet was the only one capable of bringing us out of the mire in which the politicians and their mediocrity had driven us ... Chilean woman true to heart never let us forget.

Another Chilean also remembered the military coup and the time leading up to it, but from quite a different viewpoint:

How can I forget that September, when a friend came to the house to borrow the telephone to tell his family that his father was dead. How can I forget the 13th of September 1973 when all the businesses could open and sell the hoarded merchandise, tears ran down my cheeks since just a few days earlier I had been in a line, trying to buy sugar and oil. How can I forget my elementary school teacher who was tortured until she went crazy just because she had leftist ideas. How can one forget all the dead people we saw floating down the Mapocho river and how we ran away when the patrol came to break up our gathering ... The Chilean Generals, the people who have power, and those who don't understand poverty and justice are those who forget that God lives, and that sooner or later, whatever they do, it will be judged by divine justice.

As online forums open up spaces in the Chilean public sphere, they become part of the transition and reconciliation process. In this chapter I will look at the forum as a public space and argue that two consequences of these online interchanges are the formation of public opinion and the expression of collective memories. The chapter is divided into four main sections. The first part presents the methods and theoretical framework for the study, as well as a brief synopsis of the Pinochet case. The second part looks at the characteristics of this online public space. The third part examines the consequences of online debate: opinion formation and development of collective memories. The fourth part reflects on collective memories in the age of new communication technologies.

THE PINOCHET CASE FORUM: THEORY AND METHODS

On 16 October 1998 Scotland Yard, acting on an international arrest and capture warrant from Spain, detained Pinochet in a London hospital where he was recovering from a hernia operation. Spain was pursuing legal action against Pinochet for genocide and terrorism against Spanish citizens during the Chilean military regime. The protests and celebrations began almost immediately. Within days Chile appeared to be polarised along the same Yes–No dividing lines that had resulted in Pinochet's defeat in the October 1988 plebiscite.

The decade-old divisions that had appeared to be nicely covered up and mended were suddenly just as pertinent and decisive. During this time, Chile experienced what Alexander Wilde (1999) calls 'irruptions of memory', or public events that evoke the political past and demonstrate that these memories are still part of the people's present experience. Wilde argues that the arrest of Pinochet ranks as the 'most evocative of all the irruptions of memory during the Chilean transition' (489).

Essential to the transition to a democratic government is the idea of 'reconciliation', or the process whereby individuals, groups or countries come to terms with past events and resolve the problems associated with them. During the transition, said Chilean scholar Osvaldo Sunkel (1993), 'the prevalent disposition among the most important political streams and social actors has been to attenuate, moderate and reduce controversies, to avoid addressing them, shelving them instead for the future' (2). The arrest of Pinochet forced politicians and others to address directly problems that had been 'shelved for the future'.

Chileans were given ample time to debate reconciliation issues since Pinochet's arrest precipitated an extensive legal battle in the British Courts. In the first three months of the online debate, readers sent in 1,670 letters; about 64 per cent of the forum letters were anti-Pinochet, 26 per cent were pro-Pinochet, and the remainder (10 per cent) dealt with issues not directly supporting or criticising Pinochet and his arrest. The Law Lords of the House of Lords ruled in March 1999 that Pinochet did not have diplomatic immunity, which allowed the extradition proceedings to begin. However, in March 2000 the British government found that Pinochet was mentally unfit to stand trial in England and he was sent back to Chile. In Chile Pinochet faced more than 150 lawsuits and a legal process to strip him of his immunity as a senator-for-life. After a protracted series of court cases, his immunity was revoked, but he was declared mentally incompetent to stand trial.

In both practice and theory, communication plays an essential role in these processes of reconciliation, transition and democrat-isation. A useful way of discussing communication processes in society is to use the concept of the public sphere as developed by Jürgen Habermas. This concept describes how communication works, while at the same time contrasting it with an ideal situation, showing both possibilities and problems. The public sphere is defined as communication networks in civil society that have deep links to people's everyday experiences. Communication takes place in social spaces, which can be physical places or abstract locations where people are linked together through the mass media. In the political public sphere, people publicise, thematise, dramatise and propose solutions to social problems, and in the process bring them into the political system so they can be addressed by the government and parliamentary organisations (Calhoun (ed.) 1992; Habermas 1989, 1998).

The internet facilitates these communication networks, while continuing to make public spaces more abstract or 'virtual'. Since the mid-1990s people in Chile used the internet to create spaces for public debate on political and social topics. The newspaper *La Tercera* produces what continues to be one of the most popular internet news sites in Chile, as seen in number of visits per day and surveys.[1] Other major newspapers, such as *El Mercurio*, and media have also developed successful news Web sites with online forums and chat rooms. The study is based on the content and textual analysis of 1,670 letters sent to *La Tercera Internet*'s Pinochet case forum between 16 October 1998 and 23 January 1999.[2]

CHARACTERISTICS OF AN ONLINE PUBLIC SPACE

In writings about the public sphere it is possible to identify four broad issues associated with public spaces. The first is a question of access to the space. The second issue is the freedom people have to communicate in that area. Closely based on these access and communicative freedoms is the third issue – the structure of deliberation. These three elements shape the actual talk that occurs in the space. It is possible to identify consequences of this talk, such as the formation of public opinion, the shaping of collective memories, the creation of identities, and so on.

The question of access can be seen as having two parts: who are the people with access to the technology? and who, of all those people, actually participates in the online forum? During the time of this study, 1 per cent to 2 per cent of the people in Chile had access to the internet. The lack of internet access within Chile was reflected in the letters sent to the online forum. The email addresses showed 26.5 per cent of the letters originated on servers in Chile, 64.8 per cent came from servers outside Chile, and 8.4 per cent were Web-based addresses, whose servers were generally located outside Chile. The letters were sent from at least 40 countries, with the largest group from Chile, followed by Canada, the United States and Sweden, in that order. The other countries represented are mostly known to have large Chilean exile communities, such as Australia and Norway. These countries also have more people with access to the internet and computers. Given these global economic barriers, internet access was limited to people who were from the upper classes or had the resources to afford computers and the internet, used the internet at work, or were university students.

With these limitations in mind, the next part of the access question is to look at who participated in the debates. The people were not politicians, public officials, or well-known figures. Rather, they were students, professionals and teachers. They were also military people, sons and daughters of Chilean exiles and ex-political prisoners. About 73 per cent of the forum participants appeared to be men, with 14 per cent appearing to be women, and 13 per cent unable to be identified in any way. I also found that almost 90 per cent of the forum participants were Chileans.

The second issue or characteristic of this online public space is the freedom of communication. Such freedom depends on factors such as the existence or absence of censorship, legal regulations and the way the forum works. Legally and formally, the online forum was open to any person who wanted to participate. There was no government censorship or other legal regulations.

Then-editor Juan Carlos Camus insisted that *La Tercera Internet* should publish all the letters, regardless of their political positions. Participants strongly believed in the value of democratic communication and often thanked *La Tercera* for the forum. Some felt the forum allowed people previously 'without a voice' to talk and share their opinions. Participants saw this talk as essential to the Chilean reconciliation process.

Does a better system exist where the people can openly write or talk without repercussions or fear? Thank God that Chile has been able to debate the problem of Pinochet. His punishment or freedom is not as important as the opportunity to openly debate the topic. Congratulations!

Compared with the access Chileans have to express their personal opinions in newspapers, magazines, television and radio, the development of the internet was a large step in expanding public spaces and the freedom to communicate.

The third characteristic of the forum is the structure of deliberation or the way people talked to each other over the forum. Participants submitted letters ranging from two words to more than 5,200 words. Most of the letters were between 150 and 700 words, though it was not at all unusual for readers to submit letters of 1,000 words or more.

About 46 per cent of the letters were directed to the general public, much like traditional letters to the editor. The letters that turned the forum into an active, vibrant interchange were those written as replies to statements made by someone inside or outside the forum. One-quarter of the submissions (25.6 per cent) were such letters, many of which mirrored verbal dialogue and debate as the participants spoke directly to other people. Through these interchanges the forum participants developed 'rules of debate' or a general standard of civility for discussion of the Pinochet case. Civil language was not always the norm, but participants repeatedly called for a higher level of discussion.

> Let's grow up. Let's be free. Let's be capable of talking without having our emotions dominate our reason. We need to grow civically and this means being able to tolerate one another as people who think differently but who have this right.

Some of the forum participants expressed the hope that civilised discussions and debates would strengthen democratic values in society and eventually help in the Chilean transition.

The fourth characteristic of a public space is that it allows for the public use of reason or rational-critical discourse. The use of reason can be seen in the debates over democracy in Chile. About 200 letters directly addressed the topic of democracy. The majority (83 per cent) contained some form of criticism of Chile's democracy. The other 17 per cent defended Chile's political system or maintained that Chile was a model of democratic government. Democracy, to the forum participants, was an everyday concern. Their experiences since 1970 and their political affiliations shaped how they defined democracy and how they viewed the Pinochet case. The discussion allowed forum participants to become acquainted with different views of what constitutes a democratic nation.

Those who defended Chile's political system often lauded the benefits of a 'protected' or 'authoritarian' democracy. These people praised Chile as a model of a free-market economy, saying that

Pinochet should be honoured for his role in establishing Chilean democracy and fighting communist forces in the world.

> they try to judge a military official who not only freed Chile from communism – that for years was a cancer of the free world – but also established the foundation of the exemplary democracy and free market system in Latin America.

The key components of a democratic country for these people are stability, order and economic progress. Human rights are not mentioned and freedom is seen only in the context of the economic free market. These writers often cited specific elements, such as the privatised social security system or the economy, to support their claim that Pinochet established an exemplary democracy in Chile.

Such letters contrasted sharply with the many people who criticised Chilean democracy. Some would simply state their opinions:

JUSTICE NOR DEMOCRACY EXIST IN THIS COUNTRY

However, many of them would use arguments and reason in an attempt to convince other readers that their position was correct. They argued that the Chilean democracy had fundamental problems. They criticised the 1980 Constitution, both its form and the way in which it was created. Related to the Constitutional questions, is the criticism of the military influence in politics. The third problem area, as pointed out by forum participants, is the presence of designated senators and senators-for-life in the Chilean Congress.

The common theme of these letters is that democracy must be founded on principles of justice; a democratic society was a just society. Justice was seen in terms of human rights, especially the location of the bodies of the detained-disappeared and trials or legal processes against those who committed abuses during the dictatorship.

> Democracy is much more than elections, a parliament, a senate, and a congress. Democracy is justice and a desperate hope of change.

Chile was not a just society because the people responsible for human rights abuses had not accepted responsibility, nor had they been tried or punished.

Perhaps through all the debates, one of the most interesting developments was the hope the forum participants had in the future –

the hope for a more democratic and just society. They were aware that such a society requires effort from all of the citizens, not just the Chilean government, or foreign governments, or other groups. Juan E. Corradi et al. (1992) suggest that the experience of repression might just help develop an understanding and appreciation of an ideal public life in democratic societies. For many of the forum writers, the lessons they learned might be even more fundamental. The dictatorship gave them a renewed appreciation of democracy and justice.

OPINIONS AND MEMORY

After describing four of the characteristics of this online public space, we can now explore some of the consequences. As mentioned before, participants shared opinions and memories when they debated the Pinochet case. This section will briefly discuss opinion formation and then turn to an analysis of memory and history in the letters.

In public sphere theory, scholars emphasise the development of opinions since these opinions can become the basis for political action and changes in government and policies. Writers in the forum expressed their opinions on just about every subject connected to the Pinochet case. One person argued that the forum plays an important role for Chileans as they construct their country's future through reconciliation with the past:

> I believe that this publication in this space begins to apply the democracy in regards to the liberty of opinion ... it is necessary to analyse what has happened, an analysis that allows us to look to the future with optimism, opening the channels of forgiveness and reconciliation, to dry one's tears, look ahead, and proudly say, 'Our dead can rest in peace, the past is left behind, it is time to go on.'

Writers agreed on the importance of the forum in analysing events and sharing their opinions. From the comments it is also evident that participants are self-conscious about their role in creating public opinion. Though some people brought set opinions to the debates, others used the forum to create, modify and develop opinions.

Besides facilitating debates over democracy and other issues, the forum provided a way for participants to share memories about the legacy of the Pinochet dictatorship. Thus, a second consequence of the debates over the Pinochet case is the development of collective memories of political events. Using the ideas of Maurice Halbwachs, sociologists James Pennebaker and Becky Banasik (1997) note that memories are collective because they are discussed and shared by people. Memories are formed and organised in a collective context, with the present needs and situation shaping how people remember past events. Studies show that in the cases of 'silent events', or events where people cannot talk or avoid talking about a major shared upheaval, the active suppression of discussion actually ingrains the event more deeply in people's memories. This seems to be the case in the Chilean situation. The number of forum submissions shows that the events of the past three decades were still a vivid part of people's lives, even for those who had been born after the military coup.

The forum letters are part of the way Chileans construct stories of the past and shape collective memories of events in order to make sense of the events surrounding Pinochet's arrest. The letters are part of the very personal level or layer of social memories that shapes the broader collective memory of the military dictatorship (see the discussion of memory in Argentina, in Jelin and Kaufman 2000). Through the new form of communication, forum participants were able to challenge official silences and express their opinions. All the letters were expressions of people's memories since they responded in some way to Pinochet's arrest. However, for this section I decided to look more closely at those letters that contained historical references, personal memories of past events, or comments about the role of memory in Chilean society. Based on these criteria, I selected 653 forum letters (or 39 per cent) for closer analysis. Of those letters, 216 (33.1 per cent) supported Pinochet, 434 (66.5 per cent) were anti-Pinochet, and the remaining three (0.4 per cent) dealt with other historical topics. These percentages mirror the anti- and pro-Pinochet divisions in the forum as a whole.

Writing in his book on history and memory Patrick Hutton (1993) said, 'We consciously reconstruct images of the past in the selective way that suits the needs of our present situation' (xxi). This can be seen in the way the Pinochetistas recount historical events and experiences to support their position. It is also evident in the human rights framework for letters written by those who oppose Pinochet and the military government. It was striking that of all the events Pinochet's supporters could have chosen to show that their feelings for the ex-dictator were not misplaced, the main strategy was to recall the problems of the Allende years. In their recounting of history,

Pinochet saved Chile from disaster and communist rule and established a model country, both economically and politically.

> It's incredible how the world laughs and talks about a betrayed man who had the guts to 'stop dead' Chilean and foreign socialists and communists that made sport of the rest of the Chileans. They charge him with deaths and more deaths and they don't understand that if it weren't for him, the dead would have been those of us who are thankful to him we live in a free country.

Many of the Pinochetistas insisted that their personal experiences under the *Unidad Popular* (Popular Unity or UP) or the military government justified their position and belief that Pinochet was Chile's great liberator. Sixty letters from the Pinochetistas included personal memories, 48 of them dating from the period 1970–3. An interesting point from these letters is that the writers, for the most part, did not dwell on the more publicised successes of the military government in areas such as economic development to justify their outrage at Pinochet's arrest. Rather, they recounted their memories of 1970–3. These memories included blaming socialists, leftists, communists, or even the 'working class' as those responsible for past and present problems in Chile.

> In the year 1973 I worked as an employee of Corfo ... I lived through all of the popular unity Government, the national disorder of the workers, the food shortages, the lines for a chicken, for a box of cigarettes, for clothing, the *alameda* [central boulevard] converted into an enormous ditch with everlasting [construction] work with the white line erased, etc. It is tiring and stressful just thinking about the hate generated among Chileans by the 'ism'. The military pronouncement was necessary for all Chileans especially the democratic sectors given the ineptness in governing of president Salvador Allende.

In these stories of the past, all people who opposed the military government were lumped together as 'communists'. The people who were killed or disappeared somehow deserved their fates because they broke the law or were involved in illegal acts.

> It's sad to read so much foolishness in this forum from the communists, no one killed any of my relatives, nor did they

disappear any of my family, the only thing I remember is that we had a curfew and we had to be in our houses at certain hours, all of my relatives and friends respected it [the law] and because of this they didn't die, and because of this they weren't sent to the National Stadium.

The letters from people who opposed Pinochet also contained many historical references and memories of life under the military government. These writers cited deaths, disappearances, torture and the military overthrow of a democratically elected government. Most of the letters were written in a framework or in terms of 'human rights abuses'. For forum readers who were too young to remember the 1970–3 period, complaints about waiting in line for bread did not have the same emotional impact as personal accounts of deaths, torture, exile and disappearances. Of the 434 letters by these writers, 125 (or 29 per cent) contained personal memories of their experiences. Incidentally, this was about the same percentage of Pinochetistas who shared personal memories (28 per cent).

Since this forum was open to people from around the world, Chileans who went into exile or who lived abroad were able to share their opinions and views. Exiles lamented that their families were not able to grow up in Chile.

I know that many believe not that much happened, but there are more of us who know the truth, the past injustices will never be forgotten and will remain written in our history for the future generations. I had to explain to my children why they were born in a country so far from Chile. I had to leave as a young girl with my heart broken, without my father, without my brother, without my brother-in-law. The worst moments were when the plane left Chile and now I relive them knowing that the author of all this is now suffering like us, and his family is suffering in a foreign country like us. Mr Pinochet, repent of your crimes in public and put an end to this tragedy.

Others gave personal accounts of people they knew who had been killed or had disappeared under the military government. These young people demand justice.

My father was arrested and disappeared in the year 1973 by the military forces in this time under the leadership of general

Pinochet, I never saw my father again I was only 5 years old and now I demand justice.

I say this because now the whole world knows that Pinochet is an Assassin, guilty of the crimes committed during 1973–1990. This isn't an invented history like many believe. (Ninel Pizarro Diaz Daughter of a Detained and Disappeared person)

A few told about their experiences in prison and subsequent exile. However, they rarely went into much detail, only sharing that they still remembered the painful experience.

In my personal life, I was exiled for more than 15 years. I suffered, like many Chileans, persecution, imprisonment and torture. This isn't hate. This is a feeling of justice.

A few talked about the problems under the UP, but blamed the military and their supporters for both the problems before and after 1973.

It is true that in 1973 there was economic chaos, food shortages, runaway inflation, distress because of the inability to find meat, milk, food. We waited in long lines from midnight in order to buy – not what you wanted – but only what they could sell you. What I can't understand is why a week after the 'pronouncement'[3] the supermarkets that had been empty were suddenly filled with all kinds of goods, as if there had been a miracle, the black market ended in one blow, the lines ended, and our bread began to arrive at our homes thank God until this day. What happened? Where was this food one month earlier when we anxiously searched for it, those of us who have always had to live on one income?

The forum participants were aware that with this technology they could share their experiences with many people around the world in a way not previously available to them. This, combined with the judicial events in the Pinochet case, provided a form of vindication or validation of their memories and experiences in Chile.

CONCLUSIONS: MEMORY AND PUBLIC SPACES

Historian Patrick Hutton (1993) suggested that the computer might make the issues of history and memory more complex since the technology offers a greater access to data and makes 'facts' more malleable. Although technology does give people greater access to data, in this case the increase is also in the number of different voices and memories now published globally. The online forum became a public space where people shared opinions and memories of the military dictatorship, creating collective memories of past events in the process.

The characteristics of this public space shape the communication of forum participants. For this reason, the first part of the chapter analysed four broad characteristics or features of the online forum: access and participation in the forum, freedom of communication, structure of deliberation and public use of reason. Since a restricted segment of Chilean population has access to the internet, this meant that wealthier, more educated people would be the ones who were sharing their opinions and memories. The international nature of the internet means that a large number of Chileans living abroad could also participate in the forum. Those who joined the online debate had a great deal of freedom to express themselves. The participants debated many topics, including the transition to democracy in Chile. I identified two consequences of their talk: formation of opinions and the sharing of memories. Opinion formation is an important concept in public sphere theory since it is through changes in discourse and public talk that people can influence the formal politics of a country. Besides its role in generating public opinion, the forum became part of the Chilean transition as people attempted to make sense of past events and to decide on appropriate actions for the future.

Chileans are now debating the 're-writing of history' of recent events. For years the official history promulgated by the military government depicted the military as the saviours of Chile from Marxism and the creators of the 15-year economic boom. 'The detention of Pinochet in London was the act that broke apart this official history', writes historian Cristián Gazmuri (2000), 'and has allowed the negative aspects of the military government, in particular everything associated with the detained-disappeared and the policies of State terrorism that occurred, to be considered topics just as or more important historically than the economic achievements'.

Pinochet's supporters appear to be threatened now that their version of the coup and military government does not seem to be so easily accepted within Chile or abroad. They argued that Pinochet's opponents had been spreading lies internationally for 25 years and that people must now learn or remember the true history. The 'correction' in history for these people entailed detailing the problems with the Allende government that justified the military coup in their minds. It is necessary to forget the past (translated to mean forgetting the human rights abuses and other problems) and look to the future, many wrote.

> I don't think this is good, because it isn't a step toward reconciliation, because this is a topic that opens the wounds of the past over and over again and what many of us Chileans want to do is think of the future, not return to the past when many people suffered.

For those who did not support Pinochet or who suffered under the military government, the retired General's arrest finally 'broke' the forgetfulness in Chile. It allowed people to share their stories and remember the events of the past. For some, it was a vindication, saying that their versions of events and their suffering were now being taken seriously. Forum participants spoke about the need to remember.

NO FORGETFULNESS, NO PARDON, ONLY JUSTICE

It has been twenty-five long years, but it appears there is light at the end of the tunnel. A light whose energy comes from the irreducible hope of justice and liberty, together with a tenacious resistance to amnesia and impunity ... From this the Pinochet case takes its importance for those of us who love justice and liberty. The [person] wanted to make a fresh start by forgetting and we stopped him and reproached him with the memory. An ancient and wise proverb says, 'The people who forget the errors of their past are obligated to repeat them.' And this well applies to my homeland Chile, also to Argentina, Uruguay, Paraguay, Brazil. While there is memory, it isn't possible to hide the truth and accept impunity. Because of this, no forgetting, no pardon, only justice.

These Chileans believe that history and memory are essential to defining the identity of a people or nation. Through remembering, these people could continue to call for justice and decry human rights abuses. Their views could be incorporated into the larger social memory and history of Chile. Both Pinochet's supporters and opponents addressed issues of remembering and forgetting. People would write about the need to forget but, in so doing, they would remember events from the past, showing that despite their proclamations the past was an integral part of their present lives. Their participation in the forum further attests to the strength of the memories. By sharing experiences, such as the human rights abuses, the personal stories became part of a collective memory of Chile's past.

It is, however, refreshing to know that, despite everything, there are in this page, beautiful and sometimes terrible testimonies of those who have faith in reconciliation. Because liberty and justice will make us free of the hate and hypocrisy, an embrace to women and men without distinction.

Through these memories and debates, some forum participants expressed the hope that the discussion will help lead to reconciliation for individuals and Chilean society.

NOTES

1. 'Un millón de personas visitó La Tercera Internet', *La Tercera* 1 September 1999 [www.tercera.cl]. For more history of internet development see Eliza Tanner 1999.
2. In the letters used in this chapter, signatures and names of the forum participants have generally been removed unless there was a specific reason for including that information. My translations keep punctuation and capitalisation as close to the original as possible, with some changes made for readability in English.
3. A reference to the 11 September 1973 military coup, using the military's own language for the event.

REFERENCES

Calhoun, Craig (ed.). 1992. *Habermas and the Public Sphere*. Cambridge, Mass.: MIT Press.

Corradi, Juan E., Patricia Weiss Fagen and Manuel Antonio Garreton (eds). 1992. *Fear at the Edge: State Terror and Resistance in Latin America*. Berkeley: University of California.

Gazmuri, Cristián. 2000. 'La verdadera vía de reconciliación', *La Tercera* 1 May [<www.tercera.cl>].

Habermas, Jürgen. 1989. *The Structural Transformation of the Public Sphere: An Inquiry into a Category of Bourgeois Society* (trans. Thomas Burger). Cambridge, Mass.: MIT Press.

Habermas, Jürgen. 1998. *Between Facts and Norms: Contributions to a Discourse Theory of Law and Democracy* (trans. William Rehg). Cambridge, Mass.: MIT Press.

Hutton, Patrick H. 1993. *History as an Art of Memory*. Hanover, N.H.: University Press of New England.

Jelin, Elizabeth and Susana G. Kaufman. 2000. 'Layers of Memories: Twenty Years After in Argentina', in T. G. Ashplant, Graham Dawson and Michael Roper (eds) *The Politics of War Memory and Commemoration*. London: Routledge.

Pennebaker, James W. and Becky L. Banasik. 1997. 'On the Creation and Maintenance of Collective Memories: History as Social Psychology', in James W. Pennebaker, Dario Paez and Bernard Rimé (eds) *Collective Memory of Political Events: Social Perspectives*. Mahwah, N.J.: Lawrence Erlbaum Associates.

Sunkel, Osvaldo. 1993. 'Consolidation of Chile's Democracy and Development: The Challenges and the Tasks', Institute of Development Studies, Discussion Paper, No. 317.

Tanner, Eliza. 1999. 'Links to the World: The Internet in Chile, 1983–1997', *Gazette 61* (Feb.):39–57.

Tanner, Eliza. 2000. *Las Grandes Alamedas: The Paradox of Internet and Democracy in Chile*. Ph.D. dissertation, University of Wisconsin–Madison.

'Un millón de personas visitó La Tercera Internet'. 1999. *La Tercera* 1 September [<www.tercera.cl>].

Walker, Igno. 1997. '¿Es Chile un país democrático?' *Revista Hoy* 13–19 January:19.

Wilde, Alexander. 1999. 'Irruptions of Memory: Expressive Politics in Chile's Transition to Democracy', *Journal of Latin American Studies* 31:473–500.

15 Reconciling Reconciliation: A Personal and Public Journey of Testifying Before the South African Truth and Reconciliation Commission

Yazir Henri

I was a 15-year-old school pupil in 1985. By 1994 I had given my youth to the armed struggle led by the African National Congress (ANC) against apartheid. My story is not unique; it is the story of thousands of youth in South Africa (SA). Today we are still searching for the bones of our friends and loved ones, haunted by their ghosts, we are still coming to terms with the horror and the extent to which the conflict we lived through undermined our dignity and humanity. These are some of the many truths behind the 'miracle' of peace in SA. Although much damage was done to property, it was people who bore the brunt of South Africa's war on colour, the violence done was not only to our skin – it was to our persons, our hearts, our souls, to our minds.

I am 30 years old now and I write this chapter in the register of someone who has experienced two wars as a teenager: the apartheid war inside South Africa which forced me into exile at the age of 16 and the war in Angola where I spent two years as a member of *Umkhonto We Sizwe* (MK), the armed wing of the ANC. When I was 19 I returned to South Africa illegally and was arrested by the South African security forces. Following the signing of the Groote Schuur 'Minutes' in the middle of 1990 between the then unbanned ANC and the apartheid government securing the release of political prisoners, I was freed after having spent seven months in detention under Section 29 of the then Internal Security Act. This Act allowed the South African authorities to hold people indefinitely without any trial or rights, it reduced those held under its authority to animals and robbed one of any sense of human dignity. It is the experience of my youth that has caused me to commit myself to the pursuit of peace and the advocacy against the morality of war which not only brings to the fore the worst of humanity, but also destroys the possibility of humanity. I am a founding member of the Western Cape Action Tour Project (WECAT) and the Direct Action Centre for Peace and Memory (DACPM). WECAT/DACPM are about my life and the lives of others like me who, out of war, have committed our lives to the pursuit of peace, hope and the promise of human dignity on South African soil.

Today Cape Town, the city in which I was born, remains deeply fractured. The legal and political framework of apartheid has been removed and, many believe, replaced by one of the world's best constitutions. Legal and political apartheid has gone but social, economic and psychological apartheid remains and will for a long time to come. As former combatants and torture survivors living in Cape Town, we continue to struggle with the duality of this legacy. Not only do we live with serious symptoms of post-war trauma, we carry this condition in a context of continued social and economic oppression.

In August 1996 I testified before the Human Rights Violations Committee (HRV) of the TRC (see related chapters in this volume for more detailed discussions on the TRC). For me, my testimony before the TRC provided a space in which to speak, to reach out, to express my anguish and painfully to face myself. Here I share what I have gained after coming into contact with this process and offer a brief personal account of my experiences through the TRC process. Hopefully, what I write will be a reminder to South Africans and people elsewhere in the world that the will to live in peace can be far stronger than the will that may give expression to other emotions of anger, bitterness, hatred and revenge.

MY SPACE!/MY SPACE?

It is said that the TRC was intended to provide a space within which people were able to speak and to tell their stories of abuse and violation. For varying reasons this did not and does not exist elsewhere in our society. For me, this space and opportunity was the most positive aspect of my contact with the TRC. The space was very positive for me because I have been able to clear my chest and my conscience. I have been able to find a new way to understand the ghosts that had left me with no place to hide and which I felt were suffocating me. My testimony has been treated mostly with openness and honesty and this has helped me to face myself openly and honestly. Yet this outcome happened largely without TRC facilitation, and has helped me to cope and slowly to reconstruct my life in real ways in spite of the official institution of the TRC.

Although the actual hearings formed only a part of the complex procedural, ideological and political processes of the TRC, the hearings were the only real contact that most people had with the Commission. Most people were unaware of the complex maze of personnel and procedures within the institutionalised framework of the TRC that constituted the basis for this artificial space controlled by the TRC Act. At the time of my hearing in August 1996, the TRC provided a space to which I could reach out in desperation. In many ways, for me, it was the 'rolling of the dice'.

Until then I had been denied an opportunity to tell my truth as I knew it and had to live – to survive – within a context of pain and silence imposed by several truths and untruths. In this context I had neither the space nor the ability to contest or counterpose perceptions about me, and the process of which I was a part. So, like many other witnesses, for reasons of my own, I sat in the witness box awaiting my chance to break my silence and face my pain publicly.

I was asking for an opportunity to be judged fairly for my role in what had happened to me in the political and psychological context of that time. However, in the immediate weeks, months and years that followed my few hours in this space, I came to realise how the complexity of the maze referred to above would colour and re-colour my experience of this space. I began to learn how the limitations and positive aspects of the process are bounded by contradictions. These contradictions can I think be learnt from if they are carefully documented and sensitively communicated to our society, as well as to other countries that are considering using the South African model as a starting point for implementing similar processes to resolve conflicts.

It has been hard and there have been times when I have felt maybe I should not have risked testifying before the Commission. It is almost as if I have been imprisoned by the TRC's inability to treat my grievances sensitively. It took me almost a complete year to recover psychologically from my testimony and the form it took publicly after having testified. I entered the TRC hearings with expectations that at least some of my requests would be taken seriously. I went to testify because I wanted the Commission to investigate the circumstances of my capture and torture. I wanted to know why I was forced to watch someone that I knew die and why I had to live in fear of my life because the South African security forces subsequently blamed me for this killing. I unequivocally requested the TRC to establish at least some semblance of the truth around what happened to me, and to free me from the threats of death that still permeate my life. It still has not done so. Instead, I have had to take the responsibility of this onto my own shoulders with no institutional support as the Commission promised. Instead of clearing my name, as I had asked, the TRC entrapped me in a cycle of victimhood that has been almost impossible to break. I went to the hearings with a broken body and a fractured mind. I left those confines with my body more broken and my mind more fractured. The space was harsh and the institution of the Commission was insensitive.

In the two years after our first national elections not only had I not visited parliament, I had had no positive contact with the ANC. There was no way that I could have expected to be sitting just a few days after my testimony in the office of the Deputy President, Thabo Mbeki, where I struggled for another hour without TRC facilitation to repeat my testimony. It was difficult to talk and answer questions asked of me by someone who was *de facto* one of the most powerful men in the country. From collapsing due to stress one week before my testimony and then collapsing after my testimony to sitting chain-smoking with the Deputy President one week later was almost impossible to handle. The fact that Thabo Mbeki decided to become involved, however, helped me immensely in my resolve to stay sane and my quest to find out what had happened to me and hopefully to clear my name from the curse of being set up as a traitor by the apartheid security forces. I desperately needed to know why the ANC had not taken any responsibility for what had happened to me – why six years later I still bore the full brunt of my torture, the death of Anton Fransch and the constant harassment of my family from the time I went into exile until long after my release from prison. The events subsequent to my arrest have scarred me forever, and I feel my life and being have been so altered that I cannot ever be the same human being again.

The meeting with Thabo Mbeki led to a series of meetings with senior ANC officials with no real results. I was forced to discontinue this process, as the emotional and psychological strain was too much for me. I had no institutional support from the TRC and was on my own. Despite the impasse with the ANC I drew immense strength from this process. The acknowledgement of my existence as a member of its former military wing at the highest political level has been crucial to me establishing within myself the honour, dignity and self-respect for having committed my youth to the liberation struggle in South Africa. Up until this point the ANC had not acknowledged even the fact that I was alive. The liberation movement's disavowal of my experience in the resistance added immensely to the trauma of my capture, imprisonment and torture. It made the fact of my having to live with this trauma everyday almost unbearable. The security forces had also arrested my father, harassed my family and threatened my mother and four-year-old nephew with death. My joining the ANC had had serious consequences for my family, consequences to which I as a 15-year-old boy had given no thought. This act of recognition by the ANC – even though it has not yielded official results – also gave recognition to the experience of my family and allowed them the possibility to be proud of me as well as of themselves.

MY TESTIMONY?

Since testifying before the HRV Committee I have been called many names, placed within several stories, given several histories and the most harmful of narratives. I have to carry them as they have now become a part of my public face. One of these narratives places me within the confines of the agonised confessor or the betrayer who should be pitied and has been constructed, since my testimony, by individual commentators, the media as well as the TRC's Final Report.

For example, in *Country of My Skull*, Antjie Krog (1998) includes a chapter called 'The Narrative of Betrayal Has to Be Re-Invented Every Time'. There she uses a version of my testimony, edited by her, to fit that particular narrative. I had no idea that she had taken my testimony, edited it herself, given it a title and so invented a chapter for her book. At the time of my testimony I had no idea what the consequences of 'public' could have meant in the context of public hearings. The fact that my testimony could be appropriated, interpreted, re-interpreted, re-told and sold was not what I expected. Given the destructive physical and mental state I was in at the time I did not foresee this eventuality. Not only do I question the intentions of writers such as Antjie Krog; I assert that their work has, in various ways and with serious personal consequences to myself, impacted negatively upon my life. Serious thought needs to be given to the ethics of appropriating testimony for poetic licence, media freedom, academic commentary and discourse analysis. Arguing these lines and 'It's on the public record' are too easy positions to take since they do not address the rights of self-authorship and the intention of the speaker, the reclamation of one's voice and one's agency. This ethical dilemma also needs to be addressed as a meta-analytical and methodological question, by theorising the relationship of the layers of listening and subjective hearing positions (proximity, relationality), mediations, disseminations of testimonies and voices of listeners and readers.

In Volume 3, Chapter 5 under the regional report of the Western Cape and beneath a section entitled 'Killing of Political Suspects', the TRC's Final Report (1998) appends my name in passing to its inconclusive finding on the death of Anton Fransch. While it is mentioned at the end of the description that the Commission's investigative body has cleared my name of the rumours spread by the security forces that I had turned against the liberation movement and had become an 'askari' (former guerrilla recruited by the security forces), my testimony is never mentioned regarding my own experiences of imprisonment and torture. In the context of the official history constructed by the Final Report my testimony appears under the name of someone who has been killed and I can never be freed from this version of the past. Instead of clearing my name, it is as if I am forever written into this death. No attempt has been made in the Final Report to look carefully at the reasons I went to testify. In the context of so many testimonies I am able to make sense of this – in the context of my own personal life it is just painful.

Other pieces that appeared in the media had titles such as 'Betrayal Was the Price of My Families Lives', 'MK Member Collapses After Admitting Betrayal' and 'Agonised Confession Moves Listeners to Applause'.

The following article describing my testimony is one example of the complex ways in which the media reduced and sensationalised my testimony to the TRC:

> The pain was overwhelming, the tension almost unbearable – as Yazir Henry struggled for nearly an hour to tell his harrowing tale to the TRC's Human Rights Committee a gamut of emotions played across his pale face. At times his fine bone features, framed by his dark hair and eyebrows were cold and disdainful, and he gazed at the audience – or perhaps a few individuals in the audience – with undisguised anger.
>
> It was an anger that was close to the surface, and it spilled over when the translator bowdlerised his recollection of an abusive Afrikaans phrase, which a security policeman had used about him

at one point in his traumatic detention. 'I said "fokking donner"!'
he shouted at the translator, who had turned his words into a
polite 'man'.

Several times he drew his lips back in anguish, baring his teeth
in a way that turned his face almost skeletal. Occasionally he
leaned his head right back onto his shoulders, trying to relieve the
appalling pain that seemed to concentrate his neck muscles. His
voice, interspersed with sobs, sighs and coughs fell and rose with
his emotions. At times Mr Henry sounded like a young Allan
Boesak, his high, clear tone ringing through the huge hall.

With other phrases his voice cracked and shattered – especially
when he referred to his comrade in arms, whom he had betrayed
to the security police just as someone else had done to him. 'I was
19, I don't think anyone in the world should have been given such
a choice.' He said of his decision to lead security police to Anton
Fransch as a quid pro quo for them not killing his mother and
four-year old nephew, 'The brutality and the tenacity with which
they questioned me, and my knowledge of what they had done to
others … made their threat to kill my family very real.'

At the end of his testimony, Truth Commission Chairman,
Desmond Tutu told him the audience had listened to his story
with 'deep reverence'. 'We hope that by having told your story,
there will be a lifting of your spirit, and that some of your
nightmares may reduce.'

Mr Henry dropped his head and wept again at the Archbishop's
words, and many in the audience rose to their feet and applauded
him. After a lengthy debriefing session with TRC staff, he later told
journalists that he had heard clapping only as a background noise.
'Nothing made sense to me. I'm extremely tired. I have so little
energy left. I just want to be judged for whom I am, that's all. I
just want to be given a chance to start life again – I've been living
in a nightmare.' It was a nightmare of concentrated pain that will
have etched itself into the consciousness of all whom heard it.
(Yeld 1996)

The media, both print and visual, took a few seconds of my testimony
and superimposed upon me the very narrative that I went to the TRC
to question. The disembodiment of my testimony has made the
struggle to reclaim my voice, memory and agency harder. The dispos-
session of my voice through a continuous recycling of my by now
unmoored testimony was compounded by the superimposition of

other voices and narratives onto my own. Taking up my pen and, in so doing, taking back my right to comment on and explain my own testimony has become an important way to intervene in the continuous dismemberment of my testimony and self.

BREAKING THE SILENCE, ENCOUNTERS WITH FREEDOM

After being released from prison in 1990, prior to testifying before the TRC in 1996 I spent six years not talking to anyone about what had happened to me; I re-invented my life. Inside this lie I attempted to survive the security police set-up after they had failed to recruit me. South Africa and my personal reality forced me to live a life of fragments and lies. My past was too dangerous to remember but I still felt it. For six years I lived in a silence that excised me from my own memory and history. My body eventually gave in to the weight of this silence, with which my psyche could no longer cope – almost as if it could not hold the heaviness that came with my mind's consistent failure at forgetting itself.

The memory of my trauma had learned to control my body's pace, my ability to talk, to eat, to sleep. This process was so harsh I felt I had to seek therapy. It was already too late and even the therapy could not prevent my gradual physical dysfunction. There seemed to be no possibility of forgetting my experience or of denying the slow death that came with the fact that my memory before 1991 didn't exist. I relived the pain of my experience every day, it possessed me and it became me. I had to forget that I had spent my youth in Angola, Zambia, and the Soviet Union, in the wars of Southern Africa, and in the hands of one of the world's most brutal security forces.

With hindsight the TRC offered me the possibility of breaking this silence. The history I reclaimed in the process was one of dignity for those of my generation who had been destroyed, symbolically if not literally, in the struggle against apartheid. It was also for myself, whose life had not only been destroyed but officially had disappeared without a trace. My life existed somewhere in the liminal space between that which is recorded officially and that which remains officially off the record. I cannot begin to explain the pain of living a life with no record, where one breathes but there is no existence.

What has made things lighter is the fact that there can no longer be any denial of my role in the resistance. This history is now undeniably mine too and its memory lives in my life now with a fire that is no longer only destructive. This makes some of the more elusive truths easier to bear. The pain of having to live with death everyday is made more bearable when one does not have to remain silent about it. At present I am integrating my story, my history, and also my testimony into my life in ways that make living without forgetting possible and honourable.

Even now I remember the energy leaving my body when the Archbishop said he had listened to my story with reverence and that he understood what I had been through. My head fell against the witness table and my knees would not carry me from his gaze. I felt the weight of his words tearing my heart from my body and my mind shouted, 'How can you say what you cannot know? ... But I am not finished! ... There is more!' The strength had left me by then and I could no longer talk. *Still* – I know I had said enough and people had listened and had heard me. I pushed away the microphone with what little energy I had left. The Archbishop had completed my testimony for me.

This telling, however, was only the beginning. The challenge since then has been to own this memory and history. I have had to avert the downward spiral of victimhood and the entrapment of the TRC's victim box to find my own humanity. This process has nurtured in me the conviction of finding peace and of transforming fear into strength and hope. I have had to dispel the guilt I was told was mine and have had to face the language of bitterness and self-destruction to find in it the words of remembrance and mourning.

DIRECT ACTION CENTRE FOR PEACE AND MEMORY: WECAT – OF PEACE AND SELF-HEALING

In the past four years I have been a part of founding several initiatives. I have been working actively to transmit the lessons not only derived from engaging in the TRC process, but also from participating in and surviving two wars and creating an environment where speaking about pain is freedom and history is the right to claim memory with honour, to live with it in dignity on one's own terms.

The Western Cape Action Tour Project started as a self-support network. It has now developed into a non-profit organisation called the Direct Action Centre for Peace and Memory with the Western Cape Action Tour Project as a core project. Initially, we met informally as former combatants and torture survivors. We found ourselves within a super-reality defined by the ongoing trauma of social, economic and psychological alienation following demobilisation, combat-related symptoms of post-traumatic stress disorder and unemployment. Our organisation grew through the realisation that we needed desperately to find a way of breaking the cycle of victimhood that society imposed upon us that we perpetuated by casting our own lives within this framework. Together we have been able to realise the collective need to value and harness our skills in political and social activism as well as in organisational planning in order to create an initiative that would address the trauma of our experience, break the prison of our victimhood.

In order to achieve these objectives, we conduct as a medium social and political heritage tours in the marginalised spaces and places of traumatic experience in Cape Town. These tours involve participants in historical encounters with the social and cultural life of communities previously engaged in the political struggle against apartheid. We merge this historical experience with an encounter with contemporary socio-economic conditions and political aspirations of post-apartheid Cape Town where the faultlines of colour, ethnicity, religion, gender and identity have never been more visible. The divisions created through almost 50 years of intense social, political and economic engineering need to be addressed and not left alone to fester. For as Cape Town remains one of the most scenic locations in the world, it is simultaneously one of South Africa's most volatile; one might even say that it is a city at war with itself.

At present the scope of our work is limited. However, from where we started in late 1997, as traumatised individuals, we have come a long way in finding ourselves. If nothing else, we have had some success in turning our lives and experiences around with no institutional or government support.

RECONCILING RECONCILIATION

Many today argue that the TRC has by and large completed its work and that South Africa must now build a new future. This thread is woven through many of the arguments supporting selective amnesia that exist today in South Africa. These arguments seek to excise from history an important part of the experience of people who had to endure the worst of apartheid. Most of these arguments prematurely support the contemporary success of the building of the 'South African Rainbow Nation'. They are constructed in ways that allow both civil society and government to shirk the responsibility of catering for the needs of millions in South Africa forced to live and survive in the ghettos and shack settlements, defined through the accident of their skin colour.

It is dangerous to make light of the reality that all is not well with the TRC process and South Africa's 'rainbow' nation-building exercise. Reconciliation in South Africa needs to take place between communities denying apartheid and their complicity in it and communities who have not as yet been given the opportunity to mourn the varying forms of loss that came with their experiences under apartheid. The challenge facing Cape Town is to find ways to mediate the colours of our barbed-wire rainbow.

Personally, my own experience with the TRC was difficult and complex but crucial to where I find myself today. Many survivors who testified did not have a positive experience. For me, what was important was that I was able to prise myself loose from the invisible hands around my throat and with the support of people around me I was able to embrace life again. It was this process that I have taken with me into my daily life and work. For me this is how the idea of supportive spaces that is so central to WECAT's philosophy developed. At WECAT we facilitate encounters around places that have witnessed immense pain. These encounters take place through dialogues that recognise the people killed there, through talking about the events that took place there, through people listening and even through those who pass by during the telling. In this process the plaque and memorial marker is human, alive and dialogic.

By moving through and talking in places that mediate the past and the present in ways that allow for the recognition of the pain, inhumanity and humanity of our past we open the possibility of experiencing the pain, inhumanity and humanity of our present. In these spaces several things occur simultaneously in different ways for different people and for many different reasons. Important aspects of our work occur on several levels. Here, I briefly identify four levels:

1. For people speaking about their loss and trauma – an opportunity to 'normalise' their experience by externalising, making it everyday in a way that also recognises the fact that there can be no forgetting but that life continues. It is almost as if one places this memory in a respectful place outside oneself. In doing that, this memory finds a place inside oneself that is not only destructive.
2. For those listening – an opportunity to listen, to learn, to share, to give respect and recognition to an experience as well as to a

person. This is an opportunity for people to express and extend their humanity to a place in a way that values the humanity of speaker, listener and place. It offers also, for some, the space to say, 'I was not a part of ...' or 'I did not know ...' or 'How could this have been?' or 'This should never happen...'.

3. This is harder to explain for it is captured by feelings and emotions, but as we collectively mediate the past the present begins to look different. It is at this point where we may be able to realise our humanity and our agency, and it is where I have had to question my own prejudice and see human beings across from me. This is where the opening occurs that makes it possible to feel that human beings should never do what was done here to other human beings, either now or in the future.

4. The level at which the actual place in which one stands or talks is transformed from an ordinary township street where the garbage does not get removed into not just any township street. The community is transformed from not just any community that happened to have settled in this particular place into a community that has been forcefully dislocated and displaced into Cape Town's geo-political backyard. The place also transforms with the realisation that where we stand was a battleground only ten years ago. Together we transform and are transformed by this place, which suddenly becomes one of recognition, commemoration, mutual learning, respect, dignity, hope and humanity.

I have been asked many times since speaking at the TRC whether I have been able to achieve reconciliation. I have found this to be a fluid and complex term meaning different things to different sectors of South African society. For some it means 'Let's move on', for others it means receiving a prosthetic limb so as to walk again, and still for others it could mean the bus fare with which to look for work. It becomes even more complex when one has lost a family member or a friend. For me, it has not been about forgiveness or revenge, but about finding a way in which I could come to terms with the torture and inhumanity that I experienced, not only in order to continue merely to survive but also to revive my hope for the future. It is for these reasons I continue to struggle with the glib use of the term 'reconciliation', especially when it is used to cover up the atrocities that have become a part of our everyday lives. In a sense I have had to reconcile myself with myself and myself with my own experience.

IN CONCLUSION: MEMORY AND RESPONSIBILITY

It is important that my criticisms are viewed in a constructive manner. I write as someone who has been touched by humanity's ability to destroy itself. As the phantoms of the conflagration stalk the peace here, it is my hope as someone living in their shadows, that we are not captured by another war.

It is my contention that, although a lot rests on the shoulders of government, each and every South African has a responsibility to ensure that the lessons of pain and suffering penetrating our daily lives are acknowledged and addressed. The price paid by witnesses who testified before the TRC is only the beginning of a process to be borne by everyone. The TRC initiated a process; it did not create nor did it heal a nation. The TRC must be understood inside its own historicity.

Crucially the space set up and controlled by the TRC was an important one that can be adapted and extended to other sectors of society. Cape Town continues to be divided by high walls, electric fencing and barbed wire. The landscape and topography is one of extreme trauma where silence speaks to the transgenerational recording of the brutality indelibly seared into the roads, streets and walls of our memory. Whole communities as well as individuals remain dispossessed of any positive sense of self-identity. Colour is still structured socially, politically and economically and defined into and through the violence of the white apartheid city. As we begin to find innovative ways of exploring sensitively our mutual humanity and bringing together people of different colour and background across these boundaries, WECAT has begun to explore the faultlines of division that are not only our legacy but also our reality. It is our aim to modify the black- and white-coloured lenses through which we view our society to become lenses that also capture the varying shades of grey.

The TRC has not provided for the continuity of its work nor has it created the foundation for equitable transformation within the social relations of power, privilege and white domination. There is almost no space left for the collective and individual working through of the trauma, anger and bitterness caused by the apartheid system. We need the time and resources to process, work through and acknowledge what happened in our city socially beyond the narrow confines of the Commission's categorisation of the victim and of apartheid. Apartheid affected everybody and everyone has a story to tell. If people who were affected are to reconstruct their lives and communities so as to consolidate a peace that has been dearly paid for, society will have to make the time to listen. People need to be given the opportunity to express their anguish and mourn their losses. It is imperative that this be addressed within a context of calm and tolerance. The peace that I have struggled so hard to find and to maintain will hopefully speak through this story that I share with you.

REFERENCES

Krog, A. 1998. *Country of My Skull*. Johannesburg: Random House.
Truth and Reconciliation Commission (TRC). 1998. *Truth and Reconciliation Commission of South Africa Report, Volumes 1–5*. Cape Town: Juta.
Yeld, Jon. *Cape Argus*, 7 August 1996.

16 Empire Dies for Irish Freedom: Silence and Amnesia in Anglo-Irish Talks

Ella O'Dwyer

The parchment of Irish history is a ground of conflict, where statement and silence are strategically deployed. As one who has engaged intimately with both conflict and language, I note the interacting dynamics involved. In the context of Anglo-Irish relations, ours has been a discourse at war. 'England's difficulty is Ireland's opportunity', another of the infinitely repeated slogans of Irish discourse. Slogan and repetition feature crucially in the Irish voice, and to the extent that our rhythm comes unstuck and our story impeded. On the other hand, if a discourse however convoluted insists on delivery, it must have something to say. Silence and statement go to form linguistic patterns at every level, where words and spaces fall in at an easy pace to allow for the logical transmission of meaning. In the conflict scenario, those words and spaces 'fall in' as strategically deployed agencies of struggle. The sad songs and bitter tales that go to tell our story form the ensuing regimental chorus. This tense discourse patrols the silent gap where memory is interned. The still moment of military cessation marks a similar pitch in the national psyche, where intervals emerge to facilitate the passage of memory.

The issues raised in this analysis assemble round the semantics of Agreement and Treaty; taking features from earlier chapters of the Anglo-Irish conflict and gathering them for shared discussion at the conference table. Agreement and Treaty are the stuff of consensus. What will clearly emerge is that a crucial divergence remains within and between the voices on these islands; a divergence as unnerving as the threat of war. The thinking expounded in this chapter identifies the contrary and very conflicting dynamics of discourse; the war of words and the linguistics of power itself.

KNOWLEDGE AND/AS POWER

Knowledge is the ultimate currency of power at any level of the politico-cultural context. The challenge of the unknown is the context against which power defines itself; a binary relationship reminiscent of most structural arrangements, from the rules of conflict to the organisation of time. A kind of power/victim analogy hovers over the vast terrain of knowledge, with neither influence impacting independently on the story of meaning. The lust for knowledge is vividly dramatised in the conduct of Empire, where power, victimage, constructions of the unknown and the loaded baggage of colonialism are key players in the contest for control. Much narrative bears the insignia of this conflict, with an emergence of the unlikely confluence of a killing creativity; a relentless association of meaning and annihilation. The ever-vulnerable subject is host to equally conflicting and destabilising drives. Imprisoned among the contrary drives of meaning, the contest for balance and control becomes the cognitive imperative.

But who gives 'a fiddler's curse about being off [his] balance, dragged to the right hand and the left, backwards and forwards' (Beckett 1979:69) at the absurd whim of reason? Molloy does; the heavily challenged passenger in *The Beckett Trilogy*. The Irishman Molloy is the ultimate expression of troubled intelligence; a however miscalculated entity, infinitely familiar and yet rarely understood. Beckett, however, understood the nature of creative annihilation and the compulsive control to which reason drives its hosts. Policing the rising chaos of Molloy's psyche were the inadequate envoys of language and logic; the necessary and compulsive application of control over fearsome tides of unconquered meaning. Silence and amnesia are the inevitable switches on the panel conducting the currents of thought, and few authors reach so intimate a sense of this modality as Samuel Beckett. The essence of his insight is delivered in the short, sharp and shocking antics of his literary entourage, Molloy, Malone and Mahood. The hero of his ensemble, one Molloy, furiously engages himself in the troubling conundrum of however to succeed in negotiating the traffic of 16 stones around his person, so that he can surely and with precision suck them each and all, on a perfectly consecutive basis. Beckett packages his subjects in the tortured and tattered garb of the anti-hero whose negotiation of reality describes the turbulence of meaning.

Molloy's eccentric response to that reality is vividly portrayed in the very involved and rigid ceremony he conducts with the pebbles he distributes 'equally between [his] four pockets' (1979:64) in an intricate attempt to suck his 16 stones consecutively. This elaborate juggling exercise engages the immediate symmetry of his physical and intellectual presence in the studiously conducted ritual. Molloy encircles his selfhood in a wheel of pockets, linking body and clothes in his careful strategy. Two trouser pockets relay the bounty to the two pockets of his overcoat, while his mouth serves as personalised pouch implicating his very person in the dance.

His mind-boggling success in this task is a kind of sorcery in itself where he indulges in the possibility of absolute control. This ludicrous conundrum is for sure the troubling question of Empire and more generally and currently the Western World; how to indulge ourselves in the possibility of absolute control, so that we can write the story of yesterday, report the incidents of today, and predict the context of tomorrow? We want to juggle the wheel of the world, and our various microscopic and cultural rituals assigned to that project meet but rarely, at conference or negotiating table.

AGREEMENT, VISION, DISCOURSE, FEAR

A controversial agreement was negotiated and contracted over the troubled relations between Ireland and England in the early 1920s in the aftermath of an Irish insurrection in Dublin. The uneasy mood of the Irish capital of the time is outlined in Rex Taylor's (1961) biography of Michael Collins. Evaluating the morale of the occupying forces on Dublin streets in 1921, Taylor's account of the life of Collins identifies the 'terror created by a force uncertain of the measure of its strength' (Taylor 1969:11). The fear or terror of uncertainty is fundamentally the fear of the unknown; the uncolonised or loose knowledge around which consensus has not been framed. The uncolonised ground of the future is contested by binarily opposed players; the disparate agencies of vision and Empire. Colonialism's compulsion to take that ground is reinforced by the thought of what vision might create within that cognitive space. A similar angst arises on the part of the vision in the face of its awesome potential as architect of the future.

The challenge of the unknown is indeed the context against which power defines itself and both concepts are vital to the shaping and making of history. The fear of the unknown and untamed possibilities of the future, however, are as nothing compared to the fear of agreement, consensus and, ultimately, the certainty of knowledge. Taylor's reference to uncertain strength is a near identification of the most unlikely of exchanges. The network of power and fear smouldering through the currents of Irish history stems from the nervous negotiations between uncertainty and vision.

Every culture has its historical moments, and Irish history has erupted sporadically with some of those rare instances of foresight and energy that take vision to the field of conflict. Laced with such historical moments and groundbreaking events, ideology consistently impacts upon and projects itself onto the story of tomorrow, with the surprising inference that history is not in fact the story of the past, but the strategic architect of the future. The visionary dynamic that pre-empts the future to become the writ of the past is housed and hosted in the historical moment of whatever cultural identity.

The terror Rex Taylor identifies in the occupying forces in relation to its own uncertain strength has its corollary in the intriguing foresight of the visionary insurgent. The historical moments with which Michael Collins engages are amongst those rare instances of foresight which unnerve the staunchest of thinkers. Laced with historical moments and groundbreaking events, ideology consistently impacts upon and projects itself onto the story of tomorrow, and the story of Michael Collins travels through the most compelling events of modern Irish history.

'The country is Ireland, the city Dublin: and the time the early months of the year 1921' states Taylor (Taylor 1961:11). Post-insurrection, therefore, as opposed to post-conflict, is the backdrop against which Taylor writes his biography, *Michael Collins*. The 1916 Rising in Ireland was one of those major historical moments which inevitably project onto and shape the future with powerful insistence, and the shape and project of the 1921 period was a direct aftermath of that all-inflaming moment. While knowledge is the currency of power, victimage and the unknown are the climate against which power defines itself, and both contexts were key players in the political processes of this, as of all chapters of the conflict in Ireland. History and vision are themselves regular victims of extenuating circumstances and external events. Chance as much as intention played vigorously on the course of events on this island, and these players took the field at every moment of engagement. By chance or by intention, the-might-have-been revolution in Ireland was thwarted at the outset, when the order to revolt was countermanded and a carefully planned gun-running intercepted. Vision, like discourse, makes passage through the most complex and intriguing terrain.

While the visionary architects of the future ought to articulate the story of today, a crucial divergence emerges between the architects of vision and the articulators of discourse. The segregation established between the makers and the writers of history reflects a deeper separation draped along the ground of meaning itself. Post-modernism poses the concept of language as maker of meaning, where discourse is perceived to orchestrate culture as a kind of hyper-reality; that is, if enough people say something long enough, it is real. Meaning, therefore, is believed to administer reality, creating it to the order of the highest bidder. If meaning is simply a matter of the fittest discourse to tell the tale, Molloy's cognitive gymnastics are hardly surprising. While Homi Bhabha (1990) argues that nation is simply a product of narration, Terry Eagleton in his *Ideology of the Aesthetic* (1990), points to the inadequacy of words in the face of a strategi-cally applied materiality. Witness the seriously challenged student and ferrier of ideas when confronted by a highly charged tank.

The country is Ireland, the city Dublin; the time the early months of the year 2000. It is again 'a time of great event' (Taylor 1961:11), with the compelling project of a united and independent Ireland vividly to the fore. Many chapters and decades have unfolded along the story of a revolution which 'smoulders and occasionally flares to intensity' (Taylor 1961:11), with again the prognosis that England's hold on Ireland is about to be relinquished. As evinced through Taylor's work, literature often revisits the present with forgotten inter-pretation, providing a context through which earlier cultural scenarios can be rewound into vivid portrayals of the present. The city that was the haunt of the spy and the informer is today the haunt of civilian surveillance, in the aspect of sundry researchers, from the speculative journalist to the infatuated academic.

The access of insight that is knowledge, therefore, remains the currency of power in a context where the lust for information has reached almost embarrassing proportions. What becomes clearer, however, is that it is not in the gift of such surveillants to know, since they miss the moment and recoil from the event. The visionary dynamic that pre-empts the future to become the writ of the past is housed in the historical moment. The makers of history, with its inflaming moments, are by extension the visionary architects of the future. The reporting surveillants, on the other hand, are the reviewers and inevitably the revisionists of the moment, with little hand in the delivery of tomorrow. A crucial divergence emerges here, a dichotomy or segregation ascending through complex layers of history and meaning, and nowhere more vividly than in the Irish politico-historical context.

This is a theme pronounced by the title of Ernie O' Malley's book *On Another Man's Wounds* (1992), and focusing on the idea of treachery as relating to post-Treaty events in Ireland. Like many another incident in Irish politics, those implicated in the notorious Arms Trial denied all knowledge and, to this day, fail to remember the facts. To quote the *Evening Herald* of, unlucky for some, Friday 13 April, 2001: 'It's not just students of history who will be eager to see the latest round of documents released under the National Archive's 30-year rule.' What the suppressed information in file S/7/70 indicates is that government authorities knew of the intended gun-running. An embryonic split at the heart of the Dublin government was postponed by the suppression of this information. 'When the chips were down,' states O' Malley in a recent television documentary, 'it was Jack Lynch, himself and several other ministers who had stood in the breach to prevent the country being led towards a sectarian civil war that would have placed the earlier civil war in shadow. That was their duty, they had done their duty.' So, in order to prevent sectarian civil war, they let Ireland into out-and-out war for the last three decades and reneged on their duties as outlined in the Proclamation of the Republic in 1916. Those implicated in the Arms Trial harvested the smell of cordite hanging over the event while criminalising the only genuine agency for resistance, the Irish Republican Army. Fianna Fáil was perceived to be *The Republican Party* and the *Provos* were further demonised, outlawed and left to serve the time.

The story of modern Irish history is one of obstructed vision and rejection; the story of the *Croppy*, an Irish rebel who was rejected by his father at the moment of his execution. Reminiscent of that story, Irish governments rejected the legacy of those who signed the Proclamation; the Irish Republican Army.

The gaping morass over which agreement is sealed marks the site of segregation, the space of silence and the inter(n)ment ground of Ireland's voice. A fundamental split sits at the heart of Irish politics, where the signatories of the Treaty were perceived to have over-written the ideological thrust. Revisionists are major players in the ideological contest and the strategy of the split is their trump card. The reviewers of the historical moment play on the fears of the participants, encouraging dissent and discouraging revolution. Many roads diverged in the ideological journey envisioned by the players on the turf of Ireland's fight for freedom. However, it is only the most powerful and empowering thrust of the historical moment that affords and facilitates the dynamic of diversion, disruption and segregation arising from obstructed ideological intention. The loaded and compelling momentum of striking historical enterprises, such as the Rising and the Treaty, are the vehicles of often disruptive and divergent energies. Packaged within the frame of one such endeavour is the uncontainable and eruptive potential of the alternative. The alternative forms part of the fall-out of events like the Treaty, though this difference is also the quarrying ground of revisionists who seek to harvest that alternative, cultivating dissention in place of change.

Contradiction and inconsistency are often demonstrated in ideology, where apparently incompatible influences compete for authority. Occasionally, as Rex Taylor describes, these incompatibilities apply to the field of combat and more often they surface at the table of negotiation. What is crucially in question here is the equally mundane attendance of fear, an entity applicable to the most surprising of contexts. In the 1920s fear of the unnamed and the unknown future was aggravated by the awesome terror entwined in the fear of power and the known. Uncomfortable relations with an unnamed future give way to the fear of vision itself, with its implied monopoly on the future.

Again who gives 'a fiddler's curse about being off [his] balance'? (Beckett 1979:69). The Irishman Molloy does. The rising crisis, erupting from the interface of reactionary and visionary thought, compels us to the often inadequate framework of tense agreement. These sporadic Treaties are of the linguistics of power; the unexhilarating though compelling steps towards resolution; stammered contracts in the delivery of discourse. Any agreement, Treaty or consensus sealed over this gaping morass is erected against impending crisis; the fearsome meeting of reaction and revolution.

VOICE

If our languages, cultures and various soul-felt endeavours engage but in one place, they do so on the eclipse or moment of vision, whatever our various choreographic presentation of that ideological dynamic. The silence and amnesia that are the 'other' and backdrop to the themes foregrounded in this volume are the troubled voices thrust against the murals and proclamations of modern Ireland. The repeats and choruses of indigenous memory as recorded in narrative, reflect patterns at the historical level, where the sad, bitter songs that go to tell our tale amount to the repeating and stammering struggle of a thwarted discourse.

Obstructing the emergence of the national voice, 'Empire Speak' has infiltrated a colonised Ireland at deep and consuming levels. The incessant repeat and re-cycle, to which the Irish are compelled in the drive to tell our story, is in itself a form of occupation. If indeed, as is evident, current discourse is an occupied ground from where the thumb prints of the past occupy the discourse of today, it is probable that the past will equally project upon and occupy the discourse of tomorrow. The most challenging task of the colonised subject is to speak at all; a dilemma long ago identified by the visionary Beckett and mirroring Molloy's troubled urge to control. Entombed in the prison house of meaning, Molloy's facility to control rests within, where he erects an internal institution no less absurd than that he contends with in the world of meaning.

The obstruction or thwarting of discourse is an expression of colonial interference at its most sophisticated level. The Irish national narrative, fiercely preoccupied with the attempt to dislodge the Empire, is inscribed with a discourse of resistance which inevitably foregrounds the reality of oppression in the national psyche. While this expression of resistance is entirely legitimate, its compelling message has weighed upon and thwarted the emergence of the national voice. Quoting Fanon's *The Wretched of the Earth*, Said (1993) adds: 'colonialism is not satisfied merely with holding a people in its grip and emptying the native's brain of all form and content. By a kind of perverted logic it turns the past of the people, and distorts, disfigures and destroys' (Said 1993:276). The side-effects of that perverted logic are eminently discernible in the silence and anonymity that are the hallmarks of a colonial imposition forever to the fore of the national consciousness; hallmarks of infiltration where 'Empire Speak' corrals us into silence and repetition.

There are few terms that transgress the borders of time, place, language and ideology. Genius like that of Beckett is near neighbour to the vision that entices gatherings such as the three-day conference that generated this collection of essays. Gather we did, and in the most surprising of contexts for people like myself, who have spent years entombed in the research ground of another fellow of the academic world, Michael Foucault. I can attest to the authority of

Foucault's work, having spent years imprisoned in the Victorian time warps of Brixton and Durham prisons. I am a Republican ex-prisoner who has served almost 14 years in prisons in England and Ireland. I was arrested in 1985 and charged with conspiracy to cause explosions in England. I was convicted and sentenced to life imprisonment and was released in 1998 under the terms of the Good Friday Agreement. Foucault got it right; a circle of surveillance called 'Empire' projects an imposed silence and anonymity upon the subject psyche. What surveillance ultimately detects is the intuitive awareness which captive silence yields to the subject. The time warp that was the Life Sentence emerged as another of those strangely precocious historical events: the loaded moment however prolonged, of vision itself. The story of meaning in the context of the historical moment is not about the past, but about the visionary's pre-emption of tomorrow. The ideological infertility of Empire, on the other hand, is about the ravaged ground of the past; and never the twain can meet. In Ireland recently, Republicans commemorated the twentieth anniversary of the death on Hunger Strike of ten of our former peers. The streets of Ireland in 1981 with their black flags and tone of grief also marked a ground of fundamental change. A line was drawn in the sand for many of us at this time and, six decades after the Treaty, Ireland again met the heightened dynamic of the historical moment.

An inheritance of intentional silence and anonymity long pursued in Ireland stamps its elusive character onto the national narrative, a parchment edited sporadically through the loaded statement of contract and agreement. A deep fear underlies that silence and an equally uneasy tension hovers around statement and agreement. A pattern of concealment and revelation is as easily traceable in Irish as in world history. The often disjointed voice of the nation therefore presents itself as an edited and erratic presentation of history. Again, the gaping morass over which agreement is sealed does not seal out that fear. Molloy, Mahood and sundry Malones do indeed give a 'fiddler's curse about being off balance' (Beckett 1979:69). What if we fall into the morass of the unknown, and what unspoken phantoms might greet us there?

Molloy juggles the runes of the world and many of those cultural icons are represented here today. Propelled along our various and often strange journeys of discovery, the motion of various cultures erupts occasionally into a cartwheel of self-command and detachment. Revolving the objects of his rigid attention around his body in a concentrated cycle of order, Molloy wheels the pursuing reader in a similarly cyclical attention to the wayward pebbles, much as I am doing with this audience. Mastering the object of consciousness in this manner is a kind of silence in itself; allowing time-out from what promises to be a painful enough identity. This is a mechanism mirroring the bureaucratic embargo on speech as witnessed in recent Irish history where our government legislated for silence as part of its controversial Offences Against the State Act (1939) rather than allow Republicans to speak.

It was offensive to government to hear the voice of history. A silencing of the national unconscious was at play here, where the painful want of identity drove governments to resort to antics as absurd as Molloy's recourse to ritual. Conversely, imposed silence kept the unspoken discourse on the national agenda. Again, engaging us in the involved and absorbing antics described above, Beckett's narrative heightens an awareness of a pivotal discontinuity in meaning and interpretation. Silence, amnesia and uncertain identity feature in Molloy's absurd antics, and in an unnervingly familiar context. The elaborate rituals to which he is compelled reflect the trappings of inadequate expression and the compulsion to control, which arises within a heightened experience of repression. The troubling feature of Beckett's work is that the Irishman Molloy's predicament bears striking resemblance to the national context.

The re-cycling and compulsive ritual, to which Molloy is reduced, suggests something of the universal speaker's condition, constrained as we are within the inadequate though necessary straitjacket of language. His particular cultural context however is both distinct and universally familiar. Oral impediment and arrested narrative are familiar themes in most colonial cultural contexts. Chinua Achebe's novel *Things Fall Apart* (1973), demonstrates the repeats and returns to which Nigeria was compelled; the narrative throwbacks of a potential discourse struggling for existence. '[T]he art of conversation' was highly regarded amongst the Ibo tribe, where the 'great talker' was the pride of the colonised Ibo (Achebe 1973:4). It is striking, of course, that Achebe furnishes his hero Okonkwo with a speech impediment. The narrator tells us that he 'had a slight stammer and whenever he was angry and could not get his words out quickly enough, he would use his fists' (Achebe 1973:4). Impeded expression intensifies and ferments until it erupts into an urgent and aggressive force for change, a transition packaged in the baggage of condition or victimage. Impediment here symbolises the broader disjunction in meaning that agreements seek to seal and conceal.

Homi Bhabha in his *Nation and Narration*, refers to 'a strange forgetting of the history of the nation's past: the violence involved in establishing the nation's writ' (Bhabha 1990:310). He goes on to demonstrate just how much forgetting is required of any nation in order to sustain itself as such. He even exposes how it is necessary for such cultural identities to remember to forget. The repetitions and recycling story of Ireland's struggle on the other hand, indicate a desperate dependence on memory. That clinging recourse to memory and repetition indicates a struggle to grasp and hold onto an embryonic discourse. After all, how can a nation remember to forget, as Bhabha would have it, when the national inheritance is one of silence. In order furthermore for one to meet what Edward Said calls the 'obligation to forget' (Said 1993:11), a discourse must exist in the first place.

The roaring silences of Ireland's discourse host its own story: history's desperate insistence on expression. The parchment of Irish history emerges as another ground of conflict, where statement and silence are strategically deployed as weapons of war. Silence is used against the interrogating Empire, while statement is of those stammered contracts in the delivery of voice. Ours has been a discourse at war, where syllable and silence are unleashed according to their military merit. Expression, like knowledge in conflict Ireland, has been on a need-to-speak basis. The critical consequence of the war of words is that the pattern has been inhaled into the Irish psyche.

Discourse is no longer a matter of the fittest narrative to tell the tale; our discourse now must re-establish itself as instrument of vision. This pattern and experience will be shared by many an emergent nation emerging from military engagement, and it is well to note that, while strategic silence and strategic expression were for long the gift of the revolutionary insurgent, they hoard the symptoms of another trauma. The loaded silences and agreements accompanying conflict project vivid tensions onto the sphere of language. Our statements of recent decades have been of tense agreement, and our silences have been the equally tension-loaded fortresses against oppression; altogether we developed a very uneasy tone.

The traditional statements, treaties and agreements, through which ideology makes passage, often mark moments of divergence in the ideological journey. The consensus of agreement often produces appendages to a given narrative, as for instance in the matter of the Treaty of 1921 in Ireland. Historical chapters prior to that time were ones engaged in the struggle for the Republic on the model of the

French Revolution. Post-Treaty Ireland was absorbed in the struggle for a United Ireland. The stillness that is the military cessation is a silent moment of remembrance for the miscarried Republic. The ideological identity of the nation split at moments like the signing of the Treaty. Amnesia took control and memory was miscarried; though never erased. One Republic was lost; long live the Republic. However overwritten by agreement and treaty, the miscarried story of revolution was never deleted.

MEMORY

The ideological identity of the nation was split by a kind of amnesia, where memory was miscarried, though never erased. To borrow one of Jonathan Culler's terms, the miscarried story was 'under erasure' (Culler 1987:153), glossed over, though never deleted. The amnesia and tensions sealed over by Treaty and Agreement are again miscarried memories under erasure. The bunkers and morass of secluded memory, however concealed, haven't gone away. Through various bouts of amnesia the national identity sometimes re-names itself, usually marrying into the predominating contract of the time. The quiet of the military cessation is imploded with the suppressed voice of memory; the return of the repressed unconscious. The loud statement of consecutive agreements, each seeking compensation for the inadequacy of its predecessor, draws attention to the shortfall in the national narrative. Our spartan instances of statement therefore amount to an expression of loss; assertions of an intuitive absence in the national discourse. That acknowledgement of absence is, of course, an awareness of the very presence – somewhere – of the miscarried story.

The presence and memory secluded behind the fortresses of agreement are the hushed rhythms of the national subconscious and the elusive traces linking the past to the future. The sense that our discourse survives however entombed is also an intuitive awareness that it will live on. This subtle awareness connects the past to the future and is the stuff of a vision propelled along the rhythm of ideology. By a peculiar enough turn of events, it turns out that the silence and amnesia, which are the hallmarks of a short-fallen discourse, become the tantalising agencies of vision.

The culture of silence and anonymity long extant in Ireland is largely the bequest of crucial events like the signing of The Treaty, an inadequate contract said to have been signed under Lloyd George's threat of 'immediate and terrible war' (Taylor 1961:149). Whether or not the agreement was indeed signed under threat, the message and lesson of that shortfallen negotiation alerted the Irish to the threat of enforced statement and signature. Disappointed ideology and inadequate contracts are amongst the influences cultivating cultural self-censorship.

History as interpretation of meaning is therefore the record of, sometimes, exhilarating endeavour, and often the acknowledgement of a deeply disappointed ideology, and this story is punctuated variously with triumphant proclamation and the silence of fear. Also ghosting that narrative are the gaps and spaces where memory is installed, secluded and erased from the narrative face of history. Conflict, like power itself, has its own victims, and often the ultimate losses are of voice, memory and identity. Disappointed ideology and shortfall agreements are some of the influences cultivating cultural self-censorship. Inadequate treaties and aggressive interrogation factored in the reclusive discourse of Irish Republicanism where the rallying cry was to say and sign nothing. Against the backdrop of an already impeded national discourse, this security all but costs us the national discourse. Furthermore, the culture of Ireland's silence presents itself in prior chapters of 'conflict Ireland'. Witness the speech from the dock of the Irish revolutionary Robert Emmet. Facing execution for his role in the 1798 Rebellion, the condemned patriot instructed; 'Let no man write my epitaph ... when my country takes her place among the nations of the earth, then, and not till then, let my epitaph be written.' A blunt silence and anonymity hankers around the cultural context of Ireland; the suspended discourse of a people unfree.

The inheritance of intentional silence in Ireland is the counter-strategy of the visionary agent. Sustaining the fortresses around voice and memory not only facilitates the survival and safe passage of vision; it also foregrounds that vision in the national psyche. The colonised quarter dumps the hardware of vision in secure, silent and anonymous places; the safe and sterile bunkers of absence. The dis-ciplining of voice is a core theme of this volume, so the contrary dynamics of presentation and concealment are the polemic framework around which this chapter emerged. I have for long been interested in the prospects for development on the journey of Empire, wondering from places like Brixton and Durham prisons, where Empire expected ultimately to go. That, however, was not a major concern of mine, since I was more than challenged by the question as to where post-colonialism would take the Irish.

The project is not to engage us in the waste ground of the past, but to commission the dynamic of truth. Truth in the revolutionary context seldom goes out alone. Truth is the very name of justice. The very repetitious and, in Spenserian terms, 'terrible yell' (Spenser 1970:54) of the Irish, is the exploding voice of inevitable freedom. It is interesting that opposites find each other and are often the vehicle of discovery taking ideological opposition to its required destination. In a peculiar turn of events, the ruthless reaction of Empire sent Ireland to revolution. Empire's difficulty in sustaining an antiquated ideology gave vision the opportunity of moulding the future. Imperialism dies for Irish Freedom. There are tantalising lessons for England to glean from the ideological passage of a nearby island, and the issues spoken of in this chapter may fall on fresher pastures of the burnt earth of colonialism. This again is part of the aspiration of resolution; an appendix to the revolutionary thrust.

ACKNOWLEDGEMENTS

A number of dynamics factor in the chapter facilitated here through the offices of Coiste na n-Iarchimí and London University, a meeting place of prolonged silence and academic discipline. Nevertheless, it is a surprising and inspiring development to find that the town and chair of Empire facilitates the opportunity of speech. There is much to be learned by all parties from conferences such as this, suggesting that something between the tortured juggling of Treaty and entreaty has at least focused us on the war of words and the resolution of contract. It is equally significant that Coiste na n-Iarchimí, the Committee for Republican Ex-prisoners, facilitated participation in the polemic debate at ideological and material levels.

REFERENCES

Achebe, Chinua. 1973. *Things Fall Apart* [1958]. London: Heinemann.
Beckett, Samuel. 1979. *The Beckett Trilogy*. London: Picador.
Bhabha, Homi. 1990. *Nation and Narration*. London: Routledge.
Culler, Jonathan. 1987. *On Deconstruction: Theory and Criticism after Structuralism*. London: Routledge and Keegan Paul.
Eagleton, Terry. 1990. *The Ideology of the Aesthetic*. Oxford: Blackwell.
O'Malley, Ernie. 1992. *On Another Man's Wounds* [1978]. Dublin: Anvil Books.
Said, Edward. 1993. *Culture and Imperialism*. London: Chatto & Windus.
Spenser, Edmund. 1970. *A View of the Present State of Ireland* [1596]. London: Oxford University Press.
Taylor, Rex. 1961. *Michael Collins: A Biography*. Ireland: Four Square Press.

Notes on Contributors

Molly Andrews is Senior Lecturer in Psychosocial Studies and Co-director of the Centre for Narrative Research at the University of East London. Her research interests include the psychological basis of political commitment, psychological challenges posed by societies in political transition, and gender and aging. She conducted the research reported in her chapter as an Associate Research Fellow at the Centre for Socialization and Human Development at the Max Planck Institute in Berlin.

Lars Buur is at present postdoctoral researcher at the Center for Development Research, Copenhagen, Denmark. He recently completed his PhD in Ethnography and Social Anthropology on the everyday work of the South African Truth and Reconciliation Commission. He has worked mainly in the areas of information management technology, human rights documentation, and reconciliation in Argentina and South Africa.

Graham Dawson was a member of the Popular Memory Group at the University of Birmingham, and now teaches Cultural and Historical Studies at the University of Brighton. He is the author of *Soldier Heroes: British Adventure, Empire, and the Imagining of Masculinities* (Routledge, 1994). A member of the editorial board of Routledge Studies in Memory and Narrative, he is a co-editor of, and contributor to, *Trauma and Life Stories* (Routledge, 1999); and *The Politics of War Memory and Commemoration* (Routledge, 2000). He is currently writing a book on the politics of memory within the Irish Troubles and peace process.

Paul Gready is a lecturer in human rights at the Institute of Commonwealth Studies, University of London, where he was one of the founders of a multi-disciplinary MA programme in human rights. His monopograph entitled *Writing as Resistance: Life Stories of Imprisonment, Exile and Homecoming from Apartheid South Africa* is shortly to be published by Lexington Press. His work experience spans human rights activism, including working for Amnesty International, and academia, and he has published in both fields. Most of his academic work combines interests in cultural studies and human rights, most recently in the context of political transition.

Joan Hackeling has recently completed her PhD in Geography at the University of California at Los Angeles (UCLA). Her dissertation research has been funded by the German Academic Exchange Service (DAAD).

Eliza Tanner Hawkins is an Assistant Professor in the Department of Communications at Brigham Young University in Provo, Utah. She received her doctorate in mass communication from the University of Wisconsin-Madison in 2000. Her dissertation was titled: '"Las Grandes Alamedas": The Paradox of Internet and Democracy in Chile'. She has published a number of articles on internet development in Latin America. Her research interests include issues of democracy, collective memory and new communication technologies in Latin America.

Yazir Henri is a former anti-apartheid activist and a former officer in Umkhonto We Sizwe, the military wing of the African National Congress. He is a poet, writer and peace activist. He has written and published on the politics of memory, trauma, identity and the South African Truth and Reconciliation Commission. He currently works with former combatants, political prisoners and torture survivors and is the Director of the Direct Action Centre for Peace and Memory.

Elizabeth Jelin is a sociologist based in Buenos Aires, Argentina. She received her PhD at the University of Texas at Austin and is currently a senior researcher at Consejo Nacional de Investigaciones Científicas y Tecnológicas (CONICET), at the Universidad de Buenos Aires. She is research director at the Instituto de Desarrollo Económico y Social (IDES) and the Academic Director of the Research and Training Program on 'Collective Memories of Repression: Comparative Perspectives on Democratization Processes in Latin America's Southern Cone' sponsored by the Social Science Research Council, New York. She has written about social movements, everyday life, human rights and citizenship. Her current work focuses on memories of repression and on social movements at the regional level.

Steven Marsh has lived in Madrid since 1989 where he has worked as a journalist, teacher and translator. He is a collaborator and researcher on the AHRB-funded international project 'An Oral History of Cinema-Going in 1940s and 1950s Spain', based at Southampton University. He recently completed his PhD on comedy in Spanish cinema during the Francoist dictatorship at Birkbeck College, University of London and is in the process of revising the thesis for book publication. He is also currently working on a manuscript concerning the cultural politics of everyday life in contemporary Madrid.

Julie Mertus is an Assistant Professor, American University, School of International Service and a Senior Fellow at the United States Institute of Peace. She was formerly a Harvard Law School Human Rights Fellow, MacArthur Foundation Fellow, Fulbright Fellow (Romania) and Counsel to Human Rights Watch. She has extensive field experience in the Balkans; she lived in Serbia for two years in the 1990s. She is the author or editor of five books, including *Kosovo: How Myths and Truths Started a War* (University of California Press, 1999); *The Suitcase: Refugees' Voices from Bosnia and Croatia* (University of California Press, 1997); and *War's Offensive Against Women: The Humanitarian Challenge in Bosnia* (Kumarian, 2000).

Carolyn Nordstrom is currently Associate Professor of Anthropology and a Fellow at the Kroc Institute of International Peace Studies, University of Notre Dame. She has been researching issues of war and peace for two decades, with a focus on Southern Africa and South Asia. Her academic books include, *A Different Kind of War Story* (1997), *Fieldwork Under Fire: Contemporary Stories of Violence and Survival* (1995), and *The Paths to Domination, Resistance, and Terror* (1992).

Ella O'Dwyer is a Republican ex-prisoner who has served almost 14 years in prisons in England and Ireland. She was released in 1998 under the terms of the Good Friday Agreement. In prison, O'Dwyer studied for an MA and PhD in English Literature, producing a thesis entitled 'The Linguistics of Power and the Structuration of Meaning'. O'Dwyer now works for Coiste na n-Iarchimí, the Committee for Republican Ex-prisoners.

Istvan Pogány is a Professor of Law at the University of Warwick. He has written extensively on human rights and constitutional issues in the post-communist states. His books include *Righting Wrongs in Eastern Europe* (Manchester University Press, 1997). He is currently completing a study of the Roma of Central/Eastern Europe.

Fiona Ross lectures in Social Anthropology at the University of Cape Town. Her recently completed doctoral dissertation examines the work of the South African Truth and Reconciliation Commission, taking women's testimonial practices as its focus. Previous research has investigated household formation in informal settlements and traced the effects of energy-use and energy-provision technologies on health and household dynamics.

Victoria Sanford is Assistant Professor of Anthropology, Residential Fellow at Kellogg (Spring 2001), and a fellow of the Kroc Institute for International Peace Studies at the University of Notre Dame. She has worked on the exhumation of clandestine cemeteries in rural Maya villages in Guatemala since 1994 and served as a research consultant to the Guatemalan Forensic Anthropology Foundation (FAFG). Her recent articles in the journals *Latin American Perspectives* (1999), *Social Justice* (2000) and *Cultural Critique* (2001) have examined the role of the truth commission, NGOs and local communities in peacebuilding efforts in Guatemala. She has recently completed *Buried Secrets: Truth and Human Rights in Guatemala* (Palgrave Macmillan, 2003).

Christine Sylvester is Professor of Women and Development Studies at the Institute of Social Studies, The Hague. Her books include *Zimbabwe: The Terrain of Contradictory Development* (Westview, 1991) and *Producing Women and Progress in Zimbabwe: Narratives of Identity and Work from the 1980s* (Heinemann, 2000); also *Feminist Theory and International Relations in a Postmodern Era* (Cambridge University Press, 1994) and the forthcoming *Feminist International Relations: An Unfinished Journey* (Cambridge University Press, 2002).

Index